CAPTAIN BILL McDONALD TEXAS RANGER

A Story of Frontier Reform

BY

ALBERT BIGELOW PAINE

WITH INTRODUCTORY LETTER BY THEODORE ROOSEVELT

A Facsimile Reproduction of the Original

Published by
State House Press
Austin, Texas
1986

9-88   MW 2200

Paine, Albert Bigelow, 1861-1937.
  Captain Bill McDonald, Texas Ranger

  Reprint. Originally published: Special subscription
ed. New York: J. J. Little & Ives, 1909.
  "A facsimile reproduction of the original."
  1. McDonald, William Jesse, 1852-1918.   2. Peace
officers—Texas—Biography.   3. Texas Rangers—
Biography.   4. Outlaws—Texas—History.   5. Frontier
and pioneer life—Texas.   6. Texas—History—1846-1950.
I. Title.
F391.M142P35   1986   976.4'06'0924 [B]   86-61298
ISBN 0-938349-02-3
ISBN 0-938349-03-1 (pbk.)
ISBN 0-938349-04-X (lim. ed.)

Design by Deborah E. Brothers

State House Press
P.O. Box 15247
Austin, Texas 78761

W. J. McDonald

CAPTAIN BILL McDONALD
TEXAS RANGER

A Story of Frontier Reform

BY

ALBERT BIGELOW PAINE

Author of "Th: Nast—His Period and
His Pictures," etc., etc.

WITH INTRODUCTORY LETTER BY THEODORE ROOSEVELT

———

" No man in the wrong can stand up
against a fellow that's in the right
and keeps on a-comin'."

BILL McDONALD'S CREED.

———

SPECIAL SUBSCRIPTION EDITION
MADE BY J. J. LITTLE & IVES CO.
NEW YORK, 1909

CONTENTS

                                                                         PAGE

FOREWORD: A letter from Theodore Roosevelt . . . 11

I.—INTRODUCING "CAPTAIN BILL" 13

II.—AN OLD-TIME MISSISSIPPI CHILDHOOD

The kind of education for a young Ranger. Presence of mind early manifested 16

III.—EMIGRATION AND ADVENTURE

A boy at the head of a household. Meeting the "Devil and his wife." An early reform 21

IV.—THE MAKING OF A TEXAN

Reconstruction and "treason." "Dave" Culberson to the rescue. Education, marriage and politics . . . 26

V.—THE BEGINNING OF REFORM

Subduing a bad man. First official appointment. A deputy who did things. "Bill" McDonald and "Jim" Hogg 33

VI.—INTO THE WILDERNESS

A New Business in a New Land. A "Sand-lapper" shows his "sand" 43

VII.—COMMERCIAL VENTURES AND ADVENTURES

Bill McDonald's method of collecting a bill; and his method of handling bad men 48

VIII.—REFORMING THE WILDERNESS

The kind of men to be reformed. Early reforms in Quanah. Bad men meet their match 55

IX.—GETTING EVEN WITH THE BROOKEN GANG

The Brooken Gang don't wait for callers. One hundred and twenty-seven years' sentence for an outlaw . . 65

X.—NEW TACTICS IN NO-MAN'S LAND

A man with a buck-board. Holding up a bad gang single-handed 69

XI.—REDEEMING NO-MAN'S LAND

Bill McDonald and Lon Burson gather in the bad men. "No man in the wrong can stand up against a fellow that's in the right and keeps on a-comin'" 78

6 *Contents*

PAGE

XII.—SOME OF THE DIFFICULTIES OF REFORM

"Frontier" law and practice. Caught in a Norther in
No-Man's Land 87

XIII.—CAPTAIN BILL AS A TREE-MAN

The lost drove of Lazarus. A pilgrim on a "paint-hoss."
A new way of getting information in the "Strip" . . 95

XIV.—THE DAY FOR "DELIVERIES"

The tree-man turns officer, and single-handed wipes out a
bad gang 106

XV.—CLEANING UP THE STRIP

Deputy Bill gets "stood off," but makes good. Bill Cook
and "Skeeter," "A hell of a court to plead guilty in!" . 115

XVI.—TEXAS RANGER SERVICE AND ITS ORIGIN

The massacre of Fort Parker; Cynthia Ann Parker's capture.
Rangers and what they are for. Their characteristics
and their requirements 126

XVII.—CAPTAIN OF COMPANY B, RANGER FORCE

Capture of Dan and Bob Campbell. Recommendations for
a Ranger Captain. Governor "Jim" Hogg appoints his old
friend on the strength of them 136

XVIII.—AN EXCITING INDIAN CAMPAIGN

First service as Ranger Captain. Biggest Indian scare on
record 145

XIX.—A BIT OF FARMING AND POLITICS

Captain Bill and his goats. The "car-shed" convention 149

XX.—TAMING THE PAN-HANDLE

The difference between cowboys and "bad men." How
Captain Bill made cow-stealing unpopular . . . 154

XXI.—THE BATTLE WITH MATTHEWS

What happened to a man who had decided to kill Bill
McDonald 165

XXII.—WHAT HAPPENED TO BECKHAM

An outlaw raid and a Ranger battle. Joe Beckham ends
his career 176

PAGE

XXIII.—A MEDAL FOR SPEED

Captain Bill outruns a criminal and wins a gold medal . 179

XXIV.—CAPTAIN BILL IN MEXICO

Mexican thieves try to hold up Captain Bill and get a surprise. Mexican police make the same attempt with the same result. President Diaz tries to enlist him . . 182

XXV.—A NEW STYLE IN THE PAN-HANDLE

Charles A. Culberson pays a tribute to Ranger marksmanship. Captain Bill in a "plug" hat 189

XXVI.—PREVENTING A PRIZE-FIGHT

The Fitzsimmons-Maher fight that didn't come off at El Paso, and why. Captain Bill "takes up" for a Chinaman 194

XXVII.—THE WICHITA FALLS BANK ROBBERY AND MURDER

Kid Lewis and his gang take advantage of the absence of the Rangers. They make a bad calculation and come to grief. Good examples of Bill McDonald's single-handed work, and nerve 199

XXVIII.—CAPTAIN BILL AS A PEACE-MAKER

He attends certain strikes and riots alone with satisfactory results. Goes to Thurber and disperses a mob . . 214

XXIX.—THE BUZZARD'S WATER-HOLE GANG

The Murder Society of San Saba and what happened to it after the Rangers arrived 221

XXX.—QUIETING A TEXAS FEUD

The Reece-Townsend trouble, and how the factions were once dismissed by Captain Bill McDonald . . . 243

XXXI.—THE TRANS-CEDAR MYSTERY

The lynching of the Humphreys and what happened to the lynchers 250

XXXII.—OTHER MOBS AND RIOTS

Rangers at Orange and at Port Arthur. Five against four hundred 260

XXXIII.—OTHER WORK IN EAST TEXAS

Districts which even a Ranger finds hopeless. The Touchstone murder. The confession of Ab Angle . . . 265

PAGE

XXXIV.—A Wolf-Hunt with the President

Captain Bill sees the President through Texas and accompanies him on the "best time of his life." Quanah Parker tells stories to the hunters 273

XXXV.—The Conditt Murder Mystery

A terrible crime at Edna, Texas. Monk Gibson's arrest and escape. The greatest man-hunt in history . . . 290

XXXVI.—The Death of Rhoda McDonald

The end of a noble woman's life. Her letter of good-by 304

XXXVII.—The Conditt Mystery Solved

Captain Bill as a "sleuth." The tell-tale handprint. A Ranger captain's theories established 308

XXXVIII.—The Brownsville Episode: An Event of National Importance

The Twenty-fifth Infantry's midnight raid . . 315

XXXIX.—Captain Bill on the Scene

The situation at Brownsville. Rangers McDonald and McCauley defy the U. S. army. Captain Bill holds a court of inquiry 323

XL.—What Finally Happened at Brownsville

How State officials failed to support the men who quieted disorder and located crime 341

XLI.—The Battle on the Rio Grande

Assassination of Judge Stanley Welch. A Rio Grande election. Captain Bill ordered to the scene. An ambush; a surprise, and an inquest. Captain Bill's last battle . 357

XLII.—The End of Rangering and a New Appointment

State Revenue Agent of Texas. The "Full Rendition" Bill enforced. A great battle for Tax Reform, and a bloodless triumph 373

XLIII.—Conclusion

Captain Bill McDonald of Texas—what he has been and what he is to-day 388

LIST OF ILLUSTRATIONS

	PAGE
PORTRAIT OF CAPT. BILL MCDONALD . . .	*Frontispiece*
FACSIMILE OF LETTER FROM THEODORE ROOSEVELT . . .	11
INTRODUCING REFORM IN THE WILDERNESS	46
BEGINNING A CAMPAIGN IN NO-MAN'S LAND	75
THE CAPTURE OF DAN AND BOB CAMPBELL	138
THE BATTLE WITH MATTHEWS AT QUANAH	173
QUELLING A LYNCHING MOB AT WICHITA FALLS . . .	211
IN CAMP WITH THEODORE ROOSEVELT	283
CAPTAIN BILL'S LAST BATTLE	367

December 19, 1908.

My dear Captain:

I am glad you are to publish your memorials. I shall always look back with pleasure to our wolf hunt in Oklahoma. Yours has been a most interesting life. You are one of the few men now living who served in that warfare against crime and on behalf of order, which has well nigh passed away with the old frontier conditions which called it into being. For a number of years you were deputy sheriff, or deputy marshal, or representative of the cattle men's associations employed by them to put a stop to cattle stealing and robbery under arms, and you served for twenty years in that unique body, the Texas Rangers. It is a career which henceforth it will be difficult to parallel.

With all good wishes, believe me,

Sincerely yours,

Theodore Roosevelt

Captain W. J. McDonald,
New Amsterdam Hotel,
New York, N.Y.

THEODORE ROOSEVELT'S LETTER TO CAPTAIN McDONALD

FOREWORD

A Letter from Theodore Roosevelt to Captain McDonald

THE WHITE HOUSE,
   WASHINGTON.

December 19, 1908.

MY DEAR CAPTAIN: I am glad you are to publish your memorials. I shall always look back with pleasure to our wolf-hunt in Oklahoma. Yours has been a most interesting life. You are one of the few men now living who served in that warfare against crime and on behalf of order, which has well-nigh passed away with the old frontier conditions which called it into being. For a number of years you were deputy sheriff, or deputy marshal, or representative of the cattlemen's associations, employed by them to put a stop to cattle stealing and robbery under arms, and you served for twenty years in that unique body, the Texas Rangers. It is a career which henceforth it will be difficult to parallel.

With all good wishes, believe me,

Sincerely yours,

THEODORE ROOSEVELT.

CAPTAIN BILL McDONALD, TEXAS RANGER

I

INTRODUCING "CAPTAIN BILL"

CAPTAIN BILL McDONALD is a name that in Texas and the districts lying adjacent thereto makes the pulse of a good citizen, and the feet of an outlaw, move quicker. Its owner is a man of fifty-six, drawn out long and lean like a buckskin thong, with the endurance and constitution of the same.

In repose, Captain Bill is mild of manner; his speech is a gentle vernacular, his eyes are like the summer sky. I have never seen him in action, but I am told that then his voice becomes sharp and imperative, that his eyes turn into points of gray which pierce the offender through.

Two other features bespeak this man's character and career: his ears and his nose—the former, alert and extended—the ears of the wild creature, the hunter; the latter of that stately Roman architecture which goes with conquest, because it signifies courage, resolution and the peerless gift of command.

His nerves are of that quiet and steady sort which belong to a tombstone and he does not disturb them with tobacco or stimulants of any kind—not even with tea and coffee. In explanation, he once said:

" Well, you see, sometimes I have to be about two-fifths of a second quicker than the other fellow, and a little quiver, then, might be fatal."

Incidentally, it may be added that Captain Bill —they love to call him that in Texas—is ranked as the best all-round rapid-fire marksman in the State, and for the " other fellow " to begin shooting is believed to be equivalent to suicide. Add to these various attributes a heart in which tenderness, strict honesty and an overwhelming regard for duty prevail, and you have in full, Captain William Jesse McDonald, formerly Deputy Sheriff, Deputy U. S. Marshal and Ranger Captain, now State Revenue Agent of Texas.

It is the story of this man that we shall undertake to tell. During his twenty-five years or more of service in the field, he reduced those once lawless districts known as the Pan-handle, No-man's Land, and, incidentally, Texas at large to a condition of such proper behavior that nowhere in this country is life and property safer than in the very localities where only a few years ago the cow-thief and the train-robber reigned supreme. Their species have become scarce and " hard to catch " there now, and the skittish officials who used to shield them have been trained to " stand hitched." The story of a reform like that is worth the telling, for it is the unwritten history of a territory so vast that if moved to the Atlantic seaboard it would extend from New York to Chicago, from Lake Erie to the Gulf of Mexico—its area equal to that of France and England combined, with Wales, Belgium, the Netherlands and Switzerland thrown in, for good measure. Furthermore, it is the story of a man who, in making that history, faced death almost daily, often under those supreme conditions when the slightest hesitancy—the twitch of a muscle or the bat of an eyelid—a " little quiver," as he put it—would have been fatal; it is the story of a man who time and again charged into the last retreat of armed and desperate murderers and brought them out hand-cuffed, the living ones, of course; it is the story of a man who, according to Major Blocksom, in his report of the Brownsville troubles in 1906, would " Charge hell with a bucket of water." In a word, it is the story of a man who has done things, who is still doing them, and whose kind is passing away forever.

II

AN OLD TIME MISSISSIPPI CHILDHOOD

THE KIND OF AN EDUCATION FOR A YOUNG RANGER. PRESENCE OF MIND EARLY MANIFESTED

IN those days when the Mississippi planter was only something less than a feudal baron, with slaves and wide domain and vested rights; with horses, hounds and the long chase after fox and good red deer; with horn and flagon and high home wassail in the hall—in those days was born William Jesse McDonald, September 28th, 1852. His father, Enoch McDonald, was the planter of the feudal type—fearless, fond of the chase, the owner of wide acres and half a hundred slaves—while his grandfather, of the clan McDonald on its native heath, was a step nearer in the backward line to some old laird who led his men in roistering hunt or bloody fray amid the green hills and in dim glens of Scotland.

That was good blood, and from his mother, who was a Durham—Eunice Durham—the little chap that was one day to be a leader on his own account, inherited as a clear a strain. The feudal hall in Mississippi, however, was a big old plantation house, built of hewn logs and riven boards, with woods and cotton-fields on every hand; with cabins for the slaves and outbuildings of every sort. That was in Kemper County, over near the Alabama line, with DeKalb, the county-seat, about twenty miles away.

It was a peculiar childhood that little " Bill Jess " McDonald had. It was full of such things as the home-coming of the hunters with a deer or a fox—sometimes (and these were grand occasions) even with a bear. Then there were wonderful ball-games played by the Bogue Chita and Mucklilutia Indians; exciting shooting-matches and horse races; long fishing and swimming days with companions black and white, and the ever recurring chase, with the bloodhounds, of some runaway slave. There was not much book-schooling in a semi-barbaric childhood such as that. There was a school-house, of course, which was used for a church and gather-ings of any sort, and sometimes the children had lessons there. But the Kemper County teaching of that day was mainly to ride well, to shoot at sight, and to act quickly in the face of danger. That was the proper education for the boy who was one day to make the Texas Pan-handle and No-man's land his hunting ground, with men for his quarry.

Presence of mind he had as a gift, and it was early manifested. There was a lake not far away where fishing and swimming went on almost con-tinuously during the summer days, and sometimes the small swimmers would muddy the water near the shore and then catch the fish in their hands. They were doing this one day when Bill Jess was heard to announce excitedly:

" I've got him, boys! I've got him! You can't beat mine! " at the same instant swinging his catch high for them to see.

That was a correct statement. They couldn't beat his catch and · they didn't want to. What they wanted to do was to get out of his neighborhood without any unnecessary delay, for the thing he held up to view was an immense deadly moccasin, grasped with both hands by the neck, the rest of it curling instantly around the lower arm. His hold was so tight and so near its head that the snake could not bite him, but the problem was to turn it loose. His friends were all ashore and at a safe distance. He did not lose his head, however, but wading ashore himself he invited them one after another to unwind that snake. Nobody cared for the job and he told them in turn and collectively what he thought of them. Then he offered the honor to a litle slave boy on attractive terms.

" Alec," he said, " ef you-all don't come an' unwind this heah snake, I'll beat you-all to death an' cut off yo' ears an' skin you alive and give yo' carcass to the buzzards."

Those were the days when a little slave-boy could not resist an earnest entreaty of that sort from the son of the household, and Jim came forward, his

face gray with gratitude, and taking hold gingerly
he unwound a yard or so of water-moccasin from
Bill Jess, who, with the last coil, flung his prize to
the ground, where it was quickly killed, it being well-
nigh choked to death already.

But even the great gift of presence of mind will
sometimes balk at unfamiliar dangers. It was about
this time that the Civil War broke out, and Enoch
McDonald enlisted a company to defend the Southern cause. The little boy left behind was heart-
broken. His father was his hero, and when by and
by the news came that the soldiers were encamped
at Meridian—a railway station about fifty miles
distant—the lad made up his mind to join them.
He set out alone afoot and being used to finding
his way in unfamiliar places he made the journey
with no great difficulty, eating and sleeping where
opportunity afforded. He arrived at Meridian one
morning, and began to look over the ground and to
make a few inquiries as to his father's headquarters.
There was a busy place, where a lot of supplies were
being unloaded from what appeared to be little
houses on wheels. They were freight cars, but Bill
Jess didn't know it. He had never seen a railroad
before, and he followed along the track with increasing interest till he reached the engine, which he
thought must be the most wonderful and beautiful
thing ever created. Then suddenly it let off steam,
the bell rang and the air was split by a screaming
whistle. It was too sudden and too strange for his

gift to work. The son of all the McDonald's and of a gallant soldier set out for the horizon, never pausing until halted by the sentry of his father's camp.

He was permitted to enter, and was directed to the drill ground, where his father, who had been promoted for bravery to the rank of Major, was superintending certain maneuvers. The little boy in his eagerness ran directly into the midst of things, and Major McDonald, suddenly seeing him, was startled into the conclusion that some dire calamity had befallen his family and only Bill Jess had escaped to tell the tale. Half sliding, half falling he dropped from his horse to learn the truth. Then gratefully he lifted the lad up behind him and continued the drill. Eunice McDonald was only a day or two behind Bill Jess, for her instinct told her where the boy had gone. They remained a few days in camp and then bade their soldier good-bye. They never saw him again, for he was killed at the battle of Corinth, October 3d, 1862, charging a breastworks at the head of his regiment, his face to the enemy, as a soldier should die.* The boy, Bill Jess, ten years old, went after his father's effects, which included two horses, both wounded. These he brought home, but his soldier father had been buried on the field, where he fell.

* Col. Rogers of Texas was killed in the same charge; Major McDonald and Col. Rogers fell side by side, within a few feet of the works.

III

A BOY AT THE HEAD OF A HOUSEHOLD. MEETING " THE
DEVIL AND HIS WIFE." AN EARLY REFORM

THE boy of ten was now the head of the household.
He had his mother and sister, and most of the
negroes still remained; but he was the " man of the
house " and was mature before his time. Except in
the matter of strength, he was a man's equal—he
could do whatever a man could do. Already he was
a crack shot, and at the age of twelve he hunted
deer, and killed them, alone. Long before, even during his father's first absence, he had followed runaway slaves with the bloodhounds and without other
assistance had captured them and marched them
back to the plantation. It was not a child's work,
and we may not approve of it to-day, but we must
confess that it constituted a special training for the
part he was to play in after years.

The war ended at last, and with it the McDonald
fortune. Slaves and cotton were gone. Only a rem-
nant of land, then worthless, remained. Eunice
McDonald, widowed, with two children—her home
left desolate by the ravages of war—knew not which
way to turn. A bachelor brother with his face set

Texasward offered to make a home for her in the new land. She accepted the offer, and in 1866 they reached east Texas and settled in Rusk County, near Henderson, the county-seat. Here the brother and sister made an effort to retrieve their broken fortunes, with moderate success. All the family worked hard, and young McDonald, now in his fifteenth year and really a man in achievements, did a man's part on the farm, attending school a portion of the year. His uncle permitted him to earn some money for himself by cutting wood and hauling it to the village, and a part of this money he laid away. Such leisure as he had, he spent in following the hounds, and presently, even as a boy, became famous for his marksmanship. Coon hunting was perhaps his favorite diversion, and frequently with his dogs he threaded the dark woods all night, alone.

But he had not as yet achieved that perfect fearlessness which distinguished him in later years, and there is still another instance recorded where his presence of mind failed to work. This latter is a curious circumstance, indeed, and should be investigated, perhaps, by the Society of Psychical Research.

He had been out on one of his long night tramps and was very tired next evening when his work was done. Coming in, he threw himself down on a lounge in the hallway and was soon sound asleep. By and by his mother came along and wakened him.

" It's bed-time, Bill Jess," she said.

He got up, walked out toward the gate, and she supposed he was awake. When he really awoke, he was a mile from there, leaning on the gate of one Jasper Smith, the father of two young ladies whom Bill Jess was in the habit of visiting. Realizing where he was, and what might happen to him if discovered just there, he set out for home down the wide public road, when suddenly a little way ahead he saw two objects perched on the top of the rail fence. At first he thought they were two men, and was not disturbed; then all at once they had left the top of that fence and in the wink of an eye, lit in the road directly in front of him.

" It was the devil and his wife," McDonald declared. " They had horns and tails, exactly like all the pictures of the devil I ever saw. Of course it might have been the devil and his brother; anyway they belonged to that family. I got by those things. I didn't debate a minute, but went home as fast as my legs could carry me, emptying my pockets as I ran, which I had always heard the darkeys say would keep off witches. There was a short way home by the grave-yard, but I didn't take it. I kept to the big road, and when I did get home, I didn't wait to go around to the door, but went right in the open window where my mother was. She said that I had imagined everything, but I hadn't. There was no imagination about it."

Curiously enough, soon after this happened a

little flock of school-children passing near the same rail fence in daylight, saw something that scared them so badly that some of them fainted. But by this time Bill Jess had gathered himself, and taking his gun he loaded it heavily and went devil hunting. However, without success.

In spite of this slight lapse, young McDonald probably considered himself a man, now. We have seen that he was already calling on the young ladies, and in the locality where he lived an ability to drink whiskey was regarded as another manly achievement. There was a small still-house located not far from his home, and he got into the habit of visiting it and of tasting the output. One day he tasted too much and did not return either in good season or condition. When his mother prepared to administer punishment, he pulled away from her and stated that he would not take a whipping. But Eunice McDonald was not one to condone such rebellion. She put away the rod and bided her time. One night when Bill Jess was fast asleep she wrapped and pinned him securely in a sheet and laid on such a thrashing as gave him a permanent distaste both for liquor and disobedience.

At another time it was attentions paid to a young lady that got him into difficulties. The young lady was the sister of his school teacher, and the latter did not approve of anything resembling attachment between the two. One day the young wooer wrote a letter in school, and passing it down the line it unluckily fell under the eye of the teacher, who captured and read it, forthwith.

" I'll settle with you at recess, sir," he said, nailing Bill Jess to the seat with his eye.

Bill Jess didn't care to have him settle. He was willing to let the account run right along, and to knock off the interest. He decided not to wait. The teacher had his back to the board, working out something hard, when Bill Jess went away. He didn't rush wildly. He didn't even run—not exactly —but he lost no time, tip-toeing out of there. Neither did he go home. He'd gone home once in disgrace, and he remembered what had happened. Eunice McDonald's combination of sheet and horse-whip offered no fresh inducements in that direction. He walked twenty miles to a saw-mill and got a job. Then, by and by, everything blew over; everybody was sorry, and he returned home to forgiveness and safety. A cyclone hit the school-house for some reason or other about this time and demolished it, Bill Jess being raked out of the debris undamaged in any particular. Perhaps this was vindication.

IV

The Making of a Texan

RECONSTRUCTION AND " TREASON." " DAVE " CULBER-
SON TO THE RESCUE. EDUCATION, MARRIAGE
AND POLITICS

But though still a boy in years, being not more than sixteen, his youth really came to an end now. It was the period of Reconstruction in the South— a time of obnoxious enforcements on the one hand, and rebellious bitterness on the other, with general lawlessness in the back settlements. The military dominated the towns and there were continuous misunderstandings between the still resentful conquered and the aggressive and sometimes insolent conquerors. Young McDonald, with the memory of his hero father, shot dead while leading his regiment against these men in blue, was in no frame of mind to submit to any indignity, real or fancied, at their hands. It happened just at this time that one Colonel Greene, a relative of the McDonalds, was murdered by negroes, who, being arrested, confessed the killing, stating that they had mistaken Greene for a mule-buyer supposed to have a large sum of money. The men were lodged in jail, but it was believed that under the " carpet-bag " military law then prevailing they would escape punishment. In later years, young McDonald was to become one of the most strenuous defenders of official procedure —one of the bitterest opponents of lynch-law the State of Texas has ever known; but he was hot-blooded in 'sixty-eight, and the situation was not one to develop moral principles. When, therefore, a mob formed and took the negroes out of jail and hanged them, there is no record of Bill Jesse having distinguished himself in their defense as he certainly would have done in later years. Indeed, it is likely that if he did not help pull a rope that night it was only because the rope was fully occupied with other willing hands.

Of course the military descended on Henderson and set in to discipline it for this concerted lawlessness. The townspeople as a whole, and the relatives of Colonel Greene in particular, resented this occupation. Charley Greene, a brother of the murdered man, in company with Bill Jess, presently got into trouble with some soldiers who were deporting themselves in a manner considered offensive, and the result was a running fight with the military in the lead. The soldiers made for their quarters in the court-house. It would have been proper to leave them alone, then—to retire flushed with victory, as the books say, and satisfied. But Greene could not rest. He persuaded Bill Jess to stay with him, and they rode up and down in front of the court-house, occasionally taking a shot at the windows, to punctuate their challenge to warfare. Finally Greene decided that they could charge the court-house and capture it. He primed himself with liquor for the onset, and refused to heed his companion's advice to abandon the campaign. The two ascended the court-house stairs, at last, with pistols cocked. Greene had one in each hand and, with them, shoved open the double doors at the head of the stairs. That was another mistake. The soldiers were " laying for him " just inside, and in an instant later his arms were pinioned, and he was a prisoner. The doors swung to, then, and Bill Jess stood outside, wondering whether he ought to charge to the rescue, wait there and be captured, or retire in good order. With that gift of logic and rare presence of mind which would one day make him famous, he decided to get out of there. He had a plan for organizing a rescue party, and did in fact get a crowd together, but in the meantime, under cover of rain and darkness, the soldiers had taken their prisoner from Henderson and he was well on the way to Jefferson, where there was a stockade. No attempt was made at the time to arrest young McDonald, though soldiers frequently loitered about his home premises, and with these he had many collisions, usually coming off victorious. He was strong, wiry and fearless, and he had then, as always, that piercing eye and a manner of going straight at things without flutter or hesitation.

Still, he was laying up trouble for himself, for

Greene's court-martial was coming off, and Bill Jess, who went over to see if he could be of any assistance, was promptly arrested while nosing about the stockade, and landed with his relative on the inside. This was a serious matter. The boy realized that it was, as soon as the gates closed behind him. He realized it still more forcibly when a few days later he and Greene were led into the court-house for military trial, and he took a look at the men who were to prosecute him for aiding in the crime of treason. Nor was he reassured when one of the lawyers present announced that he would " defend that boy's case." For there was nothing inspiring about this champion's appearance. Nothing about him except his generosity seemed worth while. He wore ill-fitting homespun clothes, smoked a common clay pipe and his long hair straggled down over his forehead. His shirt collar was carelessly unbuttoned, and his trousers, too short for him, revealed common home-knit yarn socks. Moreover, his eyes were half-closed and he had a general air of sleepy indifference which did not disappear until it came his turn to take part in the proceedings. Then suddenly the sleepy eyes became alive, the shaggy hair was tossed back, the clay pipe was laid on the table, and Dave Culberson, afterward known as an eminent lawyer and statesman, arose and made such a plea in behalf of the boy whose father had died at Corinth, and whose mother and sister relied on him to-day for protection, that only one verdict remained in the minds of his hearers when he closed. Bill Jess was acquitted, but his relative, Charley Greene, was less fortunate. He remained in a Northern prison several years before he was finally released. Dave Culberson afterward represented his district in Congress, and the boy he defended eventually served the son, Charles A. Culberson—then Governor—now, in 1909, United States Senator from Texas.

It is likely that this bit of experience with hot-headed lawlessness, and the result thereof, proved of immense value to young McDonald. From that time forward we find him a peace-maker, a queller of disturbances, a separator of combatants, even at great personal risk. He had never been a seeker after trouble and he seemed now to develop a natural talent for preserving the peace. Wherever guns are drawn, and they were drawn pretty frequently and upon small provocation in that day and locality, he stepped in without hesitation and the would-be slayers were disarmed by what seemed a veritable sleight-of-hand. In 1871, when he was nineteen years old, he decided to follow a commercial life, and with the money saved from the sale of the wood he had cut and hauled, he took a course in Soule's Commercial College, at New Orleans, graduating in 1872. Penmanship came easy to him, and upon his return to Henderson he taught a writing class. Within the year he was able to establish a small store in connection with the ferry at Brown's

Bluff on the Sabine River, between Henderson and Longview. Here, with his ferry assistant he kept bachelor's hall, not the most congenial existence, perhaps, for one with his natural leaning toward female society. At all events, he gave it up, by and by, and after a brief sojourn in Longview established himself in Wood County, at Mineola, then a newly established and busy railway terminus. This was in 1875, and his venture was a success. Soon he was considered the leading grocer of the town.

It was during this period that McDonald made the acquaintance of James S. Hogg, who in later life, as Governor of Texas, was to confer his most useful official appointment—that of Ranger Captain, thus enabling him to do much of the work which has identified his name with the State's constructive history. Hogg, then a young man, was Justice of the Peace at the county-seat, Quitman, a few miles distant from Mineola, and was also conducting a paper there. He bought his groceries of McDonald, and the account ran along in a go-as-you-please sort of a way. They were good friends, and courted together, and it was through Hogg that young McDonald met Miss Rhoda Isabel Carter, a young woman with fine nerve and force of character—just the girl for a Texas regulator's wife. And such, in due season, she was to become, for he married her in January, 1876. His friendship for Hogg continued for some time after that, but came to a

sudden end, one day, when Hogg, who had been
elected County Attorney, with characteristic con-
scientiousness prosecuted McDonald and others for
carrying concealed weapons—McDonald's possession of such a weapon having been revealed through
his aiding in the capture of a gang of boisterous
disturbers of the peace. McDonald rose and defended his own case, declaring he had quit business
to do his duty as a good citizen, and that he would
stay in jail the balance of his days before he would
pay a fine.

With his usual frank fearlessness he said some
hard things to Hogg in the presence of the court,
and though discharged, the two were estranged for
a considerable period. Then a truce was patched
up, but only for a time. Both were sharply interested in politics and on opposing sides in the con-
gressional convention. They were near coming to
blows over their differences, and were only separated
by the intervention of friends. It is not pleasant
to record this of these two worthy men, but after all
they were only human beings, and young, and then
the sequel makes it still further worth while.

V

The Beginning of Reform

SUBDUING A BAD MAN. FIRST OFFICIAL APPOINTMENT.
A DEPUTY WHO DID THINGS. " BILL " MC DONALD
AND " JIM " HOGG

But now came Bill McDonald's first official appointment and service. Living just outside of Mineola was a man named Golden, alias George Gordon, of hard character, and the owner of several bulldogs, similarly endowed. Man and dogs became a menace to travel in that neighborhood, as they lived near a public road and were allowed at large. The man was particularly quarrelsome and ugly and was said to have killed several more or less inoffensive persons. He always carried arms—the customary pistol, and a bowie knife—the latter worn in a scabbard " down his back." He was an expert at throwing this weapon, and altogether a terror to the community. Bill McDonald would naturally resent the domination of a man like Gordon, and when one day the latter came to town with one of his unruly bulldogs, and the dog set upon and injured McDonald's prized pointer, there was trouble, active and immediate. McDonald's reputation as a good man to let alone was already established at Mineola. He was known as a capable marksman—fearless, resolute and very sudden. When, therefore, he produced a six-shooter for the avowed purpose of killing the bulldog, its master, who, like every bully by trade, was a coward at heart, interceded humbly for the dog's life, promising to take the animal home and leave him there. McDonald agreed to the arrangement, but for the benefit of the community at large he promptly applied to Sheriff Pete Dowell for a commission as deputy, in order that in future he might restrain officially the obnoxious Gordon and others of his kind. The commission was promptly conferred, and thus Bill Jess McDonald, quietly and without any special manifest, stepped into the ranks of Texas official regulators, where, in one capacity or another, he was to serve so long and well.

But, however quiet his enlistment, his service was to be of another sort. Those were not quiet days, and the officer who set out to enforce the law was apt to become a busy person. Gordon very soon appeared again in Mineola, and after investing in a good deal of bad whisky, went on the war-path, flourishing a six-shooter and giving out the information that nobody could arrest him. He was in the very midst of a militant harangue when Deputy McDonald suddenly appeared on the scene, and before Gordon could gather himself, he was, by some magic " twist of the wrist," disarmed, arrested and on the way to the calaboose. He demurred and resisted, but slept that night behind lock and bars. Next morning he refused breakfast and demanded release. Deputy McDonald left him in a mixed condition of reflection and profanity, returning at noon to find him sober, subdued and hungry. Upon promise of good behavior for the future, he was taken before a justice, where he pled guilty and paid a fine. Then he took his place as the first example of a long line of wonderful cures set down to Captain Bill McDonald's credit, to-day; for he gave little trouble after that and remained mostly in retirement, to be set upon, at last, by his own dogs, who inflicted terrible wounds. His death soon afterward was thought to be the result of this attack.

But the Gordon experience was mild enough, after all, compared with the many which followed, and is only set down because it marks the beginning of a career. Indeed, an episode of larger proportions was already under way. In the timber lying adjacent to Mineola, some three hundred tie-cutters were encamped, supplying cross-ties for the I. & G. N. road. They were a drinking, lawless lot, and on Saturday nights the Mineola streets were filled with riot and disorder. The city marshal, George Reeves, and Deputy McDonald had on several occasions made arrests and such enforcement of the law had been regarded by the tie-gang as an affront to all. They sent word to the officers, at last, that they would be on hand in full force, on the following Saturday, and

that the calaboose might as well go out of commission, so far as they were concerned.

Saturday night came, and according to promise the
tie-cutters were on the street, numerous and noisy.
McDonald and Reeves were among them, keeping a
general lookout for trouble, not always together.
The saloons were full, presently, and the men getting
constantly more noisy and quarrelsome. Seeing a
commotion at the rear of a cheap hotel where a number of the men had gathered, McDonald went over
there, and found Reeves surrounded. Without hesitation he shoved a way through, with his pistol,
until he stood by Reeves's side. Reeves had arrested a man, and a general riot was imminent.
The prisoner was very drunk and disorderly and
demanding that he be allowed to go to his room
before accompanying the officer. Of course the
whole intention was to precipitate a general fight,
during which the officers were to be pummeled and
battered to a jelly. Catching the drift of matters,
McDonald said:

" All right, take him to his room, if he's got one.
I'll take care of this crowd."

There was something in the business-like confidence of that statement which impressed the crowd.
And then he had such a handy way of holding a
six-shooter. Nobody quite wanted to die first, and
Reeves started for the back entrance of the hotel
with his man. As they entered the door the fellow
reeled against the casing and fell to the ground.

Then a general stampede started, for it was called out that Reeves had struck him. McDonald said:

" Stop you fellers! The fool fell down. I'll shoot the first man that interferes! "

That was another discouraging statement from a man who had a habit of keeping his word. It seemed to the crowd that an officer like that didn't play fair. He didn't argue at all. Somebody was likely to get hurt, if they didn't get that gun away from him. Movements to this end were started here and there, but they didn't get near enough to the chief actor to be effective. Finally when Reeves and his prisoner set out for the calaboose, the crowd moved in that direction, timing their steps to a chorus of threats and profanity. Reeves and McDonald made no reply until they arrived at the lock-up; then, the disturbers being there handy, the officers began gathering them in, a dozen at a time. It was a genuine surprise-party for the tie-men. They were too much astonished for any concerted movement, and when invited at the points of those guns to step inside and make themselves at home, they did not have the bad taste to refuse.

" Step in, gentlemen; always room for one more," might have been the form of the invitation, but it wasn't. It was a Bill McDonald invitation and it was full of compliments and promises that burnt holes wherever they hit anything. The calaboose was full in a brief time and a box-car on a near-by switch was used as an annex. By the time it was full, there were no more disturbers. The outer edges had melted away. The woods were full of them. The turbulent tie-men of Texas were sober and sensible by Monday morning and allowed to go, under promise of good behavior, and upon payment of adequate fines.

Mineola suddenly became a moral town. Amusements of the old sort languished. Drunk or sober, it was humiliating to flourish a gun, only to be suddenly disarmed and marched to the calaboose by a man who acted as if he thought he was gun-proof. It was hard to understand—it was supernatural. It was better to go to the next town to flourish the gun.

But by this time Deputy Bill Jess was not satisfied with the quiet life. He had found his proper vocation—that of active enforcement of the law—and he was moved to pursue it in remoter places. A certain desperate outlaw, a white man by the name of Jim Bean, had committed crimes in Smith County, whence he had escaped to Kansas. There he had killed a city marshal and returned once more to Smith County, which adjoins Wood on the south. The officers of Smith County had surprised Jim Bean and his brother Ed, at a small station where they had gone to rob some freight cars, but the two men had handled their revolvers so desperately that they had been allowed to escape, and pursuit of them had been abandoned.

This was the kind of game that Deputy Bill always enjoyed hunting. It was worth while. He made frequent still-hunts along the Sabine River, the dividing line between Wood and Smith, hoping to locate his quarry on the side of his jurisdiction. Perhaps the men knew of these excursions and remained safely, as they believed, on the other side. At last, however, the temptation to cross the line became too strong for a hunter like Bill Jess. The impulse of the Ranger was already upon him. He crossed the Sabine River into Smith, with his Winchester on his saddle, and became an official poacher. The river bottom was overgrown in places with tall cane-brake, and he had reason to believe that the Beans were hiding, and storing their loot, in the dense growth. He had heard a rumor, too, that a certain family of swamp-dwellers (negroes) were in league with the men, and, reflecting on the matter, he concluded to visit this house, both for the purpose of investigation, and to borrow a shot-gun, which he thought might be more useful, in a man-chase through a thick cane-brake swamp, than his rifle. Arriving at the suspected house, he told in his mildest manner a tale of a wounded deer not far away, and borrowed a shot-gun, as well as the information that the men and dogs of the place were in the brakes. He now began a careful still-hunt for his game, and presently came full upon Jim Bean, who was on a horse, with a shot-gun, guarding some stolen hogs. Bean was a great burly creature, more animal than man, from having lived and slept so long in the woods and brakes. He had been shot at many times, and had been desperately wounded, but such was his natural vitality, and so hardened was he by exposure that it seemed impossible to kill him.

Before Bean could move, now, Deputy McDonald had him covered and commanded him to get off his horse or he would shoot him dead. Bean obeyed and McDonald threw his own leg over his saddle and slid to the ground, still covering Bean with his gun. Suddenly Bean made a dash for a large tree, turning to shoot just as he reached this cover. McDonald was too quick, however, and let go with two loads of buckshot, which struck Bean in several places, knocking him down. He then made off in the direction of a slough, toward thick hiding. The shot-gun was a muzzle loader and before McDonald could get it charged again he heard somebody coming through the brush. It was Ed Bean and some negroes. He was ready for them by the time they came in sight, and throwing his gun to position he commanded them to halt. Instead of doing so they turned and disappeared in the direction from which they had come. McDonald now mounted his horse and started in pursuit of the wounded Jim Bean. He found where he had crossed the slough, and presently came to the desperado's gun, which had been thrown away in his hurry. Blood-stains made the trail easy to follow. Soon a powder-horn and then a pair of boots lay in the path of flight. McDonald followed six miles to a cabin occupied by negroes. Bean was not in the cabin, but barefoot prints led into the woods. The man-hunter followed them and finally overtook their owner. It was not Bean. The officer had been tricked—Bean had escaped while his pursuer had been following this false lead. It was dark, now, and further search was hopeless. Next morning the outlaws had vanished from the country. They never returned and were heard of no more until some time after, when news came from Wise County that both the Bean brothers had been killed, resisting arrest.

While this episode did not turn out altogether successfully, inasmuch as the game got away, it had a better result in that it effected a complete reconciliation between McDonald and his old, and what was to be his lifetime friend, James S. Hogg. Certain jealous officials were bent upon making trouble for the young deputy for overstepping his authority by working outside of his own county, and especially for shooting a man in attempting an illegal arrest. McDonald held that the conditions justified his act, and was going to make his fight on that ground. But it never came to a fight, for when the matter was brought to the notice of the grand jury, Hogg, by this time District Attorney, went before that body, and regardless of the old animosity between McDonald and himself, and of the fact that they were not yet on speaking terms, declared that if the jury found an indictment against the deputy for so worthy an undertaking as that which, irregular or not, had resulted in ridding the country of a gang of outlaws, he would *nolle pros* the case—in other words, he would refuse to prosecute.

When McDonald heard of this, he went to his old friend at once.

" Jim," he said, " you're a gentleman, and I know I want to act right. Let's not be enemies any more." And they never were.

Ten years later, Jim Hogg, as Governor of Texas, would make it possible for Bill McDonald to bring down criminals in any county of that mighty State. But this is further along in our story.

VI

Into the Wilderness

A NEW BUSINESS IN A NEW LAND. A " SAND-LAPPER " SHOWS HIS SAND

HARD times came on in Mineola. Railroad building was at an end; crops failed; men who had bought goods on long credit could not pay. " Bill " McDonald, as he was now usually called, had been one to carry long lines of credit for his customers, and he was hurt accordingly. He gave up business, at last, and in 1883 invested in cattle whatever remained to him, and set his steps further westward where there was free grass. He headed toward Wichita County, which was almost an unknown land in that day, driving his cattle before him, his young wife at his side, both eager to begin a new life in a new land.

To drive cattle across the wild Texas prairies, twenty-five years ago, was an experience worth while. There were no fences, no boundaries and few roads. Settlers were far between. The climate in any season was likely to be mild; the air was pure and stimulating; society, such as it was, had not many conventions.

Yet, few and fundamental as were the conditions, they were of a sort to develop sudden situations, and

one had to be ready to face them fairly and firmly
or write himself down as unfit for the wild free
life of the range. The grass was free, but there
were always those who wanted to form a trust of its
vast areas and make trespassers of the smaller men.
McDonald had scarcely located his herd and pitched
his tent when two of these magnates notified him
that he had better move. It was a bluff, of course,
and the man who had been deputy sheriff for half
a dozen years and purified a bad community was the
wrong man to use it on. He asked in that quiet way
of his, to let him have a look at their titles, and when
they could not produce them, he added that he
thought he'd stay where he was. They began to
tell him of some of the things that were likely to
happen if he did that, but he did not seem impressed
by the information. He repeated that he would stay
where he was, and that anyone who did not wish to
be in his neighborhood had his permission to move
on, to other free grass. Perhaps they looked him
over a bit more carefully, then, and noticed the pecu-
liarity of his nose and of his eyes, and the handy
and casual way he had of picking off the heads of
rattlesnakes and such things, with a six-shooter,
while he talked. At all events they did not refer to
the matter again and even cultivated his friendship.
In a neighborhood where cattle thieves were beginning to be troublesome a man like that would be
handy to have around. They were to have an example presently of his willingness and ability to

defend the rights of ownership—a small example, but convincing.

It was no easy matter to keep a herd intact in those days. In a land of free grass, where the cost of cattle was chiefly the expense of herding, it was not likely that the moral title to the cattle themselves would be very highly regarded, especially where brands had been obliterated, or where a few strays mingled with a larger herd. The outlaw pure and simple was bad enough, but to the newcomer with a small bunch of " cows " (cattle, regardless of gender), the vast roaming herd, guarded by a veritable army of punchers whose respect for any law was small enough, was an even greater menace. McDonald knew of these conditions, and when, soon after his arrival, some of his cattle strayed away, he set out to inspect the surrounding herds. After riding some distance he came upon a large drove, evidently on its way to market. It was about noon and the men were " rounding-in " for dinner. McDonald started to address a herder, when the man turned abruptly and started off. McDonald immediately began looking through the cattle, whereupon the herder wheeled.

" What do you want in there? " he asked roughly.

" I was looking for hobbled horses," was the easy reply. The puncher made some surly comment and rode away.

McDonald, presently satisfied that his stray cattle were not with that portion of the drove, continued

his search further along and came up with the
" chuck-wagon " where dinner was being prepared.
Cow-men are hospitable and the foreman invited
him to dismount and join them. He did so, and a
little later the surly puncher came in, giving the
camp guest anything but a friendly look. In the
course of the meal the visitor was ·asked where he
was from.

" Mineola," he said, " Wood County." The surly
herder spoke up.

" These d—d sand-lappers (east-Texans) are getting too thick out here."

McDonald set down his coffee.

" The d—d skunks and prairie dogs are already
too thick," he said.

An instant later the puncher had out his pistol,
but the sand-lapper was still quicker. The puncher
was covered before he could bring his weapon to
bear. McDonald said:

" Turn it loose! Drop it! "

The herder still clutched the weapon which he was
afraid to raise. The sand-lapper stepped nearer to
him, and with a sudden movement rapped him
smartly on the head with the heavy barrel of his
six-shooter. It was a thing that as a deputy he had
done often, and it was always effective. The
puncher dropped his gun. One of his comrades
sprang to his assistance, but was covered and disarmed with amazing suddenness. The foreman interfered, now, and the beginner of the disturbance

INTRODUCING REFORM IN THE WILDERNESS.

"He was disarmed with amazing suddenness."

was led away to a brook to have his head bathed and bandaged; whereupon the sand-lapper quietly finished his dinner, thanked his host, continued the search for his missing stock, and when he had found them, set out for home. Meeting a group of punchers among which was his surly friend with a now bandaged head, he expected further trouble. Nothing happened. The sand-lapper and his missing cows had the right of way.

VII

Commercial Ventures and Adventures

BILL MCDONALD'S METHOD OF COLLECTING A BILL; AND HIS METHOD OF HANDLING BAD MEN

THE inclination to commercial enterprise still survived. At the end of a year McDonald sold his cattle and invested in the lumber business at Wichita Falls—another railway terminus, dropped down in the prairie, with a population of about two thousand, at that time. A little later he established a branch business at Harrold when the railway reached that point. Two big lumber yards were already established at Wichita Falls, and the competition was strenuous. It was a brief experience for McDonald, for he presently yearned for the freer life of the range, and soon abandoned commerce, once more, for cattle—this time for good. Yet the experience was not without valuable return, inasmuch as it established for him in Wichita Falls, quickly and permanently, a reputation of a useful kind in a country where law and order are likely to be of an elemental, go-as-you-please sort. It happened in this wise:

There was a merchant in Baylor County, Texas, to whom Lumberman McDonald sold a good bill, on time. The account ran along, until one day the county judge of Baylor, one Melvin, dropped in and stated that he had called to settle the amount for his neighbor. He gave his own check for it and McDonald supposed the matter had ended. A few days later the bank returned Melvin's check as worthless. Evidently the quiet unobtrusive life which Bill Jess had been living as a lumber merchant had given the impression that he was an inoffensive person who would pocket a loss rather than make trouble, especially with a county judge, who added to his official prestige the reputation of being a very bad man from "far up Bitter Creek." However, this impression was a mistake. McDonald ascertained that his customer had really sent the money by Melvin, to pay his bill, and considered what he ought to do. Morally, perhaps legally, he could have demanded payment a second time, on the ground that the said customer, being acquainted with Melvin, should have selected a more reliable messenger. But that was not the Bill McDonald way. What he did was to write to Melvin, demanding an explanation; adding in pretty positive terms that he expected immediate settlement. No reply came and a second and a third letter followed, each getting more definite as to phrase. Then one day Melvin and certain henchmen from Baylor appeared on the streets of Wichita Falls. McDonald who had heard of their arrival, suddenly confronted Melvin and delivered himself in whatever terms and emphasis as he had on hand at the moment. Melvin withdrew, gathered his clans and laid for McDonald in a saloon where the latter had to pass. Though previously warned of the ambush, McDonald did pass, with the result that next morning Melvin settled his bill in full, paid for a glass door that he had broken, and a fine and costs amounting to sixty-five dollars, for carrying concealed weapons. What really happened to Melvin is best told in Bill Jess's own testimony when that same morning he had, himself, been summoned to answer a charge for carrying concealed weapons, disturbing the peace, and for assault—said action being the result of Melvin's judicial pull. Arriving at the court-room the prosecuting attorney asked McDonald if he had a lawyer.

"No," he said, "I don't need anybody to defend me for knocking that scoundrel over. I'll attend to my own case, whatever is necessary."

The attorney then stated the charge to the court. Bill Jess waited until he was through and then asked permission to speak.

"Your honor," he said, rising, "I'm a busy man with no time to be fooling around this way with men who give bogus checks and steal horses and such like, but if your honor will spare about a minute I'll tell the court what happened." He then gave a history of the lumber transaction, and added the sequel, as follows:

"When I wrote him as strong a letter as I could frame up, and as would go through the mail, he

came down with a crowd of what he thought was
fighting men, and I met him and tried like a gentleman to persuade him to settle up and to convince
him what a dad-blamed rascal he was; which he
pled guilty to, and didn't deny. Then he gathers
his feeble bunch of fighters together, arms them up
with six-shooters and corrals them in Bill Holly's
saloon, that I had to pass, going home. I met
Johnny Hammond who tried to persuade me not to
take that street—said those fellows were up there
and I'd better go in some other direction. I said
I wasn't in the habit of going out of my way for
such cattle, and proceeded on up the street. When
I got in front of Bill Holly's, Melvin and his war-
riors stepped out. Melvin wanted an explanation
of my former remarks, and I gave it to him and
added some more which I would not like to mention
in the presence of the court. Then he pulled out a
big white-handled forty-five six-shooter, but being
a little slow with it, I grabbed it by the barrel and
hit him with my fist two or three times, which kind
of jarred him loose from his gun. Then I gave him
a rap on the head with it and knocked him through
Bill Holly's glass-front door, into the saloon. His
pals pulled their guns, but I covered them with the
one I took away from Melvin and they nearly broke
the furniture to pieces getting out of there. I didn't
see any more of any of them until next morning.
Then I looked up the bunch and got a check in
full, with interest, from Melvin, and made him pay

Bill Holly five dollars for his glass door. So far as carrying a gun is concerned, I had one, and I got another from this fellow here who had pulled it on me. I took it away from him and hit him with it, and I have the same here in my possession now, to turn over to the Court.''

Bill Jess reached down somewhere and drawing forth the big white handled six-shooter, laid it down in front of the court. Then suddenly turning upon Melvin who was present, he looked him straight through.

'' Melvin, is not all I have told the Court true? '' he demanded.

Melvin found himself unable to tell anything but the truth, just then.

'' Yes, sir,'' he said, quite meekly.

McDonald was discharged and Melvin paid a fine as before noted. Following this incident came another which solidified Bill McDonald's reputation for nerve, in Wichita Falls. Bill Holly, the afore-mentioned—whose name in another part of the State had been Buck Holly, which he forgot when he left East Texas, after getting into a mix-up, during which the other man died—one day absorbed an overdose of his own stock-in-trade and set forth to shoot up the town. He went afoot and let go at things generally, emptying the streets and bringing business to a standstill. The city marshal was organizing a posse to take him, and summoned McDonald, when McDonald said:

" Give me the key to the calaboose, and the'
won't be no need of a posse."

He took the key in one hand and a six-shooter in
the other; marched up to where Holly was prac-
ticing on front-doors and hardware signs; struck
the gun close up under the nose of the disturber,
and with his quick magic, disarmed him and set out
with him for the lockup. Holly begged and pleaded
and was finally locked in a room in the hotel. He
broke a window before morning and promptly paid
for it by McDonald's request. He made a fairly
quiet citizen during the remainder of McDonald's
stay in Wichita Falls.

Removing to Hardeman County was the only
thing that saved Bill McDonald from being drafted
into official service where he was. Law abiding citizens with his gifts are scarce enough anywhere, and
they were needed in the cattle districts of Texas.
There was not much law in those parts, none at all
outside of the towns. In the countries bordering
on Indian Territory and up through the Pan-handle
a man had to " stand pat " whatever his hand, and
hold his own by strength of arm and quickness of
trigger. Cow thieves and cut-throats abounded.
Officials often worked in accord with them, or were
afraid to prosecute. The man who would neither
co-operate with outlaws nor condone their offences
was already on the ground and would presently be
in the field. It was a wide field and a fruitful one
and the harvest was ripe for the gathering.

Hardeman County was a tough locality in the early eighties. It had lately been organized, and the settlers were cow-men, cow-boys and gamblers —lawless enough, themselves—and another element, which pretended to be these things, but in reality consisted of outlaws, pure and simple. The latter lived chiefly off of the herds, driving off horses and cattle and hiding them in remote and inaccessible places. Often cattle were butchered; their hides, which were marked with brand and ear-marks were destroyed to avoid identification, and the meat was sold. Men who did these things were known well enough, but went unapprehended for the reasons named. In certain sections of the Territory itself and in No-man's Land (a piece of disputed ground lying to the north of the Pan-handle, now a part of Oklahoma) matters were even worse. In these places there was hardly a semblance of law. Certainly the need of active reform—of an official crusader, without fear and above reproach—was both wide and vociferous.

VIII

THE KIND OF MEN TO BE REFORMED. EARLY REFORMS
IN QUANAH. BAD MEN MEET THEIR MATCH

IT was in 1885 that Bill McDonald disposed of his
lumber interests in Wichita Falls and at Harrold,
reinvested in cattle and set out once more for the
still farther west. He had filed on some school-land
on Wanderer's Creek in Hardeman County, about
four miles from where the town of Quanah now
stands, and in the heart of what was then the wilderness. Somewhat previous to this, McDonald, whose
reputation as a man of nerve had traveled to Harrold, was one night called upon by Ranger Lieutenant Sam Platt to assist in handling a gang of
outlaws, known as the Brooken Band, that infested
the neighborhood. The Brookens had ridden into
Harrold and were running things in pretty much
their own way. Platt and McDonald promptly
bore down upon them and a running fight ensued
as the Brookens retreated. About one hundred
shots were fired altogether, but it was dark and the
range was too great for accuracy. Nothing was accomplished, but the event marked the beginning of
a warfare between Bill McDonald and a band of

cut-throats, the end of which would be history. It was soon after this first skirmish that McDonald sold out his lumber business and set out for his Hardeman County ranch. As on his former migration he drove his cattle to the new land, and after the first hard day's drive, camped at nightfall in a pleasant spot where grass was plentiful and water handy. It seemed a good place, and man and beast gladly halted for food and rest.

But next morning there was trouble. When preparations for an early start were under headway, it was suddenly discovered that four of the best horses and a fine Newfoundland dog were missing. Investigation of the surrounding country was made, and two of the horses were found astray, evidently having broken loose from their captors. It was further discovered that the Brooken Band had a rendezvous in what was known as the Cedar-brakes, a stretch of rough country, densely covered with scrubby cedar, located about twelve miles to the south westward. McDonald naturally felt that it was again his " move " in the Brooken game, but it did not seem expedient to stop the journey with the herd and undertake the move, just then, so biding his time he pushed on, to his land on Wanderer's Creek, where he established his ranch, fenced his property, built a habitation for himself and the wife who was always ready to follow him into the wilderness; then he rode over to Margaret, at that time the county-seat, and asked Sheriff Jim Alley—a good man with his hands over full—to appoint him deputy that he might begin the work which clearly must be done in that country before it could become a proper habitation for law abiding citizens. The commission was readily granted, and from that appointment dates " that tired feeling " which the bad men of Texas began to have when they heard the sound of Bill McDonald's name.

Another word as to the kind of men with which an officer in those days had to deal. They were not ordinary malefactors, but choice selections from the world at large. " What was your name before you came to Texas? " was a common inquiry in those earlier days, and it was often added that a man could go to Texas when he couldn't go anywhere else. It was such a big State, with so many remote fastnesses, so many easy escapes across the borders. It was the natural last resort of men who could not live elsewhere with safety or profit. There is a story of a man arrested in Texas in those days for some misdemeanor, who was advised by his lawyer to leave the State without delay.

" But where shall I go? " asked the troubled offender, " I'm in *Texas, now.*"

They were the men who had borne other names before they came to Texas and who were " in Texas, now," because they could not live elsewhere and keep off of the scaffold, that Bill McDonald undertook to exterminate. He was willing to undertake the task single handed, if necessary, and in reality did much of his work in that manner, as we shall see.

With his commission in his pocket Bill Jess was not long in getting down to his favorite employment, that of man-hunting. He began quietly, for he wanted to identify some of the men nearer at hand who were in one way and another connected with the Cedar-brakes gang. Bill Brooken, a notorious outlaw, was the head of the band, and his brother Bood was one of its chief members. The Brookens were wanted not only for cattle stealing, but for train-robbing and murder, as well. A certain Bull Turner was one of their victims. Turner was said to have been one of the Brooken gang at an earlier time, but had abandoned that way of life and made an effort to become a decent citizen. The gang believed he had given information, and somewhat later when he was driving across the country with a prominent stockman—a Hebrew named Lazarus—the Brookens and half a dozen of their followers suddenly dashed out of a roadside concealment and began firing. Turner was instantly killed, and Lazarus fell over the dash-board in a wild effort to get behind something. The frightened horses, one of them wounded in the foot, ran madly all the way to town with Lazarus still clinging to the whiffletrees. He received no injury, but acquired a scare which was permanent.

With the assistance of Sheriff Alley—also short a horse, through the industries of the Brooken gang

—and one Pat Wolforth, who was acquainted with certain of the silent partners of the outlaws and stood ready to give information, several arrests were made, presently, and trouble filled the air.

Threatening letters now began to come to the new deputy, warning him against further procedure— promising him death and torture of many varieties if he did not suspend operations. Such letters always stimulated Bill McDonald to renewed enterprise. He redoubled his efforts and brought in offenders of various kinds almost daily. Cattle stealers began to migrate to other counties. Their friends and beneficiaries grew nervous.

Meantime, the railroad had reached Hardeman and the town of Quanah—named for Chief Quanah Parker, son of the historic Cynthia Ann Parker— had sprung up. It was the typical tough place and certain bad men still at large came there to proclaim vengeance and to " lay " for the men who were making them trouble. Among these disturbers was one John Davidson of Wilbarger County, on the borders of which the Cedar-brakes gang was located. Davidson was reputed to have killed several men and was believed to be an accessory of the Brooken Band, but was thus far not positively identified, and remained unapprehended. He did not hesitate, however, to boast of his always being armed and ready for men like Bill McDonald, and especially for Pat Wolforth who was getting good friends and neighbors into trouble.

Davidson appeared presently on the streets of Quanah, flourishing his firearms and making his boasts. McDonald suddenly arrived on the scene, and without any parley whatever stepped quickly up to Davidson and disarmed him so suddenly that the terror of Wilbarger stood dazed, and did not recover himself until he was half way to the office of justice, where he paid a fine. It was an unusual proceeding. It was unprecedented. The customary thing was a noisy warfare of words, followed by a general shooting, with the bad man in possession when the smoke had cleared away. This new method was prosaic. Davidson couldn't understand it at all. He tried it again the next week, with the same result. He kept on trying it, and each time settled for his amusement with a fine. Why he did not kill somebody he couldn't understand. He never seemed to get in action before Bill McDonald had his gun and was marching him to the " Captain's Office." Finally he got himself appointed Deputy Sheriff of Wilbarger and. came triumphantly to Quanah, with his commission, which he believed would entitle him to carry arms. Met suddenly, as usual, by McDonald and promptly disarmed, he flourished his commission.

" That's all right, Bill McDonald, but I'm fixed for you this time. Give me back that gun."

McDonald said:

" Your commission won't do you much good up here. If Sheriff Barker wants to appoint a man

that throws in with thieves, all right. But in Hardeman County we don't have to recognize him.''

There was never such a stubborn man, Davidson
decided, as that fool deputy, Bill McDonald. He
decided to wait until McDonald should be absent,
and then have it out with Wolforth. When the time
came, Davidson brought a gang along with him and
they followed Wolforth about with pestering remarks, until their victim suddenly grew tired of the
annoyance, and opened fire. This was unexpected
and the gang retired for reorganization. Then some
rangers, quartered at Quanah, appeared on the
scene, and Wolforth was put under arrest. He was
taken before a justice, who fixed his bond at a thousand dollars, which he was unable to raise, because
of the dread in which Davidson and his crowd were
held. It was just about this moment that Deputy
McDonald returned, and the Rangers delivered
Wolforth into his hands.

'' What's the matter, Pat? '' McDonald asked.

His co-worker explained how he had fired on the
Davidson gang, though without damage to anybody.

'' And they put you under a thousand dollar bond
for it? '' commented Deputy Bill.

'' Yes.''

'' Well, they ought to have made it a good deal
heavier for your not being a better shot. Never
mind, I'll fill your bond all right,'' and this Mc-
Donald did, immediately.

The Davidson crowd was still in town, and far

from satisfied. Davidson felt that he had support enough now to tackle even that hard-headed McDonald, and he enlisted a big butcher named Williams to stir up the mess. The gang armed themselves with long butcher knives from Williams' shop and started out to hunt up their victim. They located him in a saloon where troubles of various kinds were likely to originate and the presence of an officer was desirable. Big Bill Williams, the butcher, entered first and coming near to McDonald, slightly bumped against him. Not wishing trouble, McDonald walked away, followed by Williams who bumped against him again. Deputy Bill then walked to the other side of the room, which was unoccupied, and when Williams and his crowd started to follow, he warned them not to come any closer. At this a number of cow-men who were present saw the trouble and stepped in, and Williams and his crowd worked toward the door. Outside, the disturbers gave vent to their animosity for McDonald in violent language and opprobrious names. Suddenly McDonald himself stepped out among them and seeing a piece of scantling about four feet long lying by the door, he seized it and as Williams started toward him he gave the big butcher a lick across the face with it that flattened his features and put a habitual crook in his nose. The crowd thought Williams was killed and his supporters began to get out of the way of the scantling. But McDonald dropped it and had out his guns in a moment.

"Halt!" he said, "every one of you. Hold up there!" Then to the Rangers who at that moment appeared on the scene, "Search those men for weapons."

Search was made and the long butcher knives, intended for McDonald, came to light. A knife of the same kind was found on Williams.

"Now get a doctor quick," commanded McDonald, "that fellow looks like he's pretty badly hurt."

A doctor was found and Williams was removed. McDonald's wife, then stopping at a nearby hotel, had been an interested, not to say excited, spectator of the proceedings, and now called down a few words of encouragement and approval. Somewhat later, word was brought to Deputy Bill that what was left of the Davidson and Williams crowd had collected in Tip McDowell's saloon, where a brother of Williams tended bar, and these were declaring war to the death. McDonald promptly went down there and entered, with a revolver in each hand. The crowd of would-be assassins, about a dozen or so, took one look and made a break for the back window, climbing over chairs, counters and billiard tables—some of them almost tearing the bar down in an effort to get behind it. Deputy Bill held enough of them with the persuasion of his two six-shooters to give them some useful information in the matter of running a town like Quanah and the surrounding country, as long as he was in office.

" You thieves that have been trying to run over this country, and stealing cattle and shooting the town up," he said, " from now on are going to stop it. And you fellows like Bill Williams that are selling stolen beef, are going to stop that, too. If any one of you sells a pound of beef hereafter without showing me the hide and the brand-marks, you'll go behind the bars and I'll put you there."

There was something about the tone of that brief address that made it sink in, and from that time forward when beef was brought to Quanah the hide came with it, and they would wake up Deputy Bill McDonald to show it to him as early as three o'clock in the morning.

As for Davidson, he now became an officer of the law, in reality. Satisfied, no doubt, that the Cedarbrakes gang was doomed, he came to McDonald and offered to guide him to the den of the Brookens if McDonald would cause to be dismissed certain indictments which had been lodged against him. McDonald consulted Sheriff Barker of Wilbarger and the arrangement was made. Davidson then ascertained when his former business associates would be at their headquarters in the brakes, and the raid was planned accordingly.

IX

Getting even with the Brooken Gang

THE brakes of the Big Wichita made an ideal cover for outlaws engaged in the industry of stealing cattle and horses. There were plenty of grass and water there and the ground was so densely covered with scrub cedar as to afford any number of hiding places. Moreover, there were deep gulches and canyons that made travel dangerous to those not familiar with the region. The place was remote and not often molested.

Everything being arranged, the raiders set out—Sheriff Barker of Wilbarger, in charge—the party including two Rangers from Quanah. On drawing near the locality, Barker proposed that all but two men should halt, several hundred yards from the stronghold—a dug-out occupied by the gang when at home. To this, Deputy Bill strenuously objected. He wanted to charge forthwith, believing always in a surprise attack. Barker, however, being in his own county, was in command and was for more gradual tactics. He added that McDonald's big white hat would attract attention before they could get near enough to charge. Two men were therefore sent to reconnoiter and report. The rest lay in hiding. Presently peering through the trees they saw two other men ride up to the dug-out and go in. Deputy Bill was all excitment.

" There they are now," he said, " let's get down there and get them."

Again he was overruled. In a few minutes a number of men issued from the dug-out, mounted horses and rode away. The first two had been scouts, and had given warning. At the same moment Barker's two men came running back with the information that the Brookens were getting away.

" Of course they're getting away," said McDonald. " Do you suppose they are going to wait and hold an afternoon tea when we arrive? "

Accompanied by one of the Rangers, he started in pursuit of the outlaws, but it was impossible to follow far in that dense unfamiliar place. Returning to the dug-out they were rejoiced to find Sheriff Alley's horse, so something was accomplished, though the expedition as a whole had failed, through over-caution.

McDonald now resolved to hunt on his own hook. As deputy sheriff, he was restricted to his own county, but this handicap was speedily removed, through Ranger Captain S. A. McMurray, who had him appointed by Governor L. S. Ross as special ranger, with sheriff's rights in any county in the State.

His authority was to be still further extended, very soon. One day he received a letter from Captain George A. Knight of Dallas, Texas, U. S. Marshal of the Northern District of Texas, asking him to come to Dallas and be made U. S. Deputy Marshal, with authority to operate in Southern Indian Territory and No-man's land, where a man like him was sorely needed. McDonald went down without delay and reported at Knight's office.

" I have heard about you and your work up in Hardeman," said Captain Knight, " and I want you for a deputy. But first tell me what are your politics? "

McDonald did not hesitate. Knight was a Republican.

" Captain Knight," he said, " I am the damndest, hell-roaringest, allfiredest Democrat you ever saw. If politics has anything to do with this appointment I'd just as well go back."

" Well," said Knight, " you're pretty emphatic, but I guess you'll do. Your kind of politics seem to suit your job pretty well."

It was only a little while after this that Bill McDonald was also made Deputy U. S. Marshal of the southern district of Kansas, which enabled him to work in the remaining portion of the Territory, and now, with his four offices—two Deputy U. S. Marshalships, Deputy Sheriff of Hardeman County, and that of Special Ranger—he was qualified to undertake at any time any sort of a man-hunt in any territory likely to invite his services. He went after the Brooken gang forthwith, but this time they did not wait for him. His fame was already in their ears.

He followed them like a hound on the trail. He never recovered his two horses and his Newfoundland dog, but he broke up the gang, utterly. He brought in Bood Brooken at last and got him sentenced for five years. Bill Brooken himself escaped to Mexico, was captured there, brought back and sentenced for one hundred and twenty-seven years. He has a good deal of that time still to serve.

The life work of the boy who long ago had begun it by hunting slaves in the swamps of Mississippi was well started, now; his name as a thief-catcher was beginning to be known, and honored, and feared. Yet his more active days—his more valuable days to the community at large—still lay all ahead, and of these we shall undertake to tell.

X

New Tactics in No-man's Land

A MAN WITH A BUCK-BOARD. HOLDING UP A BAD GANG SINGLE-HANDED

SOMETHING which resembled a sense of security began to manifest itself in Hardeman and the surrounding counties. There were still cattle thieves —plenty of them—but with their rendezvous in the immediate neighborhood broken up, their work became less deliberate. They harbored now further away—in the remoter places of the Pan-handle, in the Cherokee Strip and in the fastnesses of No-man's Land. From these strong-holds they made their raids, which though more sporadic and less devastating were still a vast nuisance, particularly along the border counties, where the outlaws could run over at night, raid a herd none too well guarded, and have the stolen cattle hidden in some gully or canyon or brake in their own lawless land by morning.

No-man's Land was a favorite retreat for cattle thieves. It was that strip of public land which was set down on the map as a part of Indian Territory, but really belonged to nobody at all. Different ones of the surrounding States claimed it, and the outlaws owned it, by possession and force of arms. There was no law there and few law abiding citizens. What there were, were hard to find, and they didn't want officers to stop with them for fear of the enmity of the thieves, who were so greatly in the majority. It was a fine, sightly land—with good grass and plenty of water—level land, some of it, though there was rough country there too—with good places for outlaws to hide. Here they built their dug-outs or cabins, established their households and herded their stolen stock. Some of the cattle they butchered, peddling the meat in Kansas or the Pan-handle. Some of the beef they had the nerve and assurance to drive to market—even to ship— openly, to Kansas City or Chicago.

It was necessary that No-man's Land should be reclaimed, and it was partly for this purpose that U. S. Marshal George A. Knight had commissioned Bill McDonald his deputy. Thus far all statutory law had been disregarded in No-man's Land—all officers had been defied. When, as had happened now and then, an officer had made his way into that wilderness, he either lost his life, or had his revolver and whisky and tobacco taken away from him and was booted back across the border. It had been demonstrated that Bill McDonald had a convincing way with his words and movements, and that he had a nose for locating cow thieves. Furthermore, it was believed that he would not be likely to submit to any liberties taken with his six-shooter and to-

bacco, or to indignities of any sort. So, when the
Brookens and other established " dealers of the
range " had been evicted from Hardeman and adjoining counties, it fell to Bill McDonald to begin
the No-man's Land crusade.

He was working over in the Pan-handle in 1887
when he learned of a horse that had been stolen
somewhere below, and he set out in pursuit of the
thief. Such trail as he could find led straight for
No-man's Land and he knew that he was bound at
last for that lawless locality where U. S. deputy
marshals were favorite victims.

He was alone, but this fact did not disturb him.
He had always preferred to hunt in that way. There
was less chance of frightening the game. When he
reached Hutchinson County, which is in the second
tier from the north Texas line, he stopped at Turkey
Track Ranch and borrowed a buck-board in which
to bring home his catch. It was still seventy-five
miles to the No-man's Land line, but buck-boards
were few in the Pan-handle in those days and this
was likely to be the last chance to get one. It is
possible that Turkey Track Ranch said good-by to
that buck-board when he drove away, for while they
had heard of Bill McDonald, they also knew of the
usual fate of the U. S. deputy marshals who, with or
without a buck-board, set out on an invasion of No-
man's Land.

It was a long lonesome drive across Hutchinson
and Hansford Counties, and up through No-man's

Land, to the waters of Beaver Creek. The trail was not very difficult here, for the thief probably did not expect to be followed—certainly not farther than the border line, and had made little effort to cover his track. It was toward the end of the second or third day, at last, that the trail became very fresh, and the man in the buck-board came to a halt and set out on foot to locate his game. As silently and cautiously as an Indian he crept through the brush until he reached a place where peering through he located, some distance away on the river bank, a camp consisting of four men and the same number of horses. His man had found comrades, that was evident, and it was likely they would join in his defense. McDonald lay in the brush, watching them, as long as it was light and then crept closer, trying to identify the horse he was after, and which of the men had him in charge. He had no intention of beginning operations that night, for he had long since made up his mind that the proper time for a surprise attack is in the early morning. Men have not gathered themselves, then, and have not been awake long enough to be fearless, and quick of thought and action. His purpose now was to know his ground exactly, so that with daylight he could act with a clear understanding.

He was obliged to wait until daylight before he could be sure of his ground; then, awake and watching, he saw the different men go to look after their horses. He located a bay horse that answered to the description of the stolen animal, and identified the man who had him in charge. He crept back to his buck-board now, got in and drove up leisurely to the outlaw camp, looking as inoffensive and guileless as any other fly with a horse and buck-board, driving straight into the spider's den.

" Good-morning, boys," he said pleasantly, " you-all look mighty comfortable with that fire going. I lost my way and laid out last night. Mebbe you-all can tell me something about the trails around here. There don't seem to be none that I can find."

They invited him cordially to get down and warm himself and said they would show him the trail. McDonald stepped out and walked over to the fire, still talking about the country and the weather, working over close to the man he wanted. The deputy wore a short overcoat, and he had a pair of hand-cuffs in the left side-pocket. He got just in front of his man at last and reached out his right hand as if to shake hands with him. Instinctively the man extended his own right hand and at that instant McDonald's left with the open hand-cuffs was out like a flash—there was a quick snap, a sudden movement—a slight-of-hand movement it was— then another quick snap and the horse thief, dazed and half stupefied stood gazing down at the manacles on his wrists, while Bill McDonald, a gun in each hand, quietly regarded the other three members of the camp.

The captive was first to break the silence.

" Boys," he said, " what does this mean? "

One of the men turned to McDonald.

" Yes," he said, " what does this mean? Who are *you* and what are you going to do with that man? "

"I'm Deputy U. S. Marshal McDonald, of Texas," was the cheerful reply, " and I'm going to take this man with me and put him in jail."

" What for? "

" For stealing that bay horse out there."

The outlaw advanced a step.

" And you'll just about play hell doing it! " he said.

" All right, I am ready to start the game right now," said McDonald.

The men whispered a little among themselves. Their saddles were off to one side and their Winchesters lay across them, all there together. They wore six-shooters also, but they realized who their man was, now, and they were careful to make no movement toward them. Presently one of the men said:

" You say you are going to put that fellow in jail? "

" That's what I'm going to do."

" Well, now let's see about that."

The men were starting in as if to make an argument. One of the party began working a little in the direction of the guns. The idea was to distract the officer's attention for a moment and get the drop

BEGINNING A CAMPAIGN IN NO-MAN'S LAND.

"Three pairs of hands went up."

on him. It was a good game, but it failed to work in this instance. McDonald brought his guns exactly to bear on the men in front of him.

" Throw up your hands! " he commanded, " every one of you quick! Throw them up, you scoundrels! "

Three pairs of hands went up. That command from Bill McDonald has almost never been disobeyed. Perhaps it is the tone of the voice that makes it convincing. Perhaps it is the curious look in those needle-pointed eyes of his; perhaps it is something more than these—something psychologically imperative. Whatever it is, it has filled the air of Texas with hands, from Red River to the Rio Grande.

" Now, face the other way! " was the next command.

The men faced about, their hands still high above their heads. With one six-shooter still on them, McDonald went up behind each man and disarmed him, sticking the revolvers in his own belt. Then he went over and took the cartridges out of the Winchesters. He now marched his men to where the horses were hitched, secured the stolen one and tied him to the buck-board. Then he ordered his prisoner to get in and proceeded to shackle him to the slats of the vehicle. The other three men, meantime, were kept in a group, a rod or so ahead in the direction of Texas.

" Now, march for Texas, you devils! " McDonald

said, when he was seated beside his prisoner. The procession started, the men complaining that they had done nothing, and that he had no right to take them back, even if he were authorized to take the other man.

Deputy Bill said:

" You fellows have been in the habit over here of resisting and killing officers, or driving them out, and doing as you please. I just want to show you how easy it is to take your kind. Come, move right along there, now. I don't know what you've done, but you probably stole all those horses back yonder."

The men now began to beg for their horses, complaining that the animals left behind would stay there and starve. McDonald really had no intention of taking them all the way back with him. He had no warrants for them, and besides he did not care to march and camp with that number unless necessary. His purpose was to get them far enough away so that they would not be likely to try to overtake him and catch him asleep when he should halt for the night. He made no concessions however, until they were well along toward the Texas line. Then he said:

" Now, if you fellows think you can behave yourselves and want to go back and tend to your horses, I may let you go back on that account. But you can make up your minds, and you can tell your friends about it, that I'm not afraid of any of you, and I'm going to clear you dam'd thieves out of this country. I'm going to show you that there's one man you won't kill nor run out. Now, will you do what I tell you?''

The men protested that they were good citizens, and that if he would let them off they would undertake missionary work in the cause of law and order. He let them go, then, and handed back their unloaded arms, promising them another fate, if he ever caught them in mischief. He watched them disappear behind the first rise; then, whipping up, he made the best time he could for Turkey Track Ranch, where he rested a day, delivered the borrowed buck-board, taking his prisoner next morning to jail.

XI

Redeeming No-man's Land

It was natural that other work in No-man's Land should follow this first experiment. It having been demonstrated that Bill McDonald could go into that infested place and not only come out alive, but bring back his man, other and more extensive contracts were laid out for him. There were several bad gangs there to be broken up before legitimate settlers could live there, and it was decided that McDonald was the man for the job.

McDonald on his part was ready for the undertaking, it being of a sort which he found always most congenial. Deciding that it was a good thing to have a reliable partner in the handling of a gang, he selected for his associate another deputy marshal— one Lon Burson of Henrietta—a quiet athletic fellow with plenty of grit and endurance.

"I could always rely upon Lon," McDonald said, in speaking of that period, long after; "I believed I knew just what he would do, every time, and he never failed me." It may be added that Burson on his part had complete faith in McDonald, and that their ideas of conducting a campaign were in exact accord.

They began on what was thought to be one of the worst gangs, a band of nine who had established on Beaver Creek a general headquarters from which they conducted a miscellaneous business in crime— stealing cattle and horses, robbing trains and shooting down bank officials when occasion offered, frequently crossing over into adjoining States for that purpose.

McDonald had laid out the plan of attack, which was to arrive on the scene at his favorite early hour—daybreak—and then to do no parleying or long distance firing, but to charge at once and storm the works. His theory was—and is to-day—that the criminal cannot stand up against the man who is not afraid of him and does not hesitate.

" If you wilt or falter he will kill you," he has often said, " but if you go straight at him and never give him time to get to cover, or to think, he will weaken ninety-nine times in a hundred. No man in the wrong can stand up against a fellow that's in the right and keeps on a-comin'. I made up my mind to that long ago, and I've never made a mistake yet."

Here in homely vernacular is expressed a mighty truth. Crime is always coward and cannot stand against the conviction of right. Error cannot survive in the face of truth that does not falter and " keeps on a-comin'."

McDonald and Burson proceeded in the saddle to Higgins, in Lipscomb County—a station on the Santa Fe Railroad, and their last base of supplies. Here they chartered a big three-seated hack in which to bring back their prisoners, should their raid prove successful. They put their own horses to this vehicle, loaded their saddles in behind and continued their journey.

It was toward evening when they arrived in the neighborhood of the outlaw den and camped in a secluded place, to wait for morning. The house stood in the edge of the prairie, near Beaver Creek and was easy of access. It was made of logs and seemed to be a deserted ranch place, probably built by some adventurous person who had long since departed for a locality where there was more law, even if less grass.

One of the band—an early riser—had just gone out to round up the horses when the two deputies, mounted, made their approach, next morning. He discovered them when they were about four hundred yards away and made for the house, McDonald and Burson following at full speed. The outlaw was a little in advance, and his eight companions were out in front with their Winchesters when the officers bore down on them.

" Go round the house, Lon, and come in from behind. I'll 'tend to them on this side," said McDonald as they dashed up.

This maneuver was immediately put into action

and in less than a minute later the deputies were on the spot, their game between them. In another instant both deputies had slid from their horses and were in the midst of the confused, half awake outlaws.

" Drop them guns! Drop 'em, and put up your hands! " commanded McDonald—his own gun and Burson's leveled.

There was not even an attempt at resistance. The bandits were simply dazed, overwhelmed by the suddenness and vigor of the onslaught. Heretofore, attacks—always made by a posse—had begun with scouting and skirmish and ended with a running fight, usually at long range. The plan of two mere deputies coming straight upon them and demanding sudden and complete surrender was wholly new. As before remarked, there was something about it terribly convincing—almost supernatural.

McDonald kept the men covered, now, while Burson secured their weapons. Then, hand-cuffed and shackled, they were marched to the big hack, crowded into it and driven fifty miles to Higgins; thence by rail to the United States Commissioner at Wichita Falls.

McDonald, as usual, was sociable enough with his prisoners, once secure, and delivered to them his customary homily, as they drove along.

" I just want to show you fellows, up here, how easy it is to take you," he said affably. " You-all have got the notion that you can run this country your own way, and that there ain't any officers that can come up here and make you behave. Now, you-all are mightily mistaken. I'm going to put every one of you fellows in jail and a lot more like you. You know well enough it ain't right to act like you-all have been doing—driving off other men's cattle and robbing trains and shooting men that you had the drop on. You might know you'd get into trouble. The United States has made laws against such business as that, and them laws cover this country the same as anywhere else and every one of your kind up in here is going to find it out.''

The gang was landed safely in Wichita Falls. Some of them were eventually convicted; the rest either became better citizens or sought quieter territory for their industries. The cleaning up of No-man's Land had begun.

The work of active reform was not allowed to languish. News of the first successful raid traveled quickly, and State Senator Temple Houston—son of Governor Sam Houston—notified McDonald that the Sheriff of Hansford County was in need of assistance to cope with a bad gang which had a rendezvous just across the border from Hansford, in No-man's Land. These bandits had been carrying on the usual business of horse and cattle stealing and general highway robbery. Unlike some of the officials, the sheriff of Hansford, though not noted for reckless bravery, was in no way in league with the thieves and desired only their extermination.

His jurisdiction, however, extended no farther than the Texas line, and thus far no State or federal officer had rendered any assistance. As a result, the band, becoming very bold, had pitched their camp just over the line, and had defied arrest, declaring they would shoot the first man that stepped across.

When Bill McDonald got the word from Senator Houston, he immediately sent over for Lon Burson and then proceeded to Canadian, Hemhill County, where Houston lived. Here they learned more fully what work was cut out for them, and presently continued their journey over into Hansford, where, from the sheriff, they secured the names of the offenders, as far as possible, and a partial list of their misdeeds. Complaints were now filed against six men, the usual commodious hack was secured; also, a light buggy for possible side excursions, and McDonald and Burson, accompanied by the sheriff as a guide, drove through the gray of early morning, to the line which divided Hansford County from No-man's Land.

Arriving at the border, the sheriff pointed out where the robber den—a log building—was located, not more than eight hundred yards beyond. Then he said he would wait there until they got back.

" Come right along with us," said McDonald, " we need you to identify the men."

But the officer said " No," that the men knew him, and it might alarm them if they saw him coming. Besides, he had no authority over there.

" Never mind that," urged McDonald, " I'll risk the consequences, and I'll make you one of a deputy's posse, which fixes your authority all right."

But the sheriff still said " No," that he didn't care for any more authority than he had—that anything new in that line might make him proud. He said he thought he would enjoy sitting there in the hack where he would have a good view of what happened to them when they tackled that outfit.

McDonald and Burson, therefore, set out in the light buggy, driving leisurely across the intervening space. Arriving near the log-house, they discovered that five men were up, and sitting sleepily on the ground in front of their cabin, their Winchesters leaning against the wall behind them. Evidently they did not look for any attack, and even when they saw the approaching buggy, their wits were not sufficiently collected to suspect that these might be officers; nor could they realize that any two men in a buggy would drive over to attempt their capture. In another instant they were covered.

" Get up from there and throw up your hands! " was the word of greeting they received. " And don't try to touch them guns. The first man that tries it I'll kill him."

The five men rose—it was polite to do so—also, they refrained from offering any discourtesy in the matter of the guns. McDonald now called the roll of the names he wanted, and curious as it may seem, each man answered to his name. One man of the six wanted, being missing, the officers proceeded to hand-cuff and shackle the five captured men, and marched them back to the hack, where the sheriff of Hansford was waiting.

Of course the sheriff didn't believe it was true. He had had such dreams before and thought he would wake up, presently, at home, in bed. When he convinced himself at last that he was not asleep, he offered to aid in the search for the sixth man. He was well acquainted with the Territory trails, and McDonald decided to send Burson to Hansford with the hack-load and to proceed with the buggy and the sheriff after Number Six of the gang who, it appeared, had a place of his own some twenty miles away.

Number Six was out looking after his cattle— about thirty in number—the result of industry— when McDonald and the sheriff of Hansford arrived, and not expecting official guests, was unprepared. He had, in fact, "no more gun than a rabbit," as Deputy Bill said afterward, and his capture was child's play. That night the gang complete set out for Wichita Falls, to be tried later in the United States Court at Dallas.

Raids followed each other rapidly. One gang of cattle thieves after another was gathered in, and took up the march for Dallas and trial. Outlawing in No-man's Land became an unpopular occupation. Men of more legitimate enterprise began to wonder if the time was not coming, by and by, when they could do business on or within the borders of that territory without the protection of a company of soldiers. The fame of Bill McDonald was on every man's tongue, and those who had not seen him, especially the outlaws still at large, usually conceived him to be a very terrible person: large, bushy, heavy of voice and fierce of mien. Yet he was just the opposite of all these things. He was slender, quiet, blue-eyed, and gentle of voice—only, he had that gift of command—that look, and that manner of speech with law-breakers which they did not disobey. The time came presently in No-man's Land when his name alone and a rumor that he was coming was sufficient to cause a gang to contemplate emigration. Perhaps they believed he bore a charmed life, and it was useless to resist him. If so, they were hardly to be blamed for such a conviction.

XII

Some of the Difficulties of Reform

" FRONTIER " LAW AND PRACTICE. CAUGHT IN A NORTHER IN NO-MAN'S LAND

IT is neither necessary nor possible to give a full
history of all the raids that during the brief period
of little more than a year broke up organized lawlessness in that stray corner of the nation and re-
deemed an abandoned land. The general plan was
the same in all. The early morning hour; the hack
and the Winchester; the surprise attack, and the
pleasant drive home with the guests duly hand-
cuffed and shackled; these were features common to
each episode. Though conducted against desperate
men, it was a bloodless warfare. Nobody was killed
—scarcely a gun was fired. Bill McDonald's career
was not to be always like that. There was to be
shooting enough and blood-letting too, but the No-
man's Land campaign was peculiar in the absence
of these customary attributes of border warfare.

Yet there are one or two aspects of the happen-
ings of that period which may not be overlooked
here. As before suggested, the administrators of
the law were not always to be relied upon. Some of
them were actually in league with the law-breakers;

others were honest enough, but afraid of them. But there was still another sort, who being both honest and courageous lacked information. Sometimes this resulted in curious complications which were annoying and discouraging to an officer. Often, the results were rather humorous in their nature. The following is an illustration of frontier jurisprudence.

McDonald had heard of a cow thief in No-man's Land who was working on his own hook—a sporadic case, as one might say—and went over to arrest him. He descended upon him in an unexpected moment, and though the outlaw strenuously protested that it being Sunday the law of arrest did not hold good, Deputy Bill conveyed him across the border and down into Roberts County where the cattle had been stolen and where there was a justice of the peace—it being hardly worth while to take a single prisoner to Wichita Falls. McDonald's idea was that the justice would have authority to bind his prisoner over until such time as the grand jury of that district should meet and indict him in regular form.

Now, Roberts County was a wild desolate place in those days. There was no town anywhere about, and few people. There had been no previous call for administration of the law of any sort, and up to that time no case had come before this justice of the peace. On the arrival of McDonald with his prisoner, his honor convened court with a sort of a helpless look. His office was merely a title, so far as he was concerned, and the wide realm of the law was to him an unexplored country. He had a copy of the "Revised Statutes," however, which he now took down and examined, perhaps for the first time. With McDonald's help he found the section which related to cattle stealing, and the penalty. Regular procedure, with indictments and trial by jury were as nothing to him. He only knew that he had been elected to his office, and that his duty was to administer the law as laid down. He read the law as pointed out, and assumed a judicial severity.

"You own up that you stole them cattle?" he said to the prisoner.

The prisoner nodded.

"Then as justice of the peace of this county I hereby send you to the penitentiary for ten years."

McDonald gasped.

"Judge," he said, "I don't believe that's quite regular."

"Why; ain't that the law?"

"Well, yes, but you see he's entitled to trial, an' mebbe it would be just as well to bind him over under a good heavy bond, and if he can't raise it send him to jail over in Canadian until the grand jury meets. Of course I only mention that as being the usual way of doing things."

The justice looked a little disappointed.

"Why, yes, of course, if you want it that way," he said, "but the man's guilty and I thought you'd like to put the thing through as quick and easy as possible, and save expense. Oh, well, any way to suit you. I'll make his bond heavy enough, any-way.'' He paused to think, perhaps trying to im-agine a sum large enough for a man who had plead guilty to the heinous crime of cattle stealing. '' I'll put him under a heavy bond—a *good heavy bond*—I'll make it three hundred dollars! ''

It will be seen that an official who was given to inspirations such as these could become a trial, even with the best intentions in the world; and there were others who added arrogance to their ignorance, and connivance at crime. Nor were the raids into No-man's Land altogether pleasure excursions even though Deputies Bill McDonald and Lon Burson, with their headlong tactics and general disregard of death, had things pretty much their own way when it came to the final show-down. There were long wearying journeys in a trailless land and long night vigils when bone and muscle and nerve were racked and the whole body cried out for sleep. The onset might be swift and reckless, once begun, but the preparation for that moment was cautious and slow and often beset with difficulties. The few dwell-ers in No-man's Land really desirous of getting rid of the outlaws, were afraid to reveal their anxiety, to give anything resembling information, or even to offer shelter to the officers. They knew that to manifest any interest on the side of law and order would incur the enmity of the gangs and bring down reprisal swift and bloody. McDonald and

Burson realized this, and, however severe the conditions of weather and weariness, faced them, rather than impose any risk upon men whose only offense was to dwell among very bad neighbors.

At one time the deputies were after a gang of five men, wanted for murder and theft, and were driving from Higgins into No-man's Land, with hack and team, their saddles loaded in behind, as usual. It was late in the year, now, and suddenly in the swift Texas fashion a norther came down, with piercing wind and fine driving snow. If the reader has never seen a Texas norther, or a Dakota blizzard, he will hardly understand their predicament. The wind leaps up in a wild gale almost in an instant; the air from being balmy takes on a sudden bitterness that wrings the body and numbs the heart and pinches the very soul. Then the snow comes, fine and blinding—sharp and hard as glass. No living being was ever created that could survive long in the face of a storm like that. Cattle know when a norther is coming and find shelter in canyons, or gather into thick bunches in the open, their heads to the center. Birds speed away to the south, ahead of it, or find shelter in hollows and crannies until the demon has passed by. A storm like that always means death. The Texas norther and the Dakota blizzard have strewn the prairies with bones.

McDonald and Burson in the face of such a tempest tried to press on, hoping to find a shelter of some sort—anything that would break the terrible wind. But everywhere was only the wide prairie, level as the sea and lost now in the swirling drift. Night was coming on rapidly, and unless a place for camp was found soon, their case would be hopeless, indeed. It seemed to them that they had drifted for hours, battling against the norther—though it probably was less than one hour—when they came upon some stacks of prairie hay, which indicated the habitation of men. Without seeking further, they made for the shelter of the stacks, burrowed themselves and their horses into them, allowing the latter to feed liberally from the hay. There they remained all night and until the afternoon of the next day, the men without food. The storm abated then, and the officers undiscouraged, pressed on, reaching the outlaw camp late in the afternoon, instead of at their favorite morning hour.

The surprise was quite as complete, however, for the last thing that those bandits expected was that two officers should suddenly appear out of that white devastation to take them to jail. They were too much astonished to attempt resistance and were on their way to Wichita Falls that night, following the road which earlier in the year so many of their kind had taken.

Indeed it was this capture at the end of 1888 that marked about the close of the heaviest work in that particular section. The year's crusade had demonstrated that No-man's Land was not big enough to hold a band of cow thieves and two deputies like Bill McDonald and Lon Burson at the same time. It was no encouragement to a band of hard-working outlaws, just as they had got their plant established and things well under way to be suddenly pounced down upon and put out of business by two men who had no regard for the customary rules of fighting, but just rushed right in with a lot of impertinent orders and an assortment of hand-cuffs and always had a big hack ready to start at a moment's notice for Wichita Falls.

" What is the use? " one of the freebooters is said to have complained, " A fellow no more than gets started when these dam' fools come in and upset everything."

What *was* the use? Such of the No-man's Land fraternity as still remained unhung and out of jail set out for other fields of labor. Some of them located in the more barren districts of New Mexico and Arizona. Some of them settled in the further places of what was then known as the Cherokee Strip, where they joined with congenial spirits in that territory, and pretending to be engaged in agriculture—for they were in a more settled country —Indian country—continued their old business at the new stand. These we shall meet again presently, for if they had said good-by to Bill McDonald, he had not said good-by to them. It would require new tactics to deal with the new conditions—to identify the outlaw in the pretended agriculturist, and to get evidence for his conviction. It would require the development of another talent in Bill McDonald's make-up, and that talent was ready for cultivation, as we shall see.

XIII

Captain Bill as a Tree-man

THE LOST DROVE OF LAZARUS. A PILGRIM ON A " PAINT
HOSS " A NEW WAY OF GETTING INFORMATION
IN THE " STRIP "

MEANWHILE, the ranch on Wanderer's Creek had
suffered. Compelled to be absent most of the time,
McDonald was unable to give his herd personal protection, and now and again bunches of his cattle
were driven off by outlaws from across the border.
His brave wife, facing the problem of the wilderness
with only a few hired helpers, did her best, but was
not always able to prevent these raids. The thieves
would seem to have taken especial delight in watching for the times when Deputy Bill was absent and
then descending on his herds, mainly for the booty,
no doubt, but also by way of retaliation. It was a
dangerous thing for them to do, and though they
were certain to pay for it in the end; the double
temptation of profit and revenge was not to be
resisted.

But while the ranch did not prosper, its owner
was in no immediate danger of bankruptcy. With
his success in breaking up the gangs in Hardeman
and adjoining counties, and in No-man's Land, Mc·

Donald's fame had grown amazingly. As a thief-
taker he was regarded as a past-master. That an
outlaw could neither intimidate nor elude him, and
that when he was feeling well he could whip any
number of them single-handed, before breakfast,
was the current belief. The Cattle-men's Association—a combination of law abiding ranchmen, one
of the strongest organizations ever known—invited
his special attention to their herds and contributed
a monthly acknowledgement of one hundred and
fifty dollars, which with his numerous fees made his
income an ample one—often as large as five hundred
dollars a month—sometimes double this amount.

Among the members of the association was Sam
Lazarus, who was with Bull Turner when he was
shot by the Brookens, and who came into town on
the whiffletrees, undamaged, but a good deal shaken
up as to nerves. Soon after McDonald's arrangement with the cattlemen, Lazarus was sending a
herd of perhaps a thousand head into Kansas, driving them across the Territory. Pat Wolforth, whose
name may also be recalled in connection with the
Brookens, was in charge of this herd, and when just
beyond the Territory line, in a very lonely district,
met with misfortune. One evening near nightfall
the cattle suddenly became frightened, doubtless
through some device of the outlaws, and Wolforth
and his men found it impossible to control them. A
general stampede followed and Lazarus's cattle
were scattered over the prairies and through the

fastnesses of the Strip—a prey to the spoilers lying in wait on every hand. It was a heavy disaster and there seemed little hope of much in the way of recovery. The spring round-up might gather in a few stragglers, but for the most part the herds of Lazarus were believed to be beyond all hope of restoration.

Bill McDonald took no such view of the situation. With Pat Wolforth he immediately visited the scene of the stampede, and began looking for cattle with the " Diamond-tail " brand, such being the symbol of the Lazarus herd. It was a ticklish undertaking. Some of the cattle had been butchered, and these of course were lost. Others had been absorbed by the herds of men who though not regularly engaged in cow stealing were in nowise particular as to whose cows they got and welcomed anything that browsed unguarded on the range. Still others had been collected in " pockets "—small gullies or canyons—where they were retired from general circulation, guarded, as a rule, by one or two ostensible cowboys.

McDonald began by prevailing upon the honest ranchmen in that section to join at once in a general round-up by which means a great number of cattle could be collected and distributed to their rightful owners. The result was fairly satisfactory and a good many of Lazarus's cattle were recovered, though not always without disputes and a display of firearms, especially where the brands had been grown over by the long winter-coat of hair. Such cases were settled first and tried afterward. In other words, McDonald and Wolforth possessed themselves of the cattle and then at their leisure " picked the brand," which is the range idiom for picking the hair from around the brand with a pocket-knife, so the brand may be seen. If the brand proved to be other than that of the Lazarus herd, the cattle were turned over to their true owners. When the round-up was over the cow-hunters took up the search in other directions.

It mattered little to McDonald and Wolforth where they found the Diamond-tail brand—they took the cattle, peaceably if possible, forcibly if necessary. They conducted the campaign with an enthusiasm and vigor which did not invite argument. Large herds they searched without ceremony and if any cattle of their brand were found, they were " cut out " with few formalities and with scant courtesy. When they came upon bunches of the Diamond-tail brand in secluded places, they did not pause to present any credentials except their Winchesters which they carried always ready for instant action, and set out at once with the cattle; also, sometimes, with the astonished cowboys as well. It was a sudden and energetic procedure and resulted in the recovery of the greater number of the lost drove of Lazarus.

It resulted further in a definite plan by Bill McDonald for the discouragement of cattle stealing in the Territory, and for the capture of the most actively engaged in that industry. As set down in a foregoing chapter, the outlaws in the Cherokee Strip were not likely to be congregated in a single rendezvous, as had been the case in No-man's Land, but were scattered as individual squatters through neighborhoods more or less friendly to their business, or at least not bold enough openly to oppose it. Indeed, the back country was very sparsely settled, and the Indians and half-breed whites and negroes were not especially interested in law and order, even where they were not directly concerned in opposing these things. Along the rivers—the Cimmaron, the Canadian, the Washita and the North Fork of the Red River, the country was rugged, and the hiding places for plunder were good. The prairies were nice and level with fine land and plentiful grass. White men had no legal right of residence there, except where they were intermarried with the Indians, and those who acquired citizenship in this manner were not likely to be any more desirable than those others whose occupation was itself an infringement on the law.

" Did they raise anything there, Bill? " McDonald was asked in discussing the conditions, long afterward.

" Just raised hell! " the old Ranger answered drily.

Nearly all, however, made a pretense of agricultural employments; for after all, the country, unlike No-man's Land, was really under a regular form of government; legitimate settlement was considerable, and there was a semblance, at least, of law and order. Also, there were towns of considerable size, and railroads—the latter affording liberal returns now and then when some train was waited upon in a lonely place and the express messengers, mail agents and passengers were invited at the point of six-shooters to contribute to a highway development fund. The writer of these chapters was himself a resident of Kansas during this earlier period, and he recalls now what an uninteresting month it was when an M. K. & T. or Santa Fe or Rock Island train did not come up out of the Territory with passengers telegraphing home for money and the express and mail cars full of bullet holes.

Bill McDonald decided to break up this sort of thing, and set about it in a way suggested by his own peculiar genius. It was necessary first to identify the men who were really concerned in these various employments, for in a country where all were " settlers," even if unofficial ones, it was not worth while working at hap-hazard and bothering men whose only offense might be that of squatting. Investigation must be conducted openly and yet in a way to avoid suspicion. His gentle manner and seemingly inoffensive personality suited him for just such an undertaking, and he prepared and " made up " carefully for the part.

Returning to Quanah and Wanderer's Creek, he

bought a " paint horse " (a spotted pony); an old
tenderfoot saddle, such as a plainsman would never
use, and a book with pretty pictures of fruit in it
—a regular nurseryman's plate-book—the kind of
a book fruit-tree salesmen always carry. Then
dressed as unlike an officer, or a cow-man, or a
Texan as possible, with these properties he set out
—to all appearances a genial, garrulous, easy-going
tree-man, inviting orders and confidences—willing
to sit around all day and whittle and swap knives
and yarns, and to express any kind of interest or
sympathy necessary to encourage a man to tell his
business ventures and those of his neighbors.

It was a pleasant excursion, enough. No fruit-
tree man had been through that section before—
none ever had dared, or perhaps thought it worth
while, to go. McDonald's excursion proved that
profit awaited the seller of trees who should first
make that wilderness his territory. He had expected
not much in the way of sales, for he did not imagine
that men engaged in driving off and slaughtering
other men's cattle, and in waylaying trains and robbing banks would have any special taste for horticul-
ture. This was an error of judgment. Most of these
bad men had been fairly good boys at home at some
time in the past, and the sight of those luminous
plates presenting fruit of extravagant size and
coloring, made their mouths fairly water at the
thought of its cultivation by the doorway of their
own dug-outs or sod houses or log cabins. They

turned the pages lovingly, and lingered over the wonderful plums and pears and peaches, and as they turned they talked and somehow almost without realizing it they told a great many things about themselves and neighbors which no well-trained and properly constructed outlaw should tell, even to a sympathetic and simple-hearted fruit-tree man who wrote down the orders and listened and chuckled at some of the yarns, while he encouraged further confidences.

He would drift around presently to his customer's former place of residence, and to the reason for his leaving. It was easy enough for an alert tree-man to detect a lack of complete frankness in the replies, especially if the reason had " something about a cow or horse " in it, that being the usual first admission that the isolation of the Strip had been found congenial for other reasons than those connected with its soil and climate. The tree-man did not hesitate to give a generous return for any such confidences, inventing on the spot some of his own for the purpose. The number and character of crimes he confessed to having been accused of in the States would be worth recording in this history if they could be remembered now. But, alas, like other gay bubbles, they were blown only to charm for the moment, and once vanished cannot be recalled. The tree-man would then fall to abusing laws in general and the men who enforced them, and end by declaring that he was mightily in love with that particular

section and would stay where there was little or no
chance of meeting any of those obnoxious officials,
if the boys would consider him one of them and all
stand together in time of trouble. Talk like this
would open the door for anything. The rest of the
interview was likely to run something as follows:

Picture: Two men seated on a log, or down on the
grass cowboy style, in front of a dug-out; one the
slim, mild-looking tree-man; the other a burly
person, very dirty, hairy and unkempt, bent over
a large book of gay pictures which the tree-man
leans forward to explain. Nearby, two horses are
grazing, the " paint-hoss " with the old tenderfoot
saddle and saddle-bags; the other a very good looking animal, often saddled and bridled for prompt
use.

" By gum," nods the big burly individual, staring
at a picture of such peaches as grow only in paradise, " eating peaches like them would be like holdin'
up the Santa Fe express."

" That's what," assents the salesman gayly,
" regular picnic all the time. I s'pose you fellers
in here have money to throw at the birds after that
kind of a job."

" Well, not so much after all. Too many have to
have a piece out of it. Everybody wants to help.
It has to be a pretty big basket of money to cut in
two more'n twice and leave enough to pay."

The salesman shows a sympathetic interest.

" Of course," he agrees, " it's too bad to spoil a

good bunch of money by making little piles of it. I guess you have to have a good many though for a job like that.''

'' No, two *can* do it, an' there ain't no need of more'n three. One to take care of the engineer, another to pull down on the passengers and the other man to go through 'em. It's plum easy. They give up like sinners at a camp-meetin', and the messengers and mail fellers come down pretty easy, too. If they don't we put a few shots through their cars and that fetches 'em.''

'' But you had to kill the messenger in that Rock Island job, last fall.''

'' Well, I wasn't in that mess—that was another outfit. Them boys are huntin' trouble and 'll find it some day, good an' plenty. When I put a job through, the' ain't nobody going to get killed unless they commit reg'lar suicide. You ought to come down here an' go in with *me*. You've got a per-suadin' way about you that would make a man give up anything he had and thank you for takin' it. It 'ud pay yeh better, I reckon, than ridin' a paint-hoss over the country, peddlin' trees. That reminds me—you c'n give me six o' them peaches, an' a few o' them pears an' plums an' a couple o' cherry-trees and some grape-vines—the big yaller ones—Niagaries, I think you said they was.''

And this was the drift of more than one conversation between the Cherokee agriculturists and the genial tree-man who certainly did have a '' per-

suadin' way " in making a man give up anything
he had, in the way of information. No one could
dream that this inoffensive mild-eyed pilgrim on a
paint-hoss could ever make trouble in that wilderness of lawless living and of desperate men.

So for several weeks the tree-man on his paint-
horse with his old tenderfoot saddle and his picture-
book loitered up through the Strip and on over into
the Territory, on the surface taking orders for
spring delivery, and beneath it all locating the different communities of offenders; the individuals of
the same; stolen cattle and horses, and securing
data of particular crimes. He ended his canvass at
Guthrie, a busy frontier point on the Santa Fe, with
twenty-five hundred dollars worth of orders for trees
—trees which might be bearing to this day if the
spring deliveries had been made as planned.

XIV

THE DAY FOR "DELIVERIES"

THE TREE-MAN TURNS OFFICER AND SINGLE-HANDED WIPES OUT A BAD GANG

BUT McDonald was ready now for deliveries of a different sort—deliveries of the purchasers themselves, into the hands of the law. As a preliminary step he swore out warrants for eight men—the chief operators in a very bad community located along a small creek between Guthrie and Kingfisher—about fifteen miles west of the latter. He then went with his warrants to a deputy marshal at Guthrie and invited his co-operation in making the arrests. The Guthrie deputy looked at him with curiosity, wondering perhaps if this circuit-riding Texas person was in his right mind. Clearly the fame of Bill McDonald had not yet penetrated into darkest Oklahoma. Then, when he had looked over Bill Jess's credentials, and perhaps felt his pulse, he said:

" If you can get a company of soldiers to go along I might undertake that job with you. You don't know that Sand Creek crowd—I do. No two men nor ten men could go up against that outfit and get back alive. Bring a company of regulars over here, if you want to undertake that campaign."

McDonald argued, and related what he had done in No-man's Land, but to no purpose. A sudden charge might work, over there, the deputy said, where the gangs were bunched, and were surprised before they were awake enough to fight. But it was different over here. The bad men were scattered a mile or so apart and while you might get the drop on one, there'd be a lot more left to get the drop on you, and you'd be full of lead before sunrise. No-siree, nothing less than soldiers, and plenty of them, would do that job.

McDonald went about the town trying to enlist volunteers. He realized that a scattered gang would require time to corral, and that its members would be likely to be awake and busy, before he got them all in. He did not want a company of soldiers, for such a force would scare the gang and accomplish nothing; but he did want a few quick fearless men for this work. Finally he wired U. S. Marshal Walker at Topeka, Kansas, to come on first train. Walker came, and McDonald explained the situation.

" I've got these men located, and warrants for their arrest," he said, " and now I can't get your deputies or anybody else to give me a hand on the job. It ain't just the sort of a thing I want to do alone, for we ought to get to several of these men's houses simultaneous like, an' I thought you might be able to persuade these boys to come along."

" Certainly," said Walker, " that's all right— they don't know who you are. I'm satisfied from what U. S. Marshal Knight, of Dallas, has written me that you know what you want to do, and how to go at it. I'll get the men together and explain the situation.''

They collected about a dozen deputies and posse-men, and Walker explained as agreed. It was no use. The men declared that no small force could go into the Sand Creek neighborhood and come out alive, and nothing short of a squad of trained soldiers would be of any use. McDonald looked them over scornfully. Then he turned to Walker.

'' If I had as sorry a lot of men as that,'' he said, '' I'd discharge them on the spot. I'll go out there alone, if I can get a man with nerve enough to drive a hack, and I'll bring back a load of criminals, too.''

This was regarded as a bluff. Walker returned to Topeka, and Bill McDonald's fruit-tree expedition began to look like a failure. McDonald, how-ever, was not the sort of a person to whom the words '' bluff '' and '' failure '' were likely to apply. He discovered a man presently who agreed to drive a hack, provided he would be asked to do no fighting, and would be allowed to remain out of range.

'' If you ever get 'em to the hack and tied, I'll haul 'em,'' he said, but it was clear that he expected to haul home a dead deputy marshal, instead.

They set out long before day-break, next morning, with a big three-seater—McDonald with an extra horse—and drove to the home of what was con-sidered the most desperate of the Sand Creek gang

—a very hard looking customer who lived with his wife in a dug-out in a small clearing. When they had arrived within about two hundred yards of the place, the driver declared that he was satisfied with his position and did not think it necessary by the terms of his contract to go any closer. It was full early, barely daybreak, and everything was very still. McDonald lost no time, therefore, for a whinny of the horses might rouse the occupants of the dug-out, and with his Winchester cocked stepped across the little clearing and without ceremony pushed open the door. As he did so a woman stepped directly in front of him, calling out a warning to some one behind her. In the dimness of the place McDonald saw a man on a bed in the corner reaching for a gun which lay on the mattress near him. It was no time for manners. With a quick sweep of his gun the officer pushed the woman aside and covered the man on the bed, before he could bring his weapon to bear.

" Drop it," he said. " Drop it or you're a dead man! "

There was no mistaking the sincerity of that order. The mild fruit-tree peddler, was merged completely into the resolute officer with eyes of steel and a crisp voice that uttered words of unmistakable meaning. The gun fell upon the bed. McDonald stepped forward and slipping hand-cuffs on his prisoner, ordered him to start for the hack and to make no suspicious movements. Arriving at the awaiting vehicle he invited him to step in and be shackled.

"First delivery," he said to the astonished driver. "We'll go on now and make the rest."

The next hut was perhaps a mile further along, and the sun was getting up when they arrived. As they approached, they saw the occupant standing in the doorway. He saw them about the same time, and suspected trouble. His horse was hitched to a mesquite tree, and making for it he mounted and fled. McDonald was mounted also and gave chase. The race continued for perhaps half a mile when the officer realized that his man had the better horse and would presently get into the brakes and escape. He dismounted quickly, therefore, and taking careful aim began to shoot at the ground near the flying horse in such a manner that the bullet striking the earth would go singing by, very close to the ears of the fugitive. He had long since discovered that a bullet singing in that way, close to a man's ears has an impressive and convincing sound. A man hearing a bullet sing by like that would be willing to bet any reasonable sum that the next one would hit him, especially when the command, "Halt! or I'll get you, next time," came with it. With the second shot the disturbed rider brought his horse up suddenly, dismounted and made motions of surrender. McDonald signaled him to approach, still keeping him covered. He came up in good order, and was marched toward the hack, the driver of which headed in that direction, now that the danger was over.

It was thought that the sound of the shooting might have aroused the neighborhood by this time, and the thief-hunters worked more cautiously. There was no need, however. Gun-fire was of too frequent occurrence to create alarm in that locality, and the sense of immunity from the law had become too chronic to be lightly disturbed. The desperadoes had been left unmolested so long that they had become established in their security and careless of intrusion. Two men were at breakfast at the next place, and deputy Bill's Winchester covered them before they fairly realized that they had a morning visitor. These two were hand-cuffed together and marched to the hack. The driver by this time had picked up a good deal of courage and remained only a few yards behind. As for the outlaws, they were inclined to be sociable, and with the true Western American spirit discerned a certain humor in the situation.

" Hello, Jim, you been buying fruit trees too? " was the greeting of one of the men already loaded as the hand-cuffed pair came in. " What did you get, peaches or pears? "

" You go to hell, will you? You'll get a tree with a rope on it before you get out of this mess."

" That's all right—you must have bought sour grapes, I reckon, the way you talk."

" No, his got frost-bit. They'll be all right in the

spring. My apples got a little case of dry-rot, too. I wonder how Buck Dillon 'll like them blue plums o' his'n.''

McDonald, always good-natured with his prisoners, joined in the bantering.

'' I'm delivering,'' he said, '' I brought in a nice pair, this time,'' as he loaded his double capture into the hack. Truly no situation can entirely destroy the breezy Western point of view.

The next house lay across quite a stretch of prairie and the hack and its contents were discovered before the approach was near enough for effective action. McDonald on horseback immediately charged, but the outlaw suspected the nature of his visitor and mounting his horse raced away, emptying his six-shooter at his pursuer. Riding, and shooting backward disturbed his aim and his bullets flew wild. McDonald also began shooting, to bring him to a halt, not to kill. As the outlaw uncased his Winchester, however, the officer decided that it was time to bring matters to a focus. Dropping to the ground he knelt and set some bullets singing close to the ear of the fugitive. At first this only had the effect of making him sink his spurs into the pony, but at the third crack of the gun and just as Deputy Bill was taking careful aim for a shot that would be likely to save the cost of prosecution the rider dropped his gun back into the scabbard, and leaped to the ground.

'' Well, you've got me,'' he called as he came up.

" Hello, Joe, what you been buyin'? Prickly pears I reckon," was the greeting from the hack as he came nearer—the latter half of the remark due to a trickle of blood on the man's ear where the last bullet had sung its warning song a trifle too close.

" Must a struck a stone and glanced a little," commented Bill Jess as he looked at it. " I aim to make 'em miss just about three inches. They sing nicer when they don't really hit. That either glanced off of a stone or else it's mighty sorry shooting. Dad-slap it, that sorter makes me ashamed of myself. Oh, well, get in an' make yourself comfortable. I want to get along."

The boy who had been " born with a gun in his hand " as we say, and could pick cherries with a rifle was humiliated by anything that resembled bad marksmanship. Still, it was good enough under the circumstances, and was justified by the result.

That was a busy day. His favorite hour for working (day-break) was over, now, but matters were going too well to knock off on that account. There were at least three more of this gang, and he would get as many as he could.

He got them all in fact, and one extra—a bad man who happened to be visiting his brother at a bad time. The houses being a good way apart, and the work being done rapidly and with such system and neatness, the alarm had no time to spread. Deputy Bill knew the exact location of each house and of course used more caution in making the approaches as the day advanced. He stalked his game like the true hunter that he was, creeping up unnoticed until he had it covered, keeping the hack well out of view, though by this time the driver had lost all concern, except that of eagerness to see the fun, and was disappointed as were the captured fruit-tree buyers when kept out of view.

The hack went into Kingfisher next morning with every seat full and the driver sitting on the knees of two prisoners. The Sand Creek gang—one of the toughest gangs in the Territory—in the space of a single day and by a single man had been retired from active business.

From Kingfisher, their captor wired U. S. Marshal Walker at Topeka that he had his men and would proceed with them to Wichita, Kansas, as soon as he had rested a little. Within a few days the men were being distributed to the various points where they were wanted for an assortment of crimes. When McDonald and his driver returned to Guthrie, the men he had invited to assist had a downcast look. They had heard the news of the Sand Creek gang. They had heard also from Mr. Walker. Their excuses were many and various, and to a man they offered to join the next expedition.

" No," said Bill Jess, drily, " you fellows are a little too slow. My deliveries in this section are all made."

XV

Cleaning up the Strip

DEPUTY BILL GETS "STOOD OFF," BUT MAKES GOOD.
BILL COOK AND "SKEETER." "A HELL OF
A COURT TO PLEAD GUILTY IN"

THE Cherokee Strip campaign was not allowed to languish. An outlaw community about twenty-five miles north of Kingfisher, and seven miles west of Hennessey, on Turkey Creek, was raided next. In the course of his tree selling, McDonald had fallen in with a man who was peddling stolen beef. He had learned that this man was operating for the Turkey Creek gang, and that the beef he was selling was really the property of the Cherokee Strip Live-Stock Association, which, it may be mentioned, at that time had a lease on the Cherokee grazing lands for which they paid an annual rental of one hundred thousand dollars.

McDonald now went over to Kingfisher and established headquarters; took the beef peddler to Wichita, Kansas, put him in jail, and got on friendly terms with him. Then he gave his prisoner some good fatherly advice about bad company and the usual rewards of becoming the tool of lawless men. The result was a general confession and turning of State's evidence. The peddler of beef lodged information as to the identity of his employers; the exact nature of their business; the hiding place of their stolen cattle, and the locality of a deep water-hole where they had sunk the hides in order to get rid of the brands and earmarks. McDonald returned to Kingfisher, next morning, swore out warrants for the men named, and with a deputy marshal, who declared himself willing to go, set out for Turkey Creek. They went in a hack as usual and arrived before daylight at the house of one Charlie Tex, where they thought it likely they might find most of the men wanted. When they entered, however, they found only a man in bed, who declared he had just arrived in that country; that there was nobody at home, and that he knew nothing of the owner's whereabouts. They took him along, however, and proceeded to another house not far away, but found it also empty. The officers now concluded that the men had in some manner got wind of their coming and were hiding in the bottoms. They followed a way down the creek, breaking through to the prairie again, not far from the Tex house. As they did so they noticed the man with them apparently trying to signal in that direction. Then they became aware that several men with Winchesters were walking leisurely along the top of the grassy hill, either unaware of the presence of the officers, or indifferent to it.

McDonald and his associate, satisfied that these

were the men wanted, set out up the hill, briskly. Their companion discouraged this movement, insisting that they would all certainly be killed if they molested that crowd. They continued to advance, however, and presently the men with the Winchesters, without appearing to have noticed the deputies, dropped leisurely back behind the hill-top. McDonald now started running, straight up the hill, while his brother deputy set out in a sort of diagonal flank movement around it. In a moment or two he had apparently reached a place where he could see the retreating men, for he called out:

" Hey, Mack, they're right over the hill. They'll get you sure."

McDonald was too interested to stop, now. He raced to the top of the rise, his gun presented, ready for shooting, expecting to see the flash of guns as he broke the sky-line. Instead, he saw the men running for Tex's dug-out, and noticed that still another fellow was already there, pacing about, like a picket, with a gun.

McDonald did not take time to guess at their plans, but kept straight after them, supposing his companion-in-law was following. The men did not pause when they reached the house, but made for a half-built log stable, which formed a sort of pen, and leaping into it put their guns through the spaces between the logs and yelled at McDonald to stop, swearing they would kill him if he came any further.

A brave man is not necessarily a rash man, and

to establish bravery it is not necessary to throw one-self in front of a moving train or to charge alone a half-finished log stable full of outlaws who poke their Winchesters through the cracks at you and call you names. McDonald discovered now that his partner was not with him, or anywhere in the neigh-borhood, and he concluded to stop and negotiate. One might get an outlaw or two through the cracks, but on the whole it didn't seem the part of wisdom to play the game in that way.

He checked his speed when he was about sixty yards from the fort, though he continued to advance in a leisurely walk, talking persuasively meantime.

" Now you fellers better have some sense," he said. " You're going up against the United States law, and even if you killed me it wouldn't make any difference. I've got a posse coming that would be right down on you anyhow. Besides you'd have the United States army after you, and they'd take you and hang you for murder. I only want two out of your bunch anyway, this time; that's all I got war-rants for, and maybe none of you are the right ones. You'd better come out and let me look you over."

The men swore they would do nothing of the sort, and if he came a step further they would kill him.

McDonald slackened his pace a bit—some nervous man's gun might go off by accident. He could talk very well from where he was.

" Oh, pshaw! " he said. " You fellers wouldn't kill a kitten. Six of you men behind breastworks

to get away from one. Come out where I can look
at you. What kind of men are you, anyway? "

" Where's your partner? " called the outlaws.

" You see him, way up yonder, don't you? " Bill
Jess said quaintly—" on that hill. I haven't got a
rope on him; I couldn't bring him along unless he'd
come. You-all are actin' mighty sorry the way
you're doin'. Come out of there now, and quit this
foolishness."

The outlaws repeated their refusal and their
warning that if he came another step they would
shoot him dead. McDonald took out his watch.

" Well, boys," he said, " if you want to make
a fight you might as well get at it. It's time for
my men to be here. Your partner I got yesterday
said you'd likely try to start something, so I come
fixed for such fellows as you. Come, let's see what
you can do."

McDonald waved his hand as if signaling to his
companion half a mile in the rear and made a start
toward the log fort. Before he had taken two steps,
out of it piled the six outlaws and broke " lickety
brindle " for the creek bottom, like a bunch of
frightened steers. McDonald ran after them and
saw them leap on their horses that they had tethered
in the bushes and go tearing down the creek, without
stopping to look behind. Evidently they did not
doubt for a moment that the deputy had a posse,
waiting nearby, for they would not be likely to believe that he had dared to face them alone unless

assistance was close at hand. Deputy Bill, on his part was not sorry to see them go, for they had him at a serious disadvantage, and his only backing had weakened.

His companion was at the hack when he returned. The one man they had taken in charge had disappeared. Bill Jess made a few choice remarks and they set out for Kingfisher by way of Hennessey.

The following night as McDonald came out of a drug-store in Kingfisher, several shots were fired at him from the darkness. He pulled his six-shooter immediately and emptied it at the flash of the guns, running toward them as he did so. He heard retreating footsteps, but did not follow, as he discovered that he had left his cartridge belt in the hotel.

He was satisfied that the attack had been made by some of the Turkey Creek gang of the day before, trying to get rid of him, and resolved to delay no further in putting them out of business. He enlisted a man whom he knew, one Charley Meyers, and two other young men anxious for adventure, and next morning struck the trail which led, as they expected, in the direction of Turkey Creek. They followed it rapidly and toward evening came upon their game. There was no parleying this time. McDonald headed his force and they charged with a rush. Three of the men threw down their arms and surrendered—the others fired some scattering shots as they ran, and they must have kept on running, for they troubled that country no more. The Turkey and Sand Creek gangs no longer existed.*

It was while McDonald was at Kingfisher that he came in contact with Bill Cook and one " Skeeter," both of whom were later to become notorious in matters connected with the looting of banks and trains. The deputy was making some purchases in a store one evening when Cook attempted to ride his horse in the front door. McDonald grabbed the animal's bridle and set him back on his haunches, and before Cook could draw his gun—had him covered and under arrest. Immediately Cook's " side-partner," Skeeter, came up swearing vengeance, and was also suddenly disarmed and landed in jail. The incident closed there, but a sort of sequel was to come along a good many years later, as we shall see presently.

Meanwhile the work of " delivery " by the erstwhile tree-man was not delayed. Following the backward track he gathered up one undesirable citizen after another, until by the end of the season he had established official relations with no less than

---

* Somewhat later when McDonald's work, as Ranger Captain, was confined to Texas, another gang did rendezvous in this section—the gang headed by the Dalton boys (formerly deputy marshals); and for a period terrorized the surrounding country. Their crimes were daring and bloody and their end was sudden and violent. They were shot, one after another by a brave and accurate liveryman as they came out of a bank they had been looting, in daylight, in Coffeyville, Kansas. According to Bill Dalton two of the Daltons were United States deputy marshals and lived near Hennessey at the time McDonald was selling trees in that section.

fifty of his former customers, and the rest had concluded not to wait. The story of the work of that
year alone would fill a volume if fully told, but the
telling is not necessary. Having planned a campaign
along special lines it is only needful to give one or
two examples of Bill McDonald's work to see what
the rest would be in that particular field. Each
field of labor was different and called for different
treatment—requiring as much genius to conceive
the method as bravery and presence of mind to carry
it out. We have now seen what he accomplished in
reclaiming a land so lost that it was called No-man's
Land, and in cleaning up a strip of country infested
by desperadoes supposed to be invincible. We have
seen that he could do these things with thoroughness
and despatch and with little bloodshed. The old
manner of going in with a big posse and engaging in
a general fight in which men were killed on both
sides and nothing of value accomplished he had rendered obsolete. Men politically and personally opposed to Bill McDonald have referred to him in print
and in spoken word as bloodthirsty, and a desperado. Certainly the reader who has followed
these chapters thus far will find it hard to agree
with such opinions. That he was fearless almost to
the point of rashness we may believe, but that he
ever wantonly shed blood, or, with all his opportunities, deliberately took human life will be harder
to demonstrate.

"I never was a killer," he said once. "Some

fellows seem to want to kill, every chance they get, and in a business like mine there's plenty of chances. But I never did want to kill a man, and I never did it when there was any other way to take care of his case."

It may not be out of place here to refer to the method of disarming men which McDonald used. The author has been asked how this sudden and efficient action was performed. His reply is that it is just about as hard to explain as those sleight-of-hand tricks which depend on deftness and exactness of motion—the result of a natural ability combined with long practice. Bill McDonald was born " as quick as a cat," and disarming became his special sleight-of-hand trick. He could locate a man's weapon and could daze and disarm him with a sudden movement that even he himself could not convey in words, and it was this performance that saved the lives of many men, good and bad, and oftentimes his own.

It was some six years after the Kingfisher incident that McDonald was to renew relations with the " Cook-Skeeter " outfit. He had become Ranger Captain meantime and was engaged in some work in North Texas when he heard of a suspicious gang, heavily armed, camped in a vacant house in the neighborhood of Bellevue, in Clay County. Unable to go himself, he sent his sergeant, J. L. Sullivan, his nephew, W. J. McCauley and another ranger named Bob McClure, to investigate. Before the

Rangers reached the house a picket discovered them
and set out to give warning to his associates. The
Rangers overtook and captured him, but by this
time they had been discovered by the occupants of
the shanty who began firing through the cracks in
the walls.

The Rangers promptly returned the fire and
charged, shooting as they came on. The fire became
very hot, but McCauley, who had many of the characteristics of his " Uncle Bill," kicked in the door,
though the bullets were coming through it from the
other side. The outlaws now took refuge in the loft
and began shooting down through the floor, the
Rangers shooting straight up from below. The
Rangers would seem to have had the best luck in
this blind warfare for one of the men above was
wounded; another had his gun shot from his hand,
and a third had his hat shot through. One of them
came to the opening, presently, and offered his six-
shooter as a sign of surrender. Four were captured,
including the aforenamed " Skeeter," but Bill Cook,
though a member of the gang, was absent at the time,
and escaped. The captured men were taken to
Wichita Falls and one of them, a young fellow
named Turner, turned State's evidence, through Mc-
Donald's persuasive probing, and detailed their plan
for robbing the Fort Worth and Denver, next day,
giving a list of their crimes. Skeeter and the others
were taken to the United States courts at Fort Smith
for trial, and pleaded guilty. Skeeter was given

thirty years and upon hearing the verdict made his now famous remark:

" Well, this is a hell of a court for a man to plead guilty in."

XVI

Texas Ranger Service and its Origin

THE MASSACRE OF FORT PARKER. CYNTHIA ANN PARKER'S CAPTURE. RANGERS, AND WHAT THEY ARE FOR. THEIR CHARACTERISTICS AND THEIR REQUIREMENTS

The early history of Texas was written in blood and fire. Her counties preserve the names of her martyrs. Parker, Coleman, Crockett, Fannin, Travis, Bowie and a hundred others have the map for their monument; their names are given daily utterance by those for whom their deeds have little meaning.

In the beginning, after the Indian tribes—friendly at first—became hostile, the warfare was almost solely with the savages. For a full half century every settler who built his campfire on the frontier did so at the risk of his property and his scalp. Those who established homes and settlements must have been a daring race indeed, for raids upon horses and herds were always imminent and massacres were as regular as the seasons.

We have already mentioned in these chapters the name of Chief Quanah Parker (still living) for whom the town of Quanah, Texas, was named. Quanah Parker's mother was Cynthia Ann Parker, a little white girl captured by the Tehaucano Indians, during a raid on what was known as the Austin Colony, in 1836. A brief story of that raid will serve as an example of a thousand others of a similar sort. The Austin Colony settled in what in now Grimes County,* and consisted of something more than a score of persons, including women and children. The Indians who dwelt in the neighborhood seemed friendly enough until a small party of unknown settlers came along and attempted to steal their horses. Immediate trouble was the result and the loss of Tehaucano friendship for the entire settlement. When the reader considers what follows, I believe I shall be forgiven for hoping that those newcomers who stirred up the first trouble received the sort of a reward which only an Indian would know how to confer.

As the Austin Colony consisted chiefly of the Parker family, a rude fortification which they erected was called Fort Parker, a name that to-day still suggests something of shuddering horror to those who have heard its history.

It was a fair May morning when that history was made. The early risers noticed that a body of restless Indians had collected within about four hundred yards of the fort. A white flag was hoisted by the savages to signify their peaceable intentions,

* The scene of the Parker Massacre is located by some authorities, in Limestone County, somewhat further north. Accounts of the event itself also differ. The details here given are from "Texas Rangers" by A. J. Sowell, and are said to have been supplied by eye-witnesses.

and a warrior approached as if for conference. Benjamin Parker, commander of the fort, went out to meet him. He came back presently with the word that he believed the Indians intended to fight. He returned, however, to the hostile camp, where he was at once set upon and literally chopped to pieces by the savages, who then with wild yells and blood-curdling war-whoops charged on the fort. Some of the inmates had already left the stockade. Others were trying to escape. John Parker and wife and a Mrs. Kellogg were overtaken a mile away. Parker was killed and scalped, his wife was speared and Mrs. Kellogg was made captive. Other members of the colony were butchered right and left, and mutilated in the barbarous fashion which seems to give an Indian joy. Silas Parker was brutally killed and his two children, one of whom was the little girl, Cynthia Ann, were carried away. A Mrs. Plummer —daughter of Rev. James W. Parker—attempted to escape, carrying her little son in her arms. A huge painted savage, begrimed with dust and blood overtook her, felled her with a hoe, and seizing her by the hair dragged her, still clinging to her child, back amid the butchery and torture of her friends. She and the others who were living were beaten with clubs and lashed with rawhide thongs. That night such of the captives as remained alive, and these included three children, were flung face down in the dust, their hands bound behind their backs while the Indians, waving bloody scalps and shrieking, danced about them and beat them with their bows until the prisoners were strangling with their own blood. Later, they took the infant child of Mrs. Plummer and slowly choked it before her eyes. When it was not quite dead they flung it again and again into the air and let it fall on the stones and earth. Then they tied a rope around its neck and threw its naked body into the hedges of prickly pear, from which they would jerk it fiercely with demoniacal yells. Finally they fastened the rope attached to its neck to the pommel of a saddle and rode round and round in a circle until the body of the child was literally in shreds. The poor fragments were then thrown into the mother's lap. For some reason, the little girl, Cynthia Ann Parker, received better treatment, and lived. She grew up an Indian, forgot her own race and tongue, married a chief and became the mother of another chief, Quanah, surnamed Parker, to-day a friend of the white race.

It was the massacre of Fort Parker and events of a similar nature that resulted in the organization of the Texas Rangers. The Rangers were at first a semi-official body, locally enlisted and commanded, with regulations and duties not very clearly defined. Their purpose, however, was not in doubt. It was to defend life and property, and their chief qualifications were to be able to ride and shoot and stand up against the warfare of bloodthirsty savages.

" Exterminate the Indians " became a watchword in those days, and the warfare that ensued and con-

tinued for forty years, can be compared with nothing
in history unless it be with the fierce feuds of the
ancient Scottish clans.

Early in 1836 Texas fought for and gained her
independence, the only State in the Union to achieve
such a triumph. On the following year the Texas
congress recognized the Ranger movement and authorized several persons to raise Ranger companies
to scour the country and annihilate marauding
bands. Indians and low class Mexicans (" greas-
ers ") often consorted, and the work, desperate
and bloody, continued along the ever widening and
westering frontier up to within a period easily remembered to-day by men not beyond middle age.
Many names of those early Rangers have been
preserved in Texas annals and in local song and
traditions, and it would take many volumes to re-
count their deeds. Jack Hays, James and Resin
Bowie, " Big-foot " Wallace, Kit Ackland, Tom
Green " Mustang " Grey, of whom the song says:

> " At the age of sixteen
> He joined that jolly band
> And marched from San Antonio
> Out to the Rio Grand,"——

these and a hundred others are names that thrilled
the Texan of that elder day and they are still repeated and linked with tales of wild warfare and
endurance that are hardly surpassed in the world's
history of battle. A. J. Sowell, himself a Ranger
in the early seventies, when Indian outbreaks were

still frequent and disastrous, speaking of the Ranger equipment says:

" We had to furnish our own horses, clothing and six-shooters. The State furnished us carbines, cartridges, provisions, etc., and we got fifty dollars a month." *

It will be seen from the foregoing how different the Ranger service and regulations were from those of either the federal or state troops. Unlike the army they wore no uniform, and they provided, for the most part, their own equipment. They differed from State and county officials in that they were confined to no county or portion of the State, but could " range " wherever their service was needed and with little or no direction from headquarters until their mission was accomplished. It will be clearly seen that men constituting such a band must be not only brave, and quick and accurate with fire-arms, but must be men of good character and high, firm principle as well. It is the moral qualification more than any other that has given the Ranger organization its efficiency and power. A force, how-ever small, composed of men who can shoot straight and are brave, and who believe in the right, is well-nigh invincible. The Rangers, originally organized for a great and sacred purpose, the defense of homes, went forth like knights inspired by lofty motives and high resolves, and during whatever change that has come in the aspect of their duties

* "Texas Rangers," by A. J. Sowell, of Seguin, Tex., 1884.

the tradition of honor seems to have been preserved. Indeed they have been from the beginning not unlike the knights of old who rode forth without fear and without reproach to destroy evil and to redress wrong.

Speaking further of Ranger equipment Sowell says:

" In the first place he wants a good horse; strong saddle, double-girted; a good carbine (this was before the day of Winchesters); pistol and plenty of ammunition. He generally wears rough clothing, either of buckskin or strong durable cloth and a broad-brimmed hat of the Mexican style; thick overshirt, top boots * and spurs, and a jacket or short coat so that he can use himself with ease in the saddle."

And the author adds:

" A genuine Texas Ranger will endure cold, hunger and fatigue, almost without a murmur, and will stand by a friend and comrade in the hour of danger and divide anything he has got from a blanket to his last crumb of tobacco."

So much for the Ranger and his origin. As the years went by and the Indian was conquered or driven away, the Ranger's work changed, but his personality remained the same. The Ranger of

* The Ranger's boots like those of the cowboy are made with high heels to prevent his foot from slipping through the stirrup. Both the Ranger and the cowboy ride with the stirrup in the middle of the foot, it being safer and also less fatiguing on a long ride, sometimes a distance of a hundred miles between daylight and dark.

seventy years ago is the Ranger of to-day—only, his duties have altered. Long before the conquest of the savages a new element of disorder had entered the field. The desperado who had stirred up the first Indian troubles had survived and increased, to plunder his own race. The new and sparsely settled land invited every element of lawlessness and every refugee of crime. Local authorities would not or could not contend with them. It was for the Rangers, now much reduced in numbers, to solve the problem of destroying the disturber in their midst as they had driven the savage enemy from their frontiers. They were made peace officers, and became a mounted constabulary, their duties being to quell disorders, to prevent crime and to bring criminals to justice. It was new work—less romantic than the wild Indian warfare of the frontier; work full of new dangers and what was still worse it was work which instead of inviting the encouragement and enthusiasm of a community, was of a sort to incur its displeasure, for the desperadoes of a neighborhood were either the heroes or the terrors of it, and in either case to molest them was likely to prove unpopular. So it was, during this new order of things, that the Ranger service had to contend not only with the offenders but sometimes with the very people whom they were hoping to protect. This made the work hard and discouraging, as work always is hard and discouraging when it is done amid enemies who wear the guise of friends. How well

they have succeeded is told in the official reports.
W. H. Mabry, Adjutant General of Texas in 1896,
says in his report for that year, referring to the
Rangers:

" This branch of the service has been very active
and has done incalculable good in policing the
sparsely settled sections of the State where the local
officers, from the very nature of the conditions, could
not afford adequate protection. Including the mean-
derings of the Rio Grande we have about 3,000 miles
of frontier line. Part of this borders on a foreign
country, with different customs, law and language.
Only a river fordable at most any point intervenes.
But for the Ranger force, specially equipped for
continued rapid movements, this border line would
be the rendezvous for criminals of nearly every
description and class."

General Mabry then sets down the fact that the
Ranger service has increased the State revenues by
something like four hundred thousand dollars for
the year through the protection of leased frontier
State lands which otherwise could not be inhabited
and would yield no return in either rental or taxes.

In concluding he adds: " It is true that the frontier
force does not and could not cover all this territory,
but the fact that they exist and are scouting over
every foot they can travel prevents organized bands
from being established along this border line. . . .
They are circumscribed by no county limits; can
easily and rapidly move from one section to another

and criminals do not care to invite their pursuit. Specially equipped for continued rapid motion, they take up the trail and follow it with a persistency of the sleuth hound, until the criminal is either run out of the country, captured or killed.

" In every train robbery which has occurred in Texas, the robbers have been either captured or killed, whenever it was possible to carry the Rangers to the scene, so they could take the trail. The broad expanse of sparsely settled territory in this State would offer easy opportunity for such crimes, if it were not for the protection given by our mobile and active Ranger force."

XVII

"Captain of Company B, Ranger Force"

CAPTURE OF DAN AND BOB CAMPBELL. RECOMMENDATIONS FOR A RANGER CAPTAIN. GOVERNOR "JIM" HOGG APPOINTS HIS OLD FRIEND ON THE STRENGTH OF THEM

It will be seen from the foregoing, and from the chapters already published of these memoirs, that a man like Bill McDonald would be well qualified for Ranger service. Already he had been appointed a special Ranger in Company B., commanded by Captain S. A. McMurray, but his duties as U. S. Deputy Marshal, in No-man's Land and in the Cherokee Strip, had been his chief work. Nevertheless, he had, on occasion, engaged in bandit-hunting in his own State, during this period, either alone or in company with other officials, usually with good results. An instance of this kind was the capture of Dan and Bob Campbell which occurred about the time of his concluding the Cherokee Strip campaign.

With his wife, McDonald was on the way from Quanah to Fort Worth, when, at a switch now known as Iowa Park, they met a special, standing on a side-track, waiting for them to pass. It was the sort of train that is made up for an urgent purpose, consisting only of an engine and a single car, and Mc-

Donald recognized upon it the sheriff of Wichita
Falls, also the marshal and others of a posse, evidently out for action. Upon inquiry, he learned that
the Campbell boys, two well-known desperadoes of
that time, were believed to be somewhere in the
neighborhood, preparing to waylay a train. A
good reward had been offered for the Campbells and
the sheriff and his men were considerably moved.
McDonald asked if they would like his assistance,
and being assured that they would, sent word back
to his wife by the conductor of the down train that
he was going to catch some bad men, and boarding
the special already impatient to start, took the back
track toward Burke, a small station where the outlaws had been seen. When they reached there, it
was McDonald's wish to procure horses and begin
the search at that point, but the sheriff and his posse
thought better to proceed to Harrold, some twenty
miles further along, in which direction it was supposed the bandits had traveled.

Leaving word at Burke that they were to be notified in case of any fresh discoveries, the officers
again boarded the special, and upon arriving at Harrold found a telegram that the outlaws had been seen
entering a thicket not far from Burke. Horses, and
a freight car in which to load them, were immediately
secured, and the train was backed to Burke. Here
the officials separated, the sheriff directing Mc-
Donald and the guide who had located the burglars,
with a man selected from the posse, to go in one

direction, while the sheriff with the remainder of the posse, took another course; the general plan being to round in on the thicket where the outlaws were supposed to be concealed. Arriving near the place, Deputy McDonald and the two men with him discovered two horses hitched in the brush—undoubtedly the mounts of the two Campbells. It was certain now that the quarry was near by, and the three men waited a little for the sheriff and his party to come up. It became evident, however, that their tactics were of a different sort. The posse was scattering out as if they were deer-hunting, taking stands at various distant and semi-distant points, evidently expecting McDonald and his companions to go in and start up the game. McDonald noticed now that his guide was not armed, and was therefore of no further service. Turning to his other companion, he said:

" I don't like this kind of performance. I'm in favor of charging straight in on them."

His companion seemed to agree to this plan, and without further word Deputy Bill put spurs to his horse, charged straight into the thicket, and suddenly found himself almost on top of Dan and Bob Campbell. Without a breath of hesitation, he leaped to the ground, leveled at the former, who was already in the act of shooting, and commanded him to drop his gun. The order was obeyed; but Bob Campbell, who would seem to have been asleep, reached for his six-shooter, and though commanded

THE CAPTURE OF DAN AND BOB CAMPBELL.

'' He charged straight into the thicket, and suddenly found himself almost on top of them.''

not to touch it upon penalty of death, paid small attention to that order. He did not attempt to fire the weapon, but lay there on the ground with it raised, defying his would-be captor with language that was both violent and uncomplimentary. McDonald now suddenly realized that he was alone; that his companion had failed to join in the charge. Bob Campbell realized this too, and became momentarily more defiant. Then, all at once, help arrived. A dentist who had joined the sheriff's posse, had observed Deputy McDonald's single-handed charge, and now came bravely to his assistance. The Campbells both surrendered, then, for the posse was not far behind. They were taken to Wichita Falls, where the sheriff promptly claimed credit for the capture—also, the reward. Later, the Campbells broke jail, but were eventually recaptured, and served a long sentence.

Events of this sort kept Bill McDonald's name fresh in the Texas mind, and made him seem peculiarly eligible for regular service. The resignation of Captain S. A. McMurray, who had long and bravely commanded Company B became his opportunity, and he hurried to Austin to try for that command.

His old friend, James Hogg, was now governor of the State. Since the settlement of their differences so long before, there had been no discord of any kind, and each had admired the other's career, proud to remember the friendship. Arriving at the capital,

McDonald was shown into the governor's room. Greeting him, he said:

" Well, I hardly know what to call you, since you got to be governor. I don't know whether to call you ' Jim ' or ' Mister.' I'll have to call you ' Governor,' I guess, as I want to get a place."

They shook hands cordially. Governor Hogg said:

" What is it, Bill? What can I do for you? "

" Why," said McDonald, " I came down to get to be Ranger Captain—to take McMurray's place in Company B."

Hogg looked at him reprovingly.

" Why didn't you let me know sooner? " he said. " There are two other applications for the place; both from good men, with long petitions and fine endorsements."

The applicant for position forgot his old friend's title.

" Why, Jim," he said, " I never thought of it until a day or two ago. I didn't have time to get endorsements, but I can get 'em, if you want them. I have been working mostly in No-man's Land and the Territory lately, but have done work in Texas too, and I can get about any kind of endorsement you want."

Hogg laughed. He had a robust sense of humor.

" By gatlins! " he said, using his favorite expression. " That's all right, Bill, you have already got the best endorsement I ever saw."

McDonald looked puzzled.

" I don't understand," he said, " I didn't know anybody knew I wanted a place."

" All the same, you have got the endorsements," insisted Hogg.

He turned to his desk, and got out a bundle of letters.

" Look over these," he said. " You probably know some of the writers."

McDonald took the letters, and read them one after another. They were from well-known criminals, their lawyers, their friends and their associates. They had been received by Hogg while he was attorney-general, and each was a protest and a complaint against McDonald, declaring him to be a ruthless and tyrannical official, whose chief recreation was hounding good citizens for the sake of revenge or glory, enforcing laws that were not on the statute books, adding that it was not unusual for him to put the said citizen in jail, or in box-cars, declaring further that he sometimes hitched them to posts with chains, and that he was a menace to legitimate settlement and society in general.

McDonald looked over some of these documents, and grinned.

" That's so, Jim," he said, " I do put 'em in box-cars when there ain't a jail; the way I used to do back in Mineola—you recollect, when the jail was full—and I lariat 'em out with a chain and a post when there ain't a box-car handy; but I don't reckon they're innocent."

Hogg nodded.

" By gatlins! Those endorsements are good enough for me," he said. " They carry the flavor of conviction, I appoint you Ranger Captain on the strength of them."

McDonald returned to Quanah with his appointment as captain of " Company B, Frontier Battalion." The headquarters of the company were then at Amarillo, in the southern part of Potter County, near the Randall County line. This was almost the exact center of the Pan-handle, and in a locality sparsely settled, untamed, and lawless.

Since the early days of " Ranging " there had been not much change in Ranger regulations and equipment. The character of the work, however, had changed and the force had been reduced in numbers. Company B now consisted of only eight members all told. These were supposed to range over all that vast section known as the Pan-handle, and were subject to orders that might take them to any other portion of the State where their assistance was needed. The Rangers were peace-officers, their duty being to assist the local officers, rather than to take the initiative and predominate.* In the Pan-handle, however, and in many other portions of the State, the Rangers were obliged to lead, for the reason that the local officers were either incapable, indifferent, or incriminated, as we have already seen.

---

* This came into dispute somewhat later and the Twenty-seventh Legislature passed an Act confirming what had always been their custom.

The Ranger camp at Amarillo—besides the eight men mentioned—consisted of tents, furnished by the State, a wagon and mule team, a hack, and two pack-mules. Each Ranger furnished his own horse and arms; the State paid for food and ammunition, also for transportation when necessary. In Company B were enrolled Sergeants J. M. Brittain and W. J. Sullivan; Privates John and Tom Platt, Jim Green, John Bracken and John Bishop; also somewhat later, W. J. McCauley—McDonald's nephew—a daring youth—then about eighteen years old, but a natural plainsman, dashing and fearless; an ideal Ranger.

Expeditions were always made with horses. When the distance was far, the horses and pack-mules were shipped to the nearest railway-point, sometimes by special train; an engine and car being secured for such excursions. This train would stop at any point required; the horses and pack-mules were jumped from the door of the car to the ground—sometimes a distance of several feet—and when the point of attack was close by, this wild little army would sweep across the prairie or through the bushes; the pack-mules, loaded with cooking utensils and tinware, often clattering ahead—riderless, but seeming to know by instinct where to go—braying, with tail in air, constituting an advance guard of reform. It would seem that such a charge might have given the alarm and frightened every outlaw within a radius of several miles; but as a matter of fact, these charges were generally planned and undertaken with great secrecy, and the sudden clamor of such an approach was likely to create an amazement which did not subside to the point of action before the time for escape had slipped by. Speaking of it afterwards, Captain McDonald said:

" That infernal racket seemed to jar the nerve of a criminal, for I never knew a pack-mule charge where the men we wanted seemed to have either spunk enough to put up a good fight or sense enough to get away."

XVIII

An Exciting Indian Campaign

FIRST SERVICE AS RANGER CAPTAIN.   BIGGEST INDIAN SCARE ON RECORD

It was in January, 1891, that Bill McDonald received his appointment as Ranger Captain, and his first official service was not long delayed. He arrived at Amarillo about midnight, and was received with congratulations, for the news had traveled ahead of him. He was tired, however, and the hour was late, so he presently slipped away to bed. He had hardly fallen asleep when he was rudely awakened and handed a telegram which stated that the Indians had made a raid across the border, and were killing and robbing in Hall County, near Salisbury.

Captain McDonald read the telegram and laughed. There had been no Indian troubles in Texas for a number of years. White renegades there were in plenty, but Indian outbreaks had long since ceased.

" I guess the boys are trying to have some fun with me on my first night," he said, and turned in once more to sleep. But a few minutes later another telegram came; and another; this time from the superintendent of the railroad company—a Mr. Good, whom McDonald knew as a man not given to practical joking.

The Ranger Captain dressed himself, hurried over to the telegraph office and got the operator there to talk over the wire to the operator where the scare had originated. He learned that it seemed to be genuine, and that everybody was leaving the neighborhood. The operator at Salisbury ended his information with " Good-by, I'm going now myself."

Captain Bill still could not believe it a genuine Indian incursion. Hall County was in the second tier from the Territory line, and the Indians would have had to cross Childress County to get to it. He did not believe that they would undertake to do this, or that they could have accomplished it without previous alarms. Still, it was his duty to investigate. He got a special train; loaded in men, horses and pack-mules, and set out on a hunt for Indians. It was about a hundred miles to Salisbury, and they reached there early in the day. Not a soul was in sight anywhere. The inhabitants were hidden, some in dug-outs, some in haystacks, some in the tall grass. Here and there, as the train pulled in, McDonald saw a head stick out from a sod house far out on the prairie, then suddenly disappear, like a prairie-dog dropping into his hole. He set out to interview some of these wary settlers, and learned that the Indian alarm had been given by a man—a new settler just arrived in the country—who had ridden his horse to death and lost one of his children —having left him far behind somewhere—in his wild eagerness to escape the savages who, he declared, were burning and scalping not far away. Captain Bill found this man, and after a little talk with him was convinced that what he had seen was nothing more nor less than some cowboys on a round-up, disporting themselves around their camp-fire at night, as cowboys will—dancing and capering in the mad manner of young plainsmen whose ideas of amusement are elemental, and whose opportunities for social diversions are few. The man and the neighborhood, however, remained unconvinced, so it was decided to visit the scene of the disturbance.

Horses, men and pack-mules unloaded themselves from the freight car, and went racing over the prairie; the pack-mules, as usual, plunging and braying with tail in air, their tinware clattering in a manner calculated to put a whole tribe of Indians into a panic and send them capering across the eastern horizon into their own domain. But there were no Indians. It was as Captain Bill had thought; a gang of cowboys, the evening before, had rounded up some cattle; killed a beef; carried it to their camp near by, where they had built a great fire and roasted it, doing a wild war-dance of celebration, and shooting off their six-shooters in their prodigal expression of joy. Viewed from a little distance, through a sort of mirage condition which had exaggerated the whole effect, the scene to the newcomers was a horrifying picture of savages about a burning home, with the inhabitants fleeing for their lives.

The man who had just moved in had stampeded for his own safety and started a general alarm, which did not subside even when the cowboys themselves came in and testified to the truth. The panic spread throughout that section of the country and other reports of Indian outbreaks were circulated, becoming magnified until it was believed that the Indians had broken out, and were making a general raid on the Pan-handle. The inhabitants of one town, south of Amarillo, threw up breastworks, got behind them, and put out pickets in preparation for the arrival of the Indians. Every man seen loping across the prairie was reported as an Indian; and all this happened as late as 1891, when there had been no Indian outbreaks for years, and when there was scarcely a possibility of anything of the sort. It was a big joke, of course, afterward, but it seemed no joke at the time, and it was Bill McDonald's initiation as Captain of Company B.

XIX

A Bit of Farming and Politics

THERE were to be plenty of real alarms soon
enough, with plenty of desperately hard work. Before taking up this part of the story, however, it
may not be out of place to dwell briefly on certain
other labors and interests incident to this period in
Captain McDonald's career.

The ranch on Wanderer's Creek, conducted for
the most part by his plucky wife, remained one of
his possessions and in time became not unprofitable.
McDonald was one of the first to break land in that
section and when he put in a sowing of wheat it
was thought that he had gone daft. But the following year when the plowed land turned off a crop
of from twenty to thirty bushels to the acre, those
who had been first to scoff were likewise the earliest
to imitate.

Captain Bill now became chief promoter in a plan
for the irrigation of this fruitful soil—the water to
be obtained by damming Wanderer's Creek. Several years later, two men of influence and substance,
Cecil Lyon and Joseph Rice, gave able support to
this project with the result that thousands of acres

of grazing land became fertile farms—the cowman's domain passing into the hands of tillers of the soil. The town of Quanah reflected the steady agricultural increase, and what had been an antelope range when McDonald and his wife first drove their herds to that region, became a bustling city—in due time law-abiding—with a population steadily increasing to this day.

The mention of the McDonald herds opens a way here for recording an incident connected with the stocking of the Wanderer's Creek range. McDonald and his wife had decided that they would raise goats as a sort of by-product and began business in this line by introducing a flock of considerable size. However, it was a mistake. The goats were a great nuisance. They would be feeding quietly on the range, when suddenly, without warning, they would be seized with an impulse for violent exercise, and would break away and go racing over the prairie for seven or eight miles, to the brakes of the Pease River, where it was very mountainous and hilly— altogether in accord with a goat's idea of landscape. All the horses on the range were in danger of being run to death chasing goats, getting them together and bringing them back to the range. Finally it got to be a regular occupation, when there was nothing else to do, to head for the Pease River and chase goats. One of the men came in one morning when Captain Bill happened to be at home, and asked:

" Well, Cap, what shall I do to-day? "

" Oh, I don't know. Go chase goats, I reckon."

" All right; but if you want me to do that, you'll
have to get you some goats. I rode all my horses
down a couple o' days ago, hunting for them in the
brakes, and there ain't a goat to be found within
forty miles.

" D——n the goats," said Captain Bill, " I don't
care much for goats, anyhow."

There had been about two hundred of them, and
for several years afterward, hunters from other
States in these wilds used to bring down " mountain
sheep " and " antelope," which bore strong resem-
blance to the flocks which had once been Captain
Bill's.

It was not long after McDonald's appointment as
Ranger Captain that the State political campaign
came on. He had never lost his interest in politics
since the first awakening in the old Mineola days,
when he and Jim Hogg had been ranged against
each other, ready to shed blood for their candidates. Now, Hogg was governor and a candidate
for reëlection, with Bill McDonald ready to show
what he could do in the way of gratitude for favors
past and present. The convention for the nomina-
tion of the State officials was to be held at Houston,
and there was a good deal of excitement, as the
opposition was likely to be strong, with nominations
closely contested. McDonald resolved to be on hand
and ready for any condition or emergency. Arriving in Houston he learned upon investigation that

the supporters of Hogg's opponent, George Clark
of Waco, had laid a plan to pack the convention with
Clark's friends; to occupy it so fully in fact, that it
would be impossible for the regular delegates to get
seats. This would make it necessary for them to
meet elsewhere, and would cause them to be regarded as bolters from the regular convention.
Upon satisfying himself that this was to be the program, Captain McDonald promptly went to his
old friend and other leaders, and proposed to take
charge of matters. As Captain of the Rangers, he
was under the Governor's orders, and with Hogg's
sanction he could use his own methods for preserving the peace and for the prevention of scrambling
and riot.

The convention was to be held in the '' car-shed,''
a very large building, which had been seated for
the purpose. It had a wide entrance to admit cars,
and it could easily have been filled and crowded by
a mob. Captain Bill's plan was to put a good
capable fence across this wide opening, leaving a
narrow passageway for a gate, which would be completely guarded. No one unable to show credentials
as a delegate would be permitted to enter until the
delegates were in and seated.

Governor Hogg approved of the idea and issued
an order accordingly. There was no delay in carrying it out. Captain Bill got some men together,
worked all night, and by sunrise the wide gateway
of the car-shed had been narrowed down to the little

wicket-gate of official admission. It was a complete surprise to the opposition. The gang that had arranged to rush and pack the convention, regarded the barrier and the men delegated to defend it, with amazement and profanity. They began with epithets, and these they followed with more tangible missiles, such as umbrellas, old shoes, and handbags. In another part of the State they might have attempted the use of more effective ammunition. As it was, they were obliged to confine themselves to protests more spectacular than effectual. The regular delegates filed in and were seated. Then the crowds were permitted to enter in the usual way, whereupon another convention was immediately organized in the same hall, with another chairman on the same platform, and for a time two conventions were running side by side.

Captain McDonald was finally called to the platform to preserve order. There was a lively scene. The Ranger was kept busy keeping the two factions separate, taking away their knives, a few pistols, canes, umbrellas and such other weapons and missiles as they attempted to bring into action. The final result was that both Clark and Hogg were nominated, at the same time, in the same convention, and by the same political party, though the Clark followers were styled " Anti-Democrats " and bolters.

Hogg was re-elected in due time, by a good majority. The episode passed into history as the " Car-shed " Convention.

XX

Taming the Pan-handle

THE DIFFERENCE BETWEEN COWBOYS AND " BAD MEN."
HOW CAPTAIN BILL MADE COW-STEALING
UNPOPULAR

THE Texas Pan-handle is that portion of the State which lies directly south of what was No-man's Land, extending from parallels 100 to 103, east and west. Its shape suggests its name, and its name suggests limitless areas of waving grass; vast roving herds; cowboys and ponies—both of the unbridled variety; bad men whose chief business was to start graveyards, and the glad primeval lawlessness that prevails when worlds are new.

Not so many years ago the Pan-handle was distinctly a world apart, and a new one. With No-man's Land on the north, Indian Territory on the east and New Mexico on the west, civilization could come only from the south, and it did not come very fast. Indeed there was still plenty of territory to the southward to be subdued—two or three tiers of counties in fact—before the Pan-handle would be reached. So, it was a place apart—an isolated fertile land, justifying the assertion of a tramp that he had lost a hundred thousand dollars there in one year by not having cattle to eat up the grass.

The cattle came in due time, fighting back the

Apache and the Comanche, protected by Rangers from Ft. Griffin, accompanied by stockmen of every nation, cowboys of every grade and criminals of every breed. That was a wild epoch—chaotic and picturesque—a time of individual administration and untempered justice.

It was also a time of mighty domain. Ranches there were as big as some kingdoms. One, the X. I. T., covered a good portion of the northern part of the Pan-handle. Another, the Matador, spread itself into five counties. When settlement became thicker—when there were ranch-houses not more than twenty-five to thirty miles apart—official allotment of the lands was made. Then there was a grand gobble. The big stockmen fenced everything with little regard for boundaries and less for the law.

With such examples as these in high places, it is not strange that a general indifference for legal rights and possessions prevailed. Next to cattle raising, cattle-stealing was the chief industry. The cowboy proper was not concerned in such work. He was likely to be a clean-handed, straightforward, even if reckless, individual, honest according to his lights. True, loyalty to his employer might render him a trifle indifferent as to brands and marks when strays mixed with the herd, but it was the employer and not the cowboy who profited by such laxity. The cowboy was a retainer who would fight for his ranch, would die for it when circumstances seemed

to require such a sacrifice, and the increase of the
ranch herd by any means short of actual raid and
theft was a custom which bore no relation to dis-
repute. But individually the cowboy was likely to
be the soul of honor and good-nature, troublesome
only on holidays when he was moved to ride into the
nearest settlement, drink up all the whisky he could
buy, and then, with six-shooter drawn, go careering
up and down the streets, shooting in random directions, explaining meantime with noisy and repeti-
tious adjectives, that he was a bad man—a very bad
man from very far up the Creek.

On such inspired occasions he would sometimes
exclaim:

" Hide out little ones! Dad's come home drunk! "
after which he would let go a round of ammunition
and the inhabitants of that neighborhood, regardless of size, would proceed to hide out, as admonished. Sometimes a whole group of cowboys
would engage in this pastime, whereupon the rest
of the town disappeared and sat in cellars or flattened themselves under beds until the cyclone passed
by.

It was in such manner that the cowboy found
relaxations and social joy. He was not a bad man,
in spite of his declaration. He was not really hunting for trouble and would be the last to kill, without
offense.*

* "The Kansas City Journal" recently printed the following cowboy
song, with comments, offering it as a side-light on cowboy life and character. The Journal said :

"The night guards of cattle or horse herds were wont to sing to their

The truly bad man was of entirely different make-up. Always posing, and sometimes accepted, as a

charges as they slowly rode round and round them, keeping watch. If the cattle stampeded, and were then brought together again and began moving in a circle, which the punchers called 'milling,' and on all occasions of fear or uneasiness among the stock, the boys sang to them, and it had a quieting effect. These night riders were perfect horsemen and seasoned to the trail and range. Their hours were endless; the calls upon them for endurance were almost beyond human strength. Picture a night on a lonely prairie, wild, disconcerting, hoarse elements, a stampede among half-wild cattle, and it is not hard to know the task that the cowboy confronted. It is something fine to think that in such hours of danger the cattle could be 'crooned' back to normal quiet. Out of such occasions were the cowboy songs born." Then follow the words of

THE DIM AND NARROW WAY.

" Last night as I lay on the prairie,
Looking up at the stars in the sky,
I wondered if ever a cowboy
Would go to that sweet by and by;
I wondered if ever a cowboy
Would go to that sweet by and by.

The trail to that fair mystic region
Is narrow and dim so they say,
While the broad road that leads to perdition
Is posted and blazed all the way;
While the broad road that leads to perdition
Is posted and blazed all the way.

They say there will be a grand round-up,
Where cowboys like cattle must stand,
To be cut out by riders of judgment,
Who are posted and know every brand;
To be cut out by riders of judgment,
Who are posted and know every brand.

Perhaps there will be a stray cowboy,
Unbranded by anyone nigh,
Who'll be cut out by riders of judgment
And shipped to the sweet by and by;
Who'll be cut out by riders of judgment
And shipped to the sweet by and by."

man of valor, he was in nearly every case merely a boaster and a coward. He would kill when he got the drop on his man, and he built his reputation upon such murders. He passed as a cowboy, when he was merely a cow-thief; as a hero, when he was only an assassin. Driven into a corner he would fight, but his favorite method was to slay from ambush. It was seldom that his reckless disregard for human life included his own.

The Pan-handle was full of bad men in the early nineties. Most of them had graduated from other schools of crime and found here a last resort. Some of them—a good many of them—had obtained official positions and were outlaws and deputies by turns, or worked conjunctively as both. As a rule they were in one way and another associated with a gang.

Local authorities, even when conscientious, were poorly equipped to cope with such an element, and it was for Company B, Ranger Force, consisting of eight men with quarters at Amarillo, Captain W. J. McDonald commanding, to police this vast wilderness, and to capture and convert, or otherwise tame, its undesirable citizens.

Some of them would not wait to be captured; some, of course, could not be tamed alive. Others, and these were not a few, would be able to wield official influence through which they would escape conviction, regardless of the evidence.

Soon after McDonald's appointment he was notified of a marauding band that across in Hutchinson

County were committing the usual crimes. They had burned the hay belonging to a ranchman on Turkey Creek—several hundred tons in quantity—they had cut his wire fences; they had killed cows for their calves, butchered beef cattle, cut out brands—in a word they had conducted the business of cattle-stealing and general depredation on a large scale.

Taking a portion of his force, Captain McDonald went over to investigate. There seemed to be a good deal of mystery concerning the identity of the offenders; but a mystery of that sort does not stand a very good chance when it is operated upon by a man with eyes like those of Captain Bill and with a nose and pair of ears of his peculiar pattern. In a short time he had identified one member of the band in a young man prominently connected in that section. This young fellow—a dupe, no doubt, of professional cow-thieves, whose glittering reputation as bad men had dazzled him—was the son of an able and reputable lawyer, a member of the State legislature. The son, supposed to be a cowboy, had become in reality an outlaw.

Captain McDonald took him in charge one day, questioned him and secured sufficient evidence to file a complaint. The prisoner was turned over to the sheriff of Hutchinson County, and Captain Bill pursued his investigation. He located a bunch of stolen calves, herded in the brakes of the Canadian River, guarded by another member of the gang. He brought a man who had lost a number of milk cows and calves to identify the calves; no very difficult matter, for the man declared that he knew them as well as he knew his own children. The cows had been killed for their calves—and the latter had been "hobbled and necked." After locating the calves, Captain McDonald investigated the canyons and after several days found the cows that had been shot and killed. One after another the missing bunches of cattle were located, and the members of the band were brought in, and lodged in jail. The case against them was clear. They were found with the stolen property; some of them did not even attempt to make denial. Their examining trial was held at Plemons, the county seat of Hutchinson County, and the settlers gathered from far and near for the event. The trial was held in a big barn of a court house, and the prisoners were bound over to the district court. The Rangers were preparing to take them to Pan-handle City, where there were safer and more commodious quarters, when the sheriff—who had already distinguished himself by setting free the prominent young outlaw first captured—appeared and demanded the prisoners, on the ground that being sheriff of that county, they could not be removed without his consent. The Ranger Captain promptly informed him that, sheriff or no sheriff, he had shown his disqualifications for office, and that these prisoners would be taken to more secure quarters than he seemed willing to provide. The officer departed, and presently mustered a crowd, armed with Winchesters. Then he appeared once more before Captain Bill, produced the law which under proper conditions might have supported him in his demand, and again declared that he would have those prisoners, or that there would be bloodshed and several Ranger funerals. Captain Bill promptly called his men together.

" We are not going to stand any foolishness," he said. " If an attempt is made to take these prisoners, cut down on any one who takes a hand in it. Come, let's move on now, and get these men in jail."

The crowd that had gathered expected battle, then and there, but nothing of the kind took place. The sheriff's armed bluff had been called. Later, he obtained a writ of habeas corpus, but it was not effective for the reason that the men had been committed under bond. At all events it was not effective so long as McDonald and his Rangers were in charge of the jail.

It was now evident that conviction of these offenders was not to be expected in that county. Most of them had official influence of one kind or another. In fact, there appeared to be nobody except those whose property had suffered who seemed concerned in bringing these bandits to justice.

With such overwhelming evidence McDonald was determined, if possible, to secure their punishment. He kept them in jail several months and eventually was instrumental in getting their cases distributed and sent to other counties for trial. Even so, they managed to evade the law. Through influence of one kind or another, and the coöperation of officials— former associates, perhaps, in the business of crime —their cases were one by one dismissed.

In spite of this miscarriage of justice, the general effect of McDonald's vigorous prosecution was wholesome. The members of that band either left for the far isolations, or decided to reform. The case is given, one of many such, as an example of what the honest official had to contend with in the early Pan-handle days. Sometimes, indeed, justice was even more openly and briskly side-tracked. Once, when Captain Bill had caught a notorious cattle-thief, red-handed; brought him to trial and secured his conviction by jury; the judge, instead of passing sentence, took the law wholly into his own hands, and administered it in a manner rather startling for its unexpectedness and originality. He delivered an elaborate oration, which no one in the court room comprehended in any large degree—himself included, perhaps—and then read a lengthy decision concerning captures made upon the high seas; closing with his own decision to the effect that the clause covered this particular case as perfectly as if it had been made for it, and that the entire proceedings were irregular, irrelevant, without warrant and without effect; concluding his amazing declaration with the statement that the prisoner was discharged.

Cases like these would have discouraged and disgruntled a man of less resolution and character than Bill McDonald. To him such things meant only renewed determination. Strong in the knowledge that unless he happened to be killed he would eventually make criminals scarce, and corrupt or weak-kneed officials unpopular in that section, he gave neither rest nor respite to those who broke the law in the field, or to those who warped and disfigured it in the courts. Individually and in groups he brought the bad men in and filled the jails with them, and the box-cars, and when neither was handy he lariated them out, set a guard, and rode off after more. When he failed to convict in one court he tried another, and when he found an honest official he kept him busy. In a recent letter written by Col. W. B. Camp of San Antonio, to Edward M. House, one of the best known citizens of Texas, the writer says:

" When he (Captain McDonald) was captain of the Rangers in Texas, and doing his most effective work, I was District Attorney of the Thirty-fifth Judicial District, in the Pan-handle, and I learned to love, respect and admire this fearless officer, who always placed duty before his own life. In those days on the frontier of Texas, it was almost worth a man's life to uphold the majesty of the law, and the five years of such experience I had in doing so teaches me the value of such men as Captain Bill

McDonald.   History should hand down his name for the coming generations by the side of the heroes of the Alamo and San Jacinto.'' *

* That Captain McDonald and his little force had the entire supervision of that vast district is shown by Adjutant-General Maby's report for 1896.   See Appendix A.

XXI

The Battle with Matthews

WHAT HAPPENED TO A MAN WHO HAD DECIDED TO KILL BILL MCDONALD

It was strange, indeed, that McDonald did not
" happen to get killed " in those busy days of the
early nineties. One of the favorite vows of tough
" pan-handlers " was to shoot Bill McDonald on
sight. But the reader will remember that there was a
suddenness and vigor about Bill McDonald's manner
and method that was very bad for a vow like that
when the moment for its execution arrived. Still,
there were those who tried to make good, and one of
these, duly assisted, came near being successful. He
would have succeeded, no doubt, if he had had time.

This man's name was John Pierce Matthews,
which became simply John Pierce after its owner
had got the drop on a steamboat captain one day in
Louisiana and shot him dead. He took the new
name with him to the Pan-handle, where in due time
he got the drop on another man, somewhere up in
the northern tier of counties, with the same result.
This was a good while before he came down to Childress County and got to be sheriff, but there were
those who had not forgotten, and among them was

Captain Bill McDonald, then stopping at Wichita Falls. Matthews, or Pierce, as he was called, frequently came down to the Falls for a spree, and on one such visit made application to join a secret society. McDonald was a prominent member of that society and Matthews did not get in. This stirred the animosity of Matthews, and he began to clean his six-shooter daily and to practise sudden and accurate firing, which he knew would be necessary in case of a show-down.

By and by there was a sheriff's convention at Houston, and on a boat excursion between Houston and Galveston, Matthews spoke disrespectfully to Governor Hogg, who was on board. McDonald, who was also present, promptly called Matthews to account, and a general settlement might have been reached then and there had well-meaning, but misguided friends of both parties not interfered, and spoiled a very pretty sheriff's-picnic newspaper story. As it was, Matthews kept on oiling his pistol and practising, meantime enlisting the sympathy of friends, to whom he confided that some day when he had a little leisure he was going to look up Bill McDonald and kill him, suggesting that they be present and take a hand; *they* being of the sort naturally interested in such an enterprise.

Matthews also had another enemy, one Joe Beckham, sheriff of Motley County, an officer of his own kind, who presently got as short as possible in his accounts, absconded, and set out for Indian Territory. Matthew had no right to go outside of his own county after a fugitive, and no business in this matter, any way, as he wanted Beckham only for a misdemeanor, whereas he was charged in his own county with felony. But Matthews had an itch for Beckham on his own account, so he picked up another enemy of Beckham, named Cook, a citizen of Motley with an ambition for Beckham's office, and the two came with peaceful attitude and fair words to Quanah where Captain Bill was then stopping, requesting the loan of a Ranger to go over into the Territory after the defaulting officer. McDonald refused, but said he would send a man as far as the Territory line—Ranger authority not extending beyond that border. He did send one Ranger McClure, who being strongly persuaded, overstepped, at the same instant, his authority and the State line; captured Beckham, whom he lost through a writ of habeas corpus; fell into a plot devised by Matthews and Cook to get rid of him, and was finally brought back to Quanah by Captain Bill, who drove a hundred miles on a bad night to get him out of the mess; after which McClure was a wiser and better Ranger.

Beckham, meanwhile, had fallen a victim to remorse, or more likely had been promised immunity, and now hurried over to Quanah and gave himself up again to Ranger McClure, Captain Bill being absent from Quanah at the time. Beckham asked to be taken to Matador, county seat of Motley, for trial, and begged McClure to see him through Childress, where he expected to be killed by Matthews and Cook.

McClure assured Beckham that he would see him safely to Matador, and they set out by rail for Childress, at which point they would take a team for the Motley county seat.

Matthews was on hand at Childress. He demanded Beckham of McClure, who refused to deliver his prisoner. Matthews then started to organize a posse to take Beckham. Word of this came to McClure who promptly gave his prisoner a revolver and told him to help defend himself. Matthews and his crowd now tried to enlist the coöperation of Sheriff Cunningham of Abilene who, as soon as he understood the situation, resigned from the Matthews force and offered to assist the McClure contingent. McClure thanked him, but said he guessed he'd go along to Matador, now, with his prisoner, as the team was waiting. Captain Bill was in Matador when Ranger and prisoner arrived, and Beckham was jailed without further difficulty. Cook got appointed sheriff, by the Commissioners' Court, but the District Judge refused to accept him and selected a man named Moses for the job, whereupon Cook refused to resign and Captain Bill was sent over to turn him out, which he did with promptness and vigor. On his way back to Quanah, waiting for a train in Childress, Matthews appeared and demanded that McDonald dismiss Ranger McClure on general charges connected with the Beckham episode. McDonald mildly but firmly refused and spoke his mind pretty freely on the subject. All of which added fuel to the old resentment which Matthews nursed and nourished in his bosom for Captain Bill.

If Matthews wanted to commit suicide he began preparing for it, now, in the right way. He gave it out openly that he was going to wander over to Quanah some day and kill Bill McDonald, just as a matter of pastime, and he sent word to the same effect by any of Captain Bill's friends that he found going that way. Perhaps he thought these messages of impending death would unnerve the Ranger Captain and interfere with his sleep. That was bad judgment. Bill McDonald needed only the anticipation of a little pistol practice like that to make him sleep like an angel child.

"I didn't talk as loud as he did—nor as much," Captain Bill said afterward. "I reckon he thought I was afraid of him."

Matthews had really cut the work out for himself, however, and had enlisted help for the occasion. He was satisfied with his target practice and the condition of his firearms, and he had taken to wearing a plug of tobacco or a Bible or something solid like that in the coat-pocket just over his heart, about where one of Bill McDonald's bullets would be apt to strike, provided the Ranger happened to get a bead on him, though he had planned against that, too.

It was in December, 1895, at last that Matthews

and his pals came down to Quanah for the declared purpose of killing a Ranger Captain. It was a cold, dreary day and they visited one saloon after another, getting a supply of courage for the job and explaining what they were going to do. Then they took to following McDonald, always in a group, evidently waiting the proper opportunity, confident enough that McDonald would not take the offensive. Finally, however, they pressed him so close that he suddenly turned and told them to quit following him or trouble would ensue. Perhaps it did not seem a good place to do the job—there being no sort of protection; perhaps there was something disquieting in the manner of Captain Bill's warning. They dropped away, for the time, and McDonald gave the matter no further thought. Men threatening to kill him was an item on every day's program.

It was nearly dusk of that bleak day, and McDonald was in the railway station, sending an official telegram to his men at Amarillo, when an old man named Crutcher, whom McDonald knew, came in with the word that Matthews wanted to see him and fix up matters without any more trouble.

Captain Bill regarded Crutcher keenly; evidently he was sincere enough.

" John says he wants to see you and fix up everything right," repeated the old man persuasively.

Captain Bill finished writing his telegram and sent it. Then turning to Old Man Crutcher he said in his slow mild way:

" Well, that all sounds mighty good to me. I never want any trouble that I can help. Come on, let's go find him."

They left the depot on the side toward the town, and as they did so they saw the sheriff of Hardeman County, whose name was Dick Coffer, with Matthews and two of the latter's friends, coming to meet them. Sheriff Coffer was a step ahead of Matthews when they started across the street. Old Man Crutcher in a friendly way put his arm through McDonald's as they advanced. When they were but four or five feet between the groups, all stopped and there was a little silence.

Then McDonald said:

" Well? "

And Matthews answered, keeping Coffer just a trifle in advance:

" Well, what is it, Bill? "

Captain Bill began quietly.

" I understand," he said, " that you have been saying some pretty hard things about me, and that you-all are going to wipe up the earth with me. Is that so? "

Matthews edged a trifle nearer to Coffer.

" No," he said, " I didn't say that, but by God I'll tell you what I did say," at the same moment pointing his left index finger in McDonald's face, while his right hand slipped in the direction of his hip pocket.

Captain Bill saw the movement and his own hand

dropped into his side overcoat pocket where in winter he carried a part of his armament. Matthews' practice in drawing, for some reason failed to benefit him. His gun seemed to hang a little in the scabbard. A second later he had jerked it free and stepping behind Coffer fired at Captain Bill over the sheriff's right shoulder. But the slight hitch spoiled his aim, perhaps, for the bullet missed, passing through McDonald's overcoat collar, though the range was so short that the powder burned his face.

The game could now be considered open. Captain Bill with a quick movement that was between a skip and a step, got around Coffer and let go two shots in quick succession, at Matthews. But the latter's breast-piece was a success. Both of McDonald's bullets struck within the space of a fifty-cent piece, just above Matthews' heart, penetrated a thick plug of Star Navy, found a heavy note-book behind it and stopped.

With a thought process which may be regarded as cool for such a moment, Captain Bill realized that for some reason he could not kill Matthews by shooting him on that side, and shifted his aim. Matthews, meantime, had again dodged behind Coffer, who now dropped flat to the ground, where it was quieter. Captain Bill was bending forward at the time, trying to get a shot around Coffer, and as the latter dropped, Matthews fired, the bullet striking McDonald in the left shoulder, ranging down through

THE BATTLE WITH MATTHEWS AT QUANAH.

"He started to cock his gun, when he received another ball in his right shoulder."

his lung to the small of his back, traveling two-thirds the length of his body for lodgment.

The Ranger was knocked backward, but did not fall. Matthews quickly fired again, but McDonald was near enough now to knock the gun aside with his own, and the ball passed through his hat-brim. Aiming at Matthews' other shoulder, McDonald let go his third shot and Matthews fell.

Meantime the two deputy assassins had opened fire, and one of them had sent two bullets through McDonald's left arm. To these he gave no attention until Matthews dropped. Wheeling now he started to cock his gun, when he received another ball, this time in his right shoulder, along which it traveled to his neck, thence around the wind-pipe to the left side. His fingers were paralyzed by this wound and he made an effort to cock his gun with his teeth; but there was no further need, for with the collapse of Matthews his co-murderers fled wildly to cover, behind the depot, nearly upsetting a box-car in their hurry, as a spectator remarked.

Captain Bill walked a few steps to the side-walk. There was a post there, and holding to this he eased himself to a sitting position. A man ran up to him.

" Cap, how about it? "

" Well, I think I'm a dead rabbit."

They gathered him up and took him to a drug-store, and they took Matthews to a drug-store across the street. By and by they carried Captain Bill home and a doctor came to hunt for the bullets.

"Don't fool around with that one in my neck, Doc," Captain Bill said. "Go after the one in the small of my back, and let out the blood. There's a bucket of it sloshin' around in there."

The doctor obeyed orders. It was proper to gratify a dying man.

"Now, Doc," the Ranger Captain said when the operation was over, and the surplus cargo had been removed, "now, I'll get well," and Rhoda McDonald, his nervy wife, who had arrived on the scene, echoed this belief.

"If Bill Jess says he'll get well, he'll do it!" she declared.

But this was a minority opinion, and that night when it was rumored that Captain Bill would not pull through, there were threats that in case he didn't, the two men who had trained with Matthews would be strung up without further notice. Some word of this was brought to Captain Bill, perhaps as a message of comfort.

"Don't you do it, boys," he said. "I'm going to get well, and even if I don't, I want the law to take its course. I'm opposed to lynching."

Matthews died in a few days. He was removed to Childress and died there. Before his death he sent word to McDonald.

"You acted the man all through," was his message. "I'm only sorry that I can't see you and apologize."

"Tell him that I'm doing all right," was the

answer returned, " and that I hope he'll get well."

The mending of Captain Bill was a slow process. For about two months he was laid up, and then with his wife he sojourned for a time at a sanitarium. After that, he was up once more, pale and stooped but ready and eager for action. In time he was apparently as fit as ever; though, in truth, the physical repairing was never quite complete.

XXII

WHAT HAPPENED TO BECKHAM

AN OUTLAW RAID AND A RANGER BATTLE. JOE BECKHAM ENDS HIS CAREER

MEANTIME the cause of the final and fatal difference between Matthews and McDonald—Joe Beckham, former sheriff of Motley—was out on bond, disporting himself in picturesque fashion. He got a change of venue, and when his case came up in Baylor County, Cook—his old rival and now his successor, by election—started over to testify; whereupon Beckham met the train and promptly shot Cook dead as he struck the platform. Beckham then mounted a fast horse and cantered away into the Territory, where he joined in organizing a new gang made up of old offenders, with a view to doing a wholesale general business in crime. In this gang were Red Buck, and Hill Loftus, both justly celebrated; also Kid Lewis—later hung. They established headquarters in a neighborhood thought to be comparatively safe, since Bill McDonald's work had been confined to Texas, and opened business with every prospect of reaping the natural reward of perseverance and industry.

They began by making a general raid on what is

now Electra, Texas, where they cleaned out some stores and knocked a storekeeper on the head; after which, they looted a country store and post office, kept by one Al Bailey, then rode away in the direction of their Territory headquarters.

Company B, Ranger Service, was promptly notified, and Captain McDonald, not yet able to undertake a hard chase, sent his nephew McCauley with Jack Harwell and two other Rangers to join the sheriff of Wilbarger County at Electra, in the pursuit. The Rangers quickly struck the trail and had followed forty miles toward the Territory at a hard gait when they spied a dug-out, not far ahead. At the same moment they met an ostensible cowboy —a " line-rider," he said, on his rounds. The dug-out, he told them, was his, and that they would find something to eat there.

The party hurried on in the hope of food and warmth, for with the coming of evening it had grown very cold, and snow was beginning to fall. They were a little surprised to see a light in the dug-out, but pushed on toward it, when suddenly a volley of shots rang out from that cover, and three horses dropped dead. Not one of the riders was injured, and they promptly returned the fire. Then followed a regular exchange of shots which kept up to some extent all that bitter cold, snowy night. When morning came, only McCauley and Harwell of the Ranger Force remained in action, the others having been driven by the cold and storm to find shelter.

The dug-out was silent enough, now, but McCauley and Harwell, nearly dead from exposure, were in no condition to charge it, alone. They were without horses, and set out for Waggoner's ranch twenty-five miles away, afoot. Red River lay between, and when they arrived there the prospect of wading that icy current was miserable enough. Nevertheless, they did it, arriving at Waggoner's ranch, frost-bitten and almost dead of hunger. The others had reached there several hours earlier.

When all were in condition again, they returned to investigate the dug-out. The place was deserted. Red Buck (wounded, as they learned later) with Hill Loftus, had been able to get away; also, Kid Lewis, for whom a telephone pole was already waiting at Wichita Falls.

Joe Beckham lay stretched upon the floor, dead.

XXIII

A MEDAL FOR SPEED

CAPTAIN BILL OUTRUNS A CRIMINAL AND WINS A GOLD
MEDAL

WE are not through with the Pan-handle, but we
will relate here an incident which belongs outside of
that district, though within the period. It seemed
always a part of Bill Jess McDonald's peculiar fortunes that wherever he went he found work suited
to his hand.

He had been in Fort Worth on official business, in
this instance, and boarded the north-bound train
just as it was pulling out of the station. As he did
so, he noticed two disreputable-looking characters
crowding against a well-dressed old gentleman, and
an instant later heard the latter exclaim, " I have
been robbed! " At the same moment the two toughs
started to leap from the car-steps.

Captain Bill's presence of mind responded
promptly. His six-shooter was out with small delay,
and seizing one of the men, he called to the other to
halt. The man detained made an attempt to strike
his captor, who promptly " bent " his gun over his
head—mildly at first, then with force, bringing the
offender to his knees. The Ranger Captain now
pulled the bell-cord; brought the train to a stand-

still; turned his prisoner over to a policeman who had appeared on the scene, and set out in pursuit of the other thief, who by this time had obtained a healthy start.

Captain Bill is built like a greyhound, with long hind legs, and a prow designed for splitting the wind. The thief was active, and making good time, but he was no match for a Ranger of that architecture. The distance between them closed up rapidly, and after a race of over a mile the fugitive, having reached what was known as " Niggertown," dived into one of the houses, causing a regular stampede among the inhabitants. Men, women, and a rabble of little pickaninnies fell out in every direction. Captain Bill, now close behind, added to the excitement as he plunged in, only to find the room vacant. A quilt, however, hung across a second doorway, and stepping over to it, his six-shooter ready for emergency, he drew the hanging quickly aside. As he did so, he was confronted by a man standing on a chair, holding in his hand a bottle filled with some transparent liquid, which he was in the act of throwing. The crack of McDonald's revolver was followed by such a sudden collapse of the would-be vitriol-thrower, that the Ranger Captain thought he had wounded him seriously, though his intention had been merely to disable the arm in action. Investigation showed, however, that the thief was only frightened; that the ball had grazed his arm, also his ear, cutting a hole through the rim of his hat.

Securing the vitriol as evidence, Captain Bill marched his man back to where he had left thief Number One, only to find that the inexperienced policeman had allowed him to escape. He did not trust him with his second capture, but personally saw him safely locked up, and then set out for home by the next train.

Not long after, a package arrived one day in Amarillo, and upon being opened, it was found to contain a handsome gold medal, contributed by a prominent jeweler and others of Fort Worth.

This decoration was engraved with Captain Mc-Donald's name and official title; and an accompanying letter stated that it was awarded as a token of appreciation of his efforts in bringing criminals to justice, and as a premium for his superior swiftness of foot on a mile and a quarter track.

XXIV

CAPTAIN BILL IN MEXICO

MEXICAN THIEVES TRY TO HOLD UP CAPTAIN BILL AND
GET A SURPRISE.   MEXICAN POLICE MAKE THE
SAME ATTEMPT WITH THE SAME RESULT.
PRESIDENT DIAZ TRIES TO
ENLIST HIM

THE First National Bank of Quanah failed in 1893, and one of the head officials, wanted for embezzlement and forgery, made his escape to Mexico, where he was arrested. Governor Hogg immediately made requisition for him, and Captain McDonald was detailed to bring him back across the line. Accompanied by one of the bank directors, McDonald set out for Mexico, only to find that his man had been set free, and was then making his way to remoter hiding. It was no difficult matter, however, to trace him, and the Ranger Captain presently overhauled him and put him in jail, there to await certain red-tape formalities incident to the deliberate Mexican official methods.

Having a good deal of time on his hands, Captain Bill spent it in sight-seeing. It was interesting enough, but he could not understand why he used up

so many handkerchiefs. They seemed to disappear
from his pockets in some magic way, and no matter
how many he set out with, he presently found his
supply entirely exhausted. He realized at last that
this curious condition was not due altogether to accident, nor to carelessness on his own part. Laying
in a fresh stock of handkerchiefs, he strolled warily
along, seemingly unconscious of those who loitered
near him, apparently absorbed in sight-seeing.
Presently, from the corner of his eye, he noticed a
Mexican passing near him make a quick movement
with his hand, and caught a glimpse of white passing
from his pocket to that of the Mexican. His sudden
grab so startled this industrious person that he did
not even attempt flight. Captain Bill thereupon
promptly recovered his handkerchief, which he found
had been lifted with a slender wire hook; an effective implement in busy and skilful hands. Without
any further preliminaries, he set out for the jail
with his prisoner, but meeting an American acquaintance to whom he explained the situation, he was
advised to proceed no further with the case.

" If you take him there, they will lock you up with
him," he said.

" Well, I guess they won't," said McDonald.

" They certainly will," insisted his friend. " The
law here is to confine the witness with the prisoner,
and there is no telling when you'll get out."

Captain Bill reconsidered, whirled his prisoner
around, gave him an impetuous kick or two, and

some advice, which perhaps reached his comprehension, though in an unknown tongue.

The man fled; it is not known whether he took the advice or not.

Captain Bill's adventures in Mexico were not over. A few nights later he visited a large casino where gambling was conducted openly, and mildly diverted himself by taking a hand at bucking the national game, monte. He played in luck, and the stakes became high. His winnings grew to a considerable sum, and there were greedy eyes in the group who watched his play. When he left the place, at last, and descended the stairway, he noticed that two men seemed to be following him. As he reached the dim hallway below, he stopped; they stopped also.

Captain Bill was pleased. This was a game he preferred even to monte, he had played it so much oftener. He stepped out into the middle of the street, where he would have a clear field of observation, and set out leisurely, as if he had not noticed anything wrong. The men following gained upon him, one dropping a little in the rear, the other working his way to the front. As they reached a dark locality, the man in front began to drop back a little, evidently getting ready to close in, while the one behind stepped up a little more lively, until he was about on a line with Captain Bill, who now noticed him throw back his serape as if to free his arm for action. No longer in doubt as to what they meant to do, the Captain brought out his " forty-five " with a swing that landed the barrel of it with full force on the head of the man in front. Wheeling, he covered the other, who, seeing his companion drop with a thud, promptly fled, the Ranger Captain close behind. They raced down the dim street, and the Mexican, trying to keep his eye on his pursuer and turn a corner at the same time, ran into a stone wall and nearly knocked his head off.

Captain Bill was satisfied with the game as it stood, and set out for his hotel. He was not to arrive there, however, without further complications. The commotion of the foot-race had aroused a squad of police—a poor lot, in greasy white uniforms—and these bore down upon him now with a good deal of excited talk and gesticulation, none of which he understood. Apparently they thought he was a bloodthirsty person, who was in the habit of knocking men over the head with his gun and chasing others into stone walls, for amusement. He explained in the best Texan he could muster that the men had been trying to rob him, but it was no use. They insisted by signs that he must come with them. When he shook his head in refusal, they began reaching for their long revolvers, which they wore in clumsy holsters.

Captain Bill knew this game, also. He had played it in No-man's Land, in the Cherokee Strip, and he was still playing it in the Pan-handle. It was his favorite and daily occupation. Before their guns were half way to any effective position, he had them covered, and in tones that are universally understood, even when they convey words of strange meaning, he warned them to desist.

Men are in the habit of obeying Bill McDonald under such conditions. The Mexican police obeyed him, and when he indicated that they were to march in front of him, they did so in a formation at once orderly and well-maintained. He directed them toward the Hotel Guadaola, where he was stopping. Arriving there, he explained to the guard, who understood English, what had happened, and instructed him to convey the information to the police, with his thanks for their courteous and prompt attention, and a request that they should meet him at the office of President Diaz at ten o'clock the following morning. The guard undertook to do this, and the police went away, dazed and muttering.

They were on hand next morning at the President's office when Captain Bill arrived. During his sojourn in the city, McDonald had come in contact a number of times with President Diaz, and a pleasant friendship had sprung up between them. Diaz, who has an excellent knowledge of English, heard the Captain's explanation now with a good deal of amusement, and after dismissing his policemen with some paternal advice, he presented Captain Bill with a pass which gave him the freedom of any portion of the city at any hour and under all circumstances.

The friendship between Diaz and Captain Bill

ripened into something like intimacy now, and a few days later, the Mexican President, in discussing the nation's troubles with Guatemala, invited the Ranger Captain's opinion of the situation, and of the force in the field.

" Well, Mr. President," said Captain Bill, " I don't think much of your Mexican soldiers, but I could take a squad of Texas Rangers and go down to Guatemala and clean up that outfit down there, capture their finances and bring their Government to terms in twenty-four hours."

The Mexican President's eyes showed his approval of this scheme.

" I think a good deal of your Texan *rurales*," he said, " but they have killed a lot of our people, too."

Captain Bill nodded.

" Only the kind that needed killing," he said.

" Very likely," assented Diaz; then added, a moment later,

" Captain, I propose that you enlist with us for the purpose you mentioned just now, and bring over five hundred of your Texas cowboys to assist in the undertaking."

Diaz waxed enthusiastic over this idea, and Captain Bill was not unwilling to enter into the scheme. The matter went so far as to get into the newspapers, but at that point it came to a sudden end. Governor Hogg and Adjutant-General W. S. Mabry —a fine soldier, who later died in the Cuban war— did not propose to have their Ranger Captain go off on any such filibustering expeditions, and promptly nipped the whole matter in the bud.

Captain Bill stayed for a considerable time in the Mexican capital, for his companion, the bank official, fell very ill, and the Captain turned nurse to pull him through. He very soon became a well-known figure in the city, being often pointed out as the man who had taken a squad of police in charge; who was going to bring his Rangers down to whip the Guatemalans, and whose skill with the six-shooter was nothing short of miraculous. This last belief was in some manner sustained one day when he visited a shooting gallery in company with an American dentist, who had taken pleasure in showing him the sights of the quaint old town.

" Captain, suppose you shoot at those targets as rapidly as you can, and see how many you'll miss," he said, when they were inside.

Without hesitation, McDonald drew his revolver and opened a perfect fusilade, hitting a target at each shot. Two Mexicans who were practising in the gallery made a wild break for the open air and safety. Soldiers and police came running in excitement and confusion to discover the cause. It was all over by this time, and the officers, seeing only Captain Bill and the dentist, stood gaping, waiting an explanation.

" It is nothing," said the dentist, in Spanish; " my friend the Captain was only practising a little to keep his hand in."

XXV

A New Style in the Pan-handle

CHARLES A. CULBERSON PAYS A TRIBUTE TO RANGER
MARKSMANSHIP.   CAPTAIN BILL IN A
" PLUG " HAT

It was during the Pan-handle period that Charles A. Culberson—son of the Dave Culberson who nearly thirty years before had cleared the boy, Bill Jess McDonald, from a charge of treason—was Attorney-General for the State of Texas.   Captain Bill was at Quanah, one day, when he received notice from Culberson that the latter was anxious to locate the 100th meridian, preliminary to beginning a suit against the United States to test the claim made by Texas for Greer County—now a portion of Oklahoma.   The Attorney General invited Captain Bill to accompany him as guide and body guard, knowing him to be familiar with the district and capable of taking care of such an expedition.

They left the railroad at Vernon, Wilbarger County, proceeded in a buck-board to Doan's Store on the Red River, and crossed over into Greer County.   It was a pleasant drive across the prairies, and Captain Bill who felt in good practice beguiled the time by bringing down prairie dogs, running rabbits, sailing hawks and the like, using his six-shooter with one hand and his Winchester with the other, riding along as they were, without stopping. To Culberson, this performance was amazing enough.

" Captain," he said, " that beats anything I ever saw. Why, I believe you could throw a nickle up in the air and hit it before it touched the ground."

McDonald smiled in his quiet way.

" Do you think so? " he said. " Well, I reckon I might, but I wouldn't want to waste a nickel that way."

Captain Bill then gave a few exhibitions of what he really could do in the way of shooting, and Culberson declared without hesitation that there was not such another marksman in the State of Texas. The Attorney General was enjoying himself immensely.

They camped that night, and next morning were continuing their journey toward Mangum, the county seat of Greer, when they began to meet men and women on horseback, evidently getting out of that section of the country without much waste of time. Captain Bill inquired the reason of this exodus and was told that a cowboy had killed an Indian over on the North Fork of the Red, and that the Indians were getting on their war-paint, preparatory to making a raid—Comanches and Kiowas.

" General," said Captain Bill, " I'll have to look into this thing. You can go on to Mangum with the team and I'll get me a horse and go over and take a hand in the trouble."

" Not at all," said Culberson, " you've undertaken to see me through this trip and I'm not going
to let you desert now, Indians or no Indians."

" But I've got to, General. This is a pleasure
trip, and that's business. Them devils are goin' to
start something over there and it's my duty as
Ranger to investigate it."

Culberson laughed.

" Now, Captain," he said, " you know very well
that all you want is to get over there where there's
a chance to give a shooting exhibition. You've got
tired of hawks and prairie dogs and want to try your
hand on Indians."

A new arrival just then furnished the information
that the offending cowboy had been jailed at Mangum, and that the Indians were likely to storm the
jail. This settled the matter, for Ranger duty and
inclination now lay in the same direction. McDonald
and Culberson drove as rapidly as possible toward
Mangum, then about fifty miles away, changing
horses once on the hard journey. The town was well-
nigh deserted, as nearly everyone who could get a
gun had gone to the scene of the killing. Captain
Bill therefore established himself as guard of the
jail where the cowboy was confined, and waited
results. Nothing of consequence happened. The
country quieted down, Culberson and Captain Bill
presently returned to Quanah.

But a few days later when the Attorney General
had arrived in Austin, Captain Bill received a pack-

age by express, prepaid. On opening it he was stupefied to find that it contained a " plug " hat of very fine quality. It was the first silk hat in the Pan-handle, where the soft wide-rimmed cowboy Stetson predominated, and it took more courage to wear it than to face an assault with intent to kill.

But Captain Bill was game. He was a " brother-in-law to the church " as he said—his wife being a member—and the following Sunday he put on the silk hat and accompanied her to meeting.

Their seat was up near the front, only a step from the pulpit—a good thing for the minister, otherwise nobody would have looked in his direction. As it was, all eyes were aimed toward Captain Bill and his hat. The congregation had seen him come in with it in his hand, and they could still observe the wonder, for it would not do to put so fine a piece of property on the floor, while to set it toppling on his lap would be to court disaster. It seemed necessary therefore to hold it in his hand, raised a little, and at a distance from his body, in order that by no chance movement the marvelous gloss of it should be marred. The people of Quanah who attended church that day were glad to be there. They are still glad. They do not remember the sermon they heard, but they do remember that hat. Even the minister wandered from his text in his contemplation of that splendid exhibition. Those of Quanah who remained away from service on that memorable Sunday have never entirely recovered from their regret. For it was their only opportunity ever to see Captain Bill in a plug hat. When services were over, the congregation crowded about for a nearer view. Cowboys stood up on the backs of the pews to look over the shoulders of those in front of them. Homesick women who remembered such things back east, shed tears. Many wanted to touch the precious thing—to stroke its silken surface, and among these were little children who insisted on rubbing the fur the wrong way.

Captain Bill got out at last and headed for home. Once there, the gift of the Attorney General was reverently damned and laid away. Somewhere in a secret stronghold, deep buried from mortal eye, it exists to this hour.

XXVI

Preventing a Prize-fight

CULBERSON became Governor in the course of time, and remembering Captain Bill's peculiar talents was wont to rely upon him for special work in any portion of the State where nerve, determination and prompt, accurate marksmanship were likely to be of value.

During February, 1896, a national sporting event —a ring contest between Bob Fitzsimmons and Pete Maher—was advertised to take place at El Paso, a busy city dropped down on the extreme western point of the Texas desert, on the banks of the Rio Grande. Governor Culberson, speaking for himself as well as for the better class of citizens in his State, announced that so long as he was in office, Texas would not go on record as a prize-fighting commonwealth, and that the fight would not take place. Thereupon there came a crisis. Certain interested citizens of El Paso had made up a purse of ten thousand dollars to bring this event to the " Paris of Texas " and these and their friends were filled

with indignation. Dan Stuart, prominent in Texas
sporting matters and promoter of this particular
event, issued a proclamation which bore not only
the announcement that the fight would take place
as advertised, but a picture of Dan himself. Also,
it was declared that there was no law in Texas
which would prevent prize-fighting, and the preparations for this particular event continued; whereupon Governor Culberson promptly called a special
session of the legislature to pass a law which would
be effective, and Adjutant-General Mabry ordered
the State Ranger Service to assemble at El Paso to
see that this law was enforced—it having been
widely reported that Bat Masterson with a hundred
fighting men would be present to see that the fight
came off. Then, when it was rumored that the contest would take place in either Old or New Mexico
—the boundaries of both being near El Paso—President Cleveland ordered the United States Marshal
of New Mexico to proceed to the vicinity of El Paso
and guard the isolated districts of that territory,
while the Governor of Chihuahua took measures to
discourage the enterprise in that State.

Things began to look pretty squally for the sporting fraternity, both in El Paso and at large, and
they were mad clear through. The city council
assembled and passed a denunciatory measure, con-
demning the Governor for asking for Rangers; the
Adjutant-General for sending them, and the Rangers
for being present.

It was no use. The Rangers went quietly about the streets, paying no attention to unfriendly looks and open threats as they passed along. Efforts were made by the principals and their friends to elude the Rangers, but with no other result than that a Ranger was appointed as a special body-guard to each of the pugilists, while a third, Captain McDonald, became the temporary associate of Dan Stuart. They had nothing particular to do—these Rangers—except to be companionable, and pleasant, and to stay with their men. Wherever Stuart and Maher and Fitzsimmons went their official attendants went with them, and even if not always welcome they were entertained with sufficient courtesy, for the person of a Ranger is sacred—besides, he is reputed to be quick and fatal.

Such sport became monotonous. The pugilists and their friends gave up the El Paso idea, and, still accompanied by the Rangers, took the train for Langtry, a point where the Southern Pacific Railway touches the Rio Grande. The State of Coahuila lay across the river, and Langtry itself was at that period the proper gateway to a pugilists' paradise, its law being administered by one Roy Bean, justice of the peace and saloon-keeper, whose sign read:

MIXED DRINKS

LAW WEST OF THE PECOS.

It is said that Bean's drinks were about on a

par with his law, and that the latter was administered with a gun. He tried court cases, granted
divorces, and handed down decisions without the
trammel of a jury or other assistance. Once when
a citizen killed a Chinaman in his place, Bean consulted the statutes, and finding nothing in reference
to the murder of a Chinaman in his saloon, discharged the prisoner as having committed no offense. At another time, when a man walking across
a high bridge over the Pecos had fallen and broken
his neck, and the matter was brought before Bean,
the dispenser of " Law West of the Pecos," discovered that the pockets of the unfortunate contained a six-shooter and forty-one dollars in money;
whereupon he fined the dead man twenty-five dollars and costs for carrying a concealed weapon, and
appropriated the forty-one dollars and the six-
shooter, in settlement. A whole chapter could be
written about Bean and his official service, but this
is not the place for it. It is the place, however, for
another incident concerning a Chinaman—a case in
which, though tried west of the Pecos, the Chinaman's rights were sustained.

The train bound for Langtry with the pugilistic
party and Rangers aboard stopped at Sanderson, a
small wayside station in the desert, for lunch.
Everybody was hungry and hurried over to a
Chinese restaurant for something to eat, and the
Chinese waiters scurried about to serve them. They
were doing their best, but it was not easy to satisfy

everybody at once. Next to Captain McDonald sat
Bat Masterson. Bat has since given up all his reckless ways and become a good citizen, but at that time
he was training with the unreformed and not feeling very well, anyhow. It seemed to Bat that a
Chinese waiter was not getting around as promptly
with food as he might and he set in to admonish
him. The Chinaman replied to the effect that he
was doing his best, whereat Masterson decided to
correct him with a table-castor. Captain Bill had
been sitting quietly, saying nothing; but as Masterson raised the castor the Ranger Captain clutched
his arm.

" Don't you hit that man! " he said.

Masterson wheeled.

" Maybe *you'd* like to take it up! "

Captain Bill regarded him steadily for an instant.

" I done took it up! " was his quiet answer.

The castor was put down. Masterson reflected
silently while he waited for his food. Perhaps that
was the beginning of his reform.

Arriving at Langtry, Stuart, Fitzsimmons and
Maher were escorted to the Rio Grande, where,
with all their fraternity, they crossed over to Mexican soil and the fight was pulled off in good order.
It was a good fight, as fights go, and Fitzsimmons
won with a knock-out landed on Maher's jaw; but
it did not take place on Texas soil.*

* For official details of the situation at El Paso, etc., see Appendix A,
Adjutant-General W. H. Mabry's report.

XXVII

KID LEWIS AND HIS GANG TAKE ADVANTAGE OF THE
ABSENCE OF THE RANGERS. HE MAKES A BAD
CALCULATION AND COMES TO GRIEF

THE absence of Captain Bill and his Rangers from
the Pan-handle, was construed by Kid Lewis as an
invitation to rob a bank. He selected the City National of Wichita Falls for his purpose and with a
partner named Crawford rode up to that institution one day about noon, and entering, demanded
the bank funds. Cashier Frank Dorsey failing to
comply with that demand, was shot dead; H. H.
Langford, bookkeeper, was wounded, and the Vice-
President of the bank escaped by having in his left
breast-pocket a small case of surgical instruments.
This deflected the ball which otherwise would have
entered his heart.

The robbers then secured whatever money was in
sight—about six hundred dollars in gold and silver
—ran out the back door, mounted their waiting
horses and galloped away. The citizens were by
this time alarmed and a number set out in pursuit,
full speed. There was a running fight, during which
Lewis' horse was shot, but an instant later he was

clear of it, and leaping behind Crawford the two went plunging away double until they met an old man driving into town with a single horse. This they appropriated forthwith, leaving their pursuers a good way behind. Still further on, they crossed Holiday Creek and came to a field where a man was plowing. They now abandoned their blown horses and at the point of a gun took his heavy Clydesdale team and once more dashed away, making for the Wichita River. Their pursuers gained on the clumsy animals and fired several more shots at the fugitives, then decided to return and organize a posse, which they raised in short order. This posse followed the track of Lewis and Crawford beyond the Wichita River, to a place where the robbers had taken to the thick brush overgrowing the river bottom. Here the trail was lost.

Captain McDonald, returning from the Fitzsimmons-Maher contest, via Fort Worth, had got as far as Bellvue in the adjoining county when he was met by a telegram, containing the news of what had happened that morning at Wichita Falls. He immediately wired the authorities at the Falls to have horses in readiness for himself and men.

The Rangers reached the city about two in the afternoon and mounting the horses, already waiting, dashed away in the direction the robbers had taken. With him, Captain Bill had Rangers McCauley, Harwell, Sullivan, Queen, and McClure—the tried, picked men whom Lewis and Crawford had been most anxious to avoid. The horses were picked, too, for speed and endurance and went at a wild headlong gait—almost too headlong for safety. A small creek that had become a bed of mud lay across the road and Captain Bill's horse, stumbling on the brink, sent him head first into the soft mixture, which literally daubed him from head to foot before he could get on his feet. His men thought for a moment that he was killed, but he rose spluttering and swearing, wholly unhurt, though fearfully disfigured, and with no time to remove his disguise. Instantly mounting, he galloped on, a sight to behold, the others respectfully restraining any tendency to mirth.

Presently they met the local posse coming back. The posse had given up the chase, but was able to furnish information. Captain Bill and his Rangers learned where the robbers had disappeared, and pressed on in that direction, the posse following.

It was now getting toward evening and would soon be dusk. It was desirable to make an end of matters by daylight, if possible, and the Rangers wasted no time. They picked their way rapidly into the thick undergrowth of the bottoms, and suddenly in a bend of the river discovered the Clydesdale horses tied close to the bank. Their riders were believed to be close by, and the Rangers expected to be fired upon at any moment. Without waiting for any such reception they charged in the direction of the horses, with no other result than that Ranger

Sullivan broke a stirrup, fell, and with a fractured rib, retired from action.

Lewis and Crawford had abandoned the horses, and their trail led down the river bank. The Rangers also left their horses at this point, for it was hard going. McDonald now took Queen and Harwell, one on either side of him, their guns in readiness while he gave his attention to the trail. The light was getting very dim where they were, but Captain Bill is a natural trailer and followed the tracks without difficulty. Here and there they found stray articles which the men had dropped in their flight. Finally the tracks led to the river where it was evident the bandits had crossed.

It was February and the water was very cold. Captain Bill had not yet recovered from the terrible bullet wounds received in the fight with Matthews, two months before, and was bent and debilitated, but he did not falter. With Queen and Harwell he plunged in and waded the icy water, chin deep, to the other side. Twice more the trail led to the river and crossed, and twice more McDonald and his men waded that bitter current, holding their firearms above their heads, their bodies literally numb with cold. It was a severe experience, but as Captain Bill said afterwards, it removed a good deal of his mud.

McDonald now made up his mind that the robbers would be likely to cross a road that had been cut through the bottoms, and head toward the Territory, which they were evidently trying to reach, believing the Rangers would not follow them across the line. He called to one of his men—Ranger Mc-Clure, who appeared just then, a little distance away —to get all the force he could and guard that road, while he, McDonald, with Queen and Harwell, would continue to beat the brush and search carefully through the bottoms. At that moment Lewis and Crawford were near enough to hear this order, and the realization that it was Bill McDonald and his Rangers who were on the trail gave them a sudden and more severe chill than the icy water they had waded.

They had been heading for the Territory, as Mc-Donald suspected, but decided to change their course toward a creek that ran parallel with the river. On their way to it they were obliged to cross an open field, and though by this time it was night—between nine and ten o'clock—a full moon had risen and they were discovered by the men guarding the road, and fired upon. They returned the fire as they ran, but no damage was done on either side. Meantime, McDonald and his two companions, nearly perishing with wet and cold, having come upon a house in their search, had stopped to try for a cup of hot coffee. At the sound of the shots they rushed out. A horse was hitched at the door and Captain Bill leaped into the saddle and hurried in the direction of the alarm. As he approached, he saw in the moonlight a crowd—the local posse—gathered on the little hill overlooking the wheatfield where the robbers had crossed. The Ranger Captain fully expected to find the captured or dead bandits in that crowd, and called out as he came up:

" Boys, where are they? Where are the robbers? "

They pointed in the direction of some brush about a quarter of a mile away.

" They went into that creek bottom, over yonder."

" Well, then, what in the devil are you all doing up here? "

Somebody answered:

" You must think we're dam' fools to go in there after those fellows. Of course we didn't go in there, and don't intend to."

" Well," said Captain Bill, " I'm going, and if any of you fellows want to go, come ahead, but I don't want any man that don't go willingly."

Ranger McCauley had ridden up.

" You can't get away from me, Uncle Bill," he said.

The two loped off in the direction of the thicket, but presently found their way barred by a wire fence. Leaving their horses they made a circuit around the enclosure and soon struck what seemed to be a road, leading into the bottom. Hurrying along they came upon Ranger McClure, who had been in charge of the posse when the shooting had occurred, and had set out alone to locate the robbers.

" Hello, Bob, where are they? " asked Captain Bill, as he and McCauley came up.

" Right over there, Cap. They ran in the brush, over by yonder big tree."

" Well, boys, we've got to get them. We'll charge in there."

They pushed rapidly into the bushes without further parley—McDonald heading for the tree, McCauley and McClure spreading out to the right.

Captain Bill made straight for the big tree pointed out by McClure, his gun ready for quick service. It was a still, moonlit place, but brushy and full of shadows, and not easy going. The crack of Winchesters might be expected at any moment.

Suddenly the Captain found himself confronted by a creek, and looking across saw two men with guns, squatting in the weeds. They appeared to be on the point of raising their guns to fire, but with McDonald's appearance and his sharp command, " Hold up there! " made from behind his own leveled Winchester, they were unable to complete the action. Their guns dropped into their laps— they seemed stupefied.

" Throw up your hands! " was the next order.

The hands went up.

" Get up from there! "

One of the men found his voice.

" We can't, Captain, our guns are lying across our laps, cocked. They'll go off if we get up."

" Get up or I'll turn you over! "

They rose hastily, their guns sliding to the ground.

"Back off there, now, and face the other way."

They obeyed like soldiers on drill.

Captain Bill stepped into the creek, about three feet deep, and waded across. He noticed a bag, doubtless containing the stolen money, and observed that the robbers had laid their cartridges out on a log for convenient use. At that moment McCauley and McClure came hurrying up, apparently ready to shoot.

"Hold up boys! It's all right," said McDonald, "I've got 'em!"

McCauley and McClure waded across and assisted in searching the prisoners. A purse of gold was found in one of the men's pockets; the sack on the ground contained silver.

"Now, let's get out of this," said McDonald, "and get where it's warm."

"You're not going to make us wade that cold creek, are you" said Lewis, shivering.

"Look here," said Captain Bill. "If you don't get across there and pretty quick, too, I'll duck you, head first. You've made me wade water up to my neck, all the afternoon."

They all crossed, then—the fifth time in the cold water that day for McDonald—and made their way to where he and McCauley had left their horses. Here they got a rope and bound the prisoners, their arms behind them. Captain Bill then called to the posse, still waiting in the road a quarter of a mile away listening for the sound of the shots that would probably bring down Rangers.

" Come on, boys," he yelled, " we've got em! "

So they came " lickety brindle," but presently stopped.

" Captain, are you sure you got 'em? "

" Yes, I've got 'em, and got 'em tied. Come on —there's no danger, now! "

The crowd tore through the brush to get over there, and some of them began abusing the captured men, declaring they had murdered the best man in Wichita Falls, and furnishing a graphic outline of what would happen to them, in consequence. What they said was all true enough, maybe, but the saying of it seemed in rather poor taste to Captain Bill.

" Look here," he said, " these men are my prisoners, now; you let them alone."

He marched Lewis and Crawford over to Mart Boger's ranch, where all got some hot coffee and something to eat. Boger also supplied a wagon in which to haul the prisoners.

It was McDonald's first intention to take the men to Henrietta, for safe keeping, but against his judgment he was persuaded to take them to Wichita Falls. He gave orders, however, that none of the crowd should leave, as he did not wish the news of the capture to travel ahead of them—realizing that a mob of citizens would be likely to gather.

On the way to the Falls the Rangers fell into conversation with Lewis; and McCauley and Harwell discussed with him the fight that he and Hill Loftus and the others had made, that night in the dug-out when Joe Beckham had been killed. Lewis explained how he and Red Buck and Loftus had managed to slip away without being seen. Then McDonald said:

" Boys, how was it you didn't shoot me a while ago, when you saw me coming through the bushes? You-all had your guns cocked and ready—and you knew you'd be hung, anyway, if you got caught. You saw me first—why didn't you shoot? "

" Cap," said Lewis, " we thought you were out of the country and wouldn't get back before we could get to the Territory. When we heard you giving orders and knew who it was, we lost our nerve, and when we saw you, we somehow got paralyzed."

When the procession had arrived within a mile or two of the Falls, Captain McDonald, realizing that some one had doubtless slipped away and carried the news, sent one of his men to have the jail door open in order that there might be no delay in entering. His suspicion was correct, for the news had traveled, and though it was then about two o'clock in the morning, several hundred men were congregated about the jail when the Rangers with their prisoners arrived. Captain Bill rode ahead and opened the way with his gun.

" Give room, here, men! " he commanded, and the way opened.

Lewis and Crawford were marched into the jail
—Rangers McCauley and Queen being left to guard
the door. The prisoners were taken to cells, carefully searched, and locked in. Captain McDonald
then descended to disperse the crowd, which had
grown noisy and ugly in its demands for the prisoners, and was apparently making ready to attack
the jail. Captain Bill addressed this assembly.

"Boys," he said, "I reckon you-all are my
friends, and if you are, you'll go home now and go
to bed. My Rangers and I captured these men and
they are our prisoners. We've got them locked up,
and they'll have a fair trial. You men didn't capture them, and you have nothing to do with them.
They're unarmed now, and can't defend themselves,
but if you make an attack on this jail I'll give the
prisoners their guns, and we'll lick this crowd. I
command you to disperse immediately. If you don't,
we'll begin business right now."

The mob dispersed. Some of the leaders wanted
to call Captain Bill away to discuss matters, but he
would have none of it, and cleared the grounds.
Then in spite of his wet, cold, weary condition, and
the terrible wounds received less than three months
before, he stayed with his men, on guard, till morning. Then a message was brought to him that Hill
Loftus had been concerned in the robbery and that
he was hiding in a dug-out near town.

Knowing that Loftus and Lewis trained together,
Captain McDonald did not discredit this report, or

suspect that it was part of a ruse to get him away from the jail. He ordered a horse from the stable at once and made ready to start.

" Aren't you going to take your men with you? " asked the men who had brought the word.

" No," said Captain Bill. " I want them to stay here."

" But Loftus is a bad man, and will have the advantage of you, being in the dug-out."

" That's all right—I can take care of him; but I do want somebody to come and show me the place."

A man volunteered to do this, and rode with Captain Bill to a dug-out some distance away, in the edge of the town. The place was empty, but another man appeared just then who claimed to have seen Loftus leave, a little while before, taking a northerly direction.

Still unsuspecting, Captain Bill set out at full speed, but after riding three miles and seeing no sign of Loftus, or his trail, he rode back to Wichita Falls. At the edge of the town he was met by his nephew, Henry McCauley, with the news that everybody who could get a gun had marched on the jail, and that no doubt Lewis and Crawford were already hung.

Captain Bill did not wait for another word. A mob of several hundred men had gathered about the jail, wild with excitement, determined to have Lewis and Crawford and to lynch them, forthwith. Suddenly this multitude saw Captain Bill bearing down

QUELLING A LYNCHING MOB AT WICHITA FALLS.

"Boys, have you still got the prisoners?"

on them—his Winchester in position for business
and fury in his eye.

" Boys," he called to his Rangers, as he dashed
up, " have you still got the prisoners? "

" Yes," they called back, " they're still in the
jail! "

Captain Bill wheeled on the mob.

" Now! " he shouted, " damn your sorry souls!
march out of here and get away from this jail, every
one of you, or I'll fill this yard with dead men! "

He had his Winchester leveled as he spoke and
those who considered themselves in range made a
wild, hasty effort to get into some safer locality.
Captain Bill swung the point of his gun a little so it
covered a good many in its orbit, and nobody knew
when it might go off. They knew if it did go off
it would hit whatever spot he selected, and nobody
wanted to own that spot. The crowd moved—some
of it hurried a good deal—and Captain Bill helped
things along with language. He escorted the mob
well into town.

The Ranger Captain now prepared to move the
prisoners to Fort Worth, but was notified by the
District Judge that this could not be done—that any
attempt to do so would result in general trouble with
the citizens of Wichita Falls. McDonald protested
that the citizens had already shown that they were
unable to take care of the prisoners in a legal way.
The judge said:

" I will appoint twenty-five men to guard the
jail."

" You mean you will appoint twenty-five men to keep me from taking Lewis and Crawford away," McDonald said:

" No, only to help you guard them."

" But if you have a guard of twenty-five men you don't need the Rangers."

The judge argued for the moral support of the Rangers. McDonald informed him that it was impossible for his force to remain in Wichita Falls, guarding prisoners; that other work was waiting for them; that there was already a requisition for them at Quanah; that furthermore they had been away from their headquarters for two weeks, besides being wet and cold and worn out from exposure and want of sleep.

" Let the others go, Captain, and you stay," urged the judge.

" Judge," said Captain Bill, " you know I'm all shot up, and it's the first time I've rode any, and what with yesterday, and last night, and to-day I'm about used up, and likely to be sick. Now, if you can take care of those prisoners with your guard, all right. If you think you can't, I'll take 'em to Fort Worth, where they'll be safe. But I'm going to get out of here to-night, unless you get an order from Governor Culberson for me to stay. It ain't far to the telegraph office, only about thirty steps— you can go and wire him, if you want to. If he says for me to stay, I will, of course. But otherwise I'm going. I've done my whole duty, now. When I get prisoners in jail, and guarded, my duty ends. Your guard of twenty-five men with your local officers can hold that jail if they want to. I could hold it alone.''

No order came to the Rangers from Governor Culberson, and they left that afternoon, when the local guard had been duly installed. That night the mob once more marched on the jail, and in spite of the armed guard and the sheriff, deputies and constables, Lewis and Crawford were taken from their cells and hung to telephones poles, close to the bank where they had committed their crime.

Citizens of Wichita Falls complained to Governor Culberson that Captain McDonald and his Rangers had gone away, leaving the prisoners to the mercy of the mob. Culberson wired to McDonald, and receiving the facts in reply, commended him throughout.

A reward of two thousand dollars for the capture of Lewis and Crawford was paid by the two banks of Wichita Falls. The local posse divided it into thirty-two equal parts, in which they generously permitted the Rangers to share.

XXVIII

CAPTAIN BILL AS A PEACEMAKER

HE ATTENDS CERTAIN STRIKES AND RIOTS ALONE WITH
SATISFACTORY RESULTS. GOES TO THURBER
AND DISPERSES A MOB

DURING the years that ended the old century and
began the new—from about 1896 to 1902, or later—
there occurred in Texas a series of strike and mob
disorders of various kinds. To quiet troubles of
this sort is the special province of the Ranger Service, and as the Pan-handle became more tractable
—more range-broken, as one may say—Captain Bill
McDonald and his little force were summoned to
points far and near to put down disturbance and to
check agitation.

It was not long after the bank murder at Wichita
Falls, and the capture of Lewis and Crawford, that
Captain McDonald was summoned there again, this
time to investigate a strike on the Fort Worth and
Denver Railroad. Things were in bad shape at the
Falls. Trains were not allowed to run, engines were
not permitted to move. Riot and bloodshed were
imminent.

Captain Bill did not think it necessary to take his
men. He went up to Wichita Falls alone, and learn-
ing where the main body of the strikers were assem-

bled, went over there. They had gathered in a hall, and were holding a secret meeting when he arrived. The Captain knocked on the door. A doorkeeper came, but refused admission.

" I am Captain McDonald, of the Rangers," said McDonald quietly, " and I'm here to talk to you men and see what the trouble is. You're all here now, and I think I'll talk to you together."

The doorkeeper went away and reported, and presently returned.

" Where are your Rangers? " he asked.

" I didn't bring any. I don't need any. I'm a pretty good single-handed talker, myself."

There was another consultation inside, and the door opened. Captain Bill went in with a friendly greeting for everybody, given in his genial natural way. Then he got up where he could see his audience.

" Boys," he said, in his slow, friendly way, " I understand you-all are acting mighty sorry over here, interfering with business and making out like you're going to tear up things generally. Now, you know me, and you know that I don't want anything that ain't right, and if a man behaves himself I'll try to get him what's right, if I can. I suppose you think you have a grievance and perhaps you have, but you'll never get it settled this way, and it's my business, as you-all know, not to have this sort of work going on. You have a perfect right to quit work, but you haven't any right to keep other men from working, or to injure people's business or to break up property. Nothing good can come out of such doings. I didn't bring any of my men along, because I didn't believe I'd need 'em, and I don't think so now, but of course if this thing goes on, I'll have to bring 'em, and then it will be too late to talk all friendly here together as we're talking now.

" I'm well acquainted with President Good of this road, and I know you can't get anything this way; and if you take my advice you'll go back to work and tell him your troubles afterward. Now, boys, that's all I've got to say, and I reckon if you listen to it you'll come out a good deal better than if you listen to one or two men that for some reason of their own are trying to stir up a lot of trouble, and will be in jail before night, as like as not."

Captain Bill went down on the street and the crowd soon followed. A good many came to him and expressed willingness to go to work. Here and there he talked to a little group in his friendly, earnest way. The strike at Wichita Falls was over.

From Wichita Falls McDonald went over to Fort Worth, where there was similar trouble, but learned that a more serious situation existed at the Thurber coal-mines, in Erath County. The miners were of many nationalities—ignorant and brutish— and they were swayed by anarchical leaders. The Ranger Captain was urged to take his men to Thurber, but decided to go alone.

Arriving at Thurber, he hunted up the mine officials, for consultation. Colonel Hunter, President of the mines, looked at Captain Bill—bent over from his wounds and battered up from illness and exposure—and shook his head.

"You should have brought your men," he said. "You can't do anything with a gang like ours, alone."

"Well, Colonel, I'm using my men in other places. I'll look around a little and do what I can, anyway."

Loitering about the town, he discovered that a number of kegs of beer were going out to a high hill, beyond the outskirts—headquarters of the striking miners. He learned that there was to be a sort of mass meeting there that night, when the leaders and chief agitators would be on hand. He decided to be present.

It was well after dark when he set out, and a good crowd had assembled when he reached the place. It was out on a mountain where the timber had been cut off, about half a mile from Thurber, and there was no light except from a misty moon. At one place there was a big log, used by the speakers to stand on, and about this the crowd and the beer-kegs were gathered. Captain Bill, unnoticed, blended with the outer edges.

It was near eleven o'clock, and a speaker had come to the conclusion that the crowd was in the proper condition to take some good radical advice —which might be followed by prompt action—so he proceeded to give it. He told them how they had been mistreated and what they should do. They were to begin by blowing up the mines and the superintendent's office, and he told them which mine to blow up first. Then he told them what they were to do to " Old Hunter," and it was clear from the faces and the muttering of the listeners that they were ready to do these things.

Captain Bill worked his way through the crowd until he was close to the speaker's log. When the agitator reached what seemed a good stopping place, the Ranger Captain suddenly stepped up beside him. The speaker stopped dead still, in his surprise. It was Captain Bill's turn.

" Men," he said, " this rascal that has been talking to you is an enemy to you and to the country. He's trying to get you to commit murder, and to get you sent to the penitentiary, or hung. You can quit work, but you can't kill people and destroy property, not in this State. These walking delegates and leaders that are telling you to do these things are just a sorry lot of damned scoundrels, and I'm going to put them where they belong, and where they're trying to get you. I'm Captain of Company B, Ranger Service, and I'm here alone, but I'll have my men here, if I need them, and I'll hang just such fellows as this man—"

Captain Bill turned to indicate his selected victim, but he was no longer there. He had melted into the crowd, and was seen no more. A man from the assembly came up and urged the Ranger Captain to desist—warning him that there were desperate men there, and that he would be killed.

"Don't mind me," Captain Bill proceeded, "that's been tried on me more than once without much success. You see I'm here yet—spared, I reckon, to give you some good advice. Now, you men had better take it and give up these meetings, and if you've got to jump onto anybody, jump onto the fellows that's trying to get you into trouble. Good-night!"

Captain Bill walked back to Thurber and next morning a messenger came to his room to tell him that there was a big crowd outside, hunting for him. He rose and dressed, and taking his Winchester went out to see what was going on. When he appeared he was waited on by some miners who wanted him to talk a little more to the men. He was told that a number of them had decided to go to work and wanted to know what kind of protection they would have. Captain Bill assured them of protection and fair treatment. Then he asked where their leaders had gone—the men who had been urging them to do murder. But they could not tell. Those ill-advisers had vanished over night. Within a brief time the men were nearly all back at work, doing better than ever before.

At other points McDonald or his Rangers quieted the strikers and prevented trouble of various kinds. Usually Captain Bill went alone. It was his favorite way of handling mob disorders, as we have seen. It is told of him in Dallas how once he came to that city in response to a dispatch for a company of Rangers, this time to put down an impending prize-fight.

" Where are the others? " asked the disappointed Mayor, who met him at the depot.

" Hell! aint I enough? " was the response, " there's only one prize-fight! "

XXIX

The Buzzard's Water Hole Gang

THE MURDER SOCIETY OF SAN SABA AND WHAT HAPPENED TO IT AFTER THE RANGERS ARRIVED

But the San Saba affair was a different matter. It was in 1897 that certain citizens of San Saba County petitioned the Governor to send Rangers to investigate the numerous murders which had been committed in that locality—the number of assassinations then aggregating forty-three within a period of ten years.

In fact, San Saba and the country lying adjacent was absolutely controlled at that time by what was nothing less than a murder society. San Saba County, situated about the center of the State, lies on the border of the great south-west wilderness, and is crossed by no railroad. In an earlier day a sort of Vigilance Committee or mob had been organized to deal with lawless characters, but in the course of time the usual thing happened and the committee itself became the chief menace of the community. Whatever worthy members it had originally claimed, either dropped out or were "removed," and were replaced by men who had a private grudge against a neighbor; or desired his property; or were fond of murder on general principles. In time this deadly organization became not only a social but a political factor, and as such had gathered into its gruesome membership—active and honorary—county officials ranging from the deputy constabulary to occupants of the judicial bench. Indeed, it seemed that a majority of the citizens of San Saba were associated together for the purpose of getting rid—either by assassination or intimidation—of the worthier element of the community.

This society of death was well organized. It had an active membership of about three hundred, with obligations rigid and severe. Their meeting place was a small natural pool of water, almost surrounded by hills. It bore the curiously appropriate name of " Buzzard's Water Hole," and here the Worthy Order of Assassins assembled once a month, usually during full moon, to transact general business and to formulate plans for the removal of offending or superfluous friends. Sentinels were posted during such gatherings, and there were passwords and signs. These were forms preserved from the original organization; hardly necessary now it would seem, since the majority of the inhabitants were in sympathy with the mob, while those who were not could hardly have been dragged to that ghastly spot. They preserved other things— they kept up the semblance of being inspired by lofty motives, and they maintained the forms that go with religious undertakings; wherefore, being duly assembled to plot murder, they still opened their meetings with prayer!

After which, the real business came up for transaction. Members in good standing would make known their desires, setting forth reasons why citizens in various walks of life were better dead, and the cases were considered, and the decrees passed accordingly. Sometimes when a man's offense was only that he owned a piece of desirable real estate, a resolution was passed that a committee of fifty should wait on that citizen and give him from three to five days to emigrate, this to be supplemented by a second committee of one whose duty it would be to call next day and make the said undesirable citizen a modest, not to say decent, offer for his holdings. It was not in human nature to resist a temptation like that. The man would be likely to go. He would accept that offer, whatever it was, and he would get out of there before night. The organization acquired a good deal of choice property by this plan. When an election was coming on, the society decided who was to be chosen for office, and who for assassination, and committees were likewise appointed to see that all was duly performed. It was a remarkable society, when you come to think about it—a good deal like Tammany Hall, only more fatal.

To break up the Buzzard's Water Hole roost, and to discourage its practices in and around San Saba, was the job cut out for Bill McDonald and his Rangers during the summer and fall of 1897.

Captain McDonald began the work by sending over three of his men—John Sullivan, Dud Barker and Edgar Neil—to investigate. There was plenty of trail and the Rangers ran onto it everywhere. It wound in and out in a hundred directions, and gathered in a regular knot around the seat of justice. Perhaps there were town and county officials who were not in the toils of the deadly membership, but if so they were not discoverable. Sullivan promptly got into trouble with the sheriff by re-jailing a man whom he found outside, holding a reception with his friends, when the State had paid a reward for his capture. Sullivan and the sheriff both drew guns, but were kept apart, and the District Judge, who seemed to have been a sort of honorary " Buzzard," holding his office by virtue of society favor, undertook to get rid of Sullivan by sending him a long way off, after some witness supposed to be wanted; though why they should want any witness, in a court like that, would be hard to guess.

Captain Bill himself now came down to look over the field. He had his hands full from the start. When he arrived, Rangers Barker and Neil were patrolling the town with guns, while a number of citizens similarly armed were collected about the streets.

" Hello, Dud," he said, " are you-all going to war ? "

" Looks like it, Cap," returned Barker.

Captain Bill looked over at the armed citizens, and raised his voice loud enought for them to hear.

" Well, Dud, if that's the best they can do," he said, " we can lick 'em. can't we ? "

" Yes, sir, if you say so, Cap."

The armed citizens showed a reluctance in the matter of hostilities and began to edge away. McDonald now got his mail and reviewed the situation, for prior to his coming he had scarcely known what the trouble in San Saba was all about. By and by he went to his hotel. It was about ten o'clock and he was sitting out in front, when he saw flashes and heard shots across the public square. The mob was shooting up the town for his benefit. Captain Bill seized his gun and went up there. The main disturbance seemed to be in and about a saloon. The Ranger Captain pushed into the place alone, compelled every man of the assembly to put up his hands and allow himself to be disarmed. He then required them to appear for examination, next morning. They did appear, and were discharged, of course, but, nevertheless, it was evident that a man who would not be scared and who was not afraid to do things, was among them. Members of the society felt a chill of uneasiness. Worthy citizens, heretofore silent through fear of their lives and property, began to take heart.

McDonald now interviewed the sheriff and county officials in general and delivered his opinion of them, individually and collectively, concluding with the statement that he would bring Sullivan back as soon as a message and steam would get him. The sheriff replied that Sullivan and he could not stay in the same town.

" Then move," said Captain Bill. " The county

will be rid of one damned rascal. It will be rid of more before I get through here."

Captain Bill went to Austin, himself, after Sullivan, so that there might be no mistake about his coming. He presented the case to Governor Culberson and got his sanction, then sent word to his men at San Saba to meet them, and he arrived with Sullivan, promptly on time. He had expected that there would be a demonstration by the sheriff and his friends, instead of which the streets of the little town were deserted. Perhaps the sheriff and his party had given out that war was imminent and this was the result.

It was clear now that to obtain evidence and convictions under such conditions as they prevailed in San Saba was going to be a long, slow job. With officials incriminated and good citizens intimidated; with witnesses ready to come forward and swear anything in defense of the murderers, knowing they would be upheld in their perjury, the securing of good testimony and subsequent justice would be difficult.

The Rangers went into camp in a picturesque spot on the banks of the San Saba River, a mile from town; pitched their tents under the shelter of some immense pecan trees; arranged their "chuck boards," staked their horses and made themselves generally comfortable. Then they posted sentinels (for a fusillade from the society was likely to come at any time), and settled down to business. Evidently they had come to stay. The society postponed its meetings.

Captain Bill now began doing quiet detective work, a labor for which he has a natural aptitude; anybody can see from the shape of his ears and nose, and from the ferret look of his eyes that this would be so. Good citizens took further courage and came to the camp with information. The Ranger Captain looked over the field and undertook a case particularly coldblooded and desperate.

A man named Brown, one of the society's early victims, had been hanged by that mob some ten or twelve years before, and his son Jim, though he had never attempted to avenge his father's death, had fallen under the ban. Jim Brown never even made any threats, but he must have been regarded as a menace, for one Sunday night while riding from church with his wife and her brother, he was shot dead from ambush; his wife, whose horse became frightened and ran within range, also receiving a painful wound.

Captain Bill secured information which convinced him that one Bill Ogle had been the chief instigator in this crime, and that the father and brother of Brown's wife were likewise members of the society and concerned in the plot. He learned, in fact, that the plan had been for Mrs. Brown's brother to ride with her, and for her father, Jeff McCarthy, to carry her baby by a different route to keep it out of danger. The brother, Jim McCarthy, was to stay close to his sister, to look after her horse and keep her out of harm's way while her husband was being murdered. It was due to the fact that Jim Mc-Carthy did not perform his work well, that the sister was wounded. McDonald in due course uncovered the whole dastardly plot.

The murderers now realized that trouble was in store for them. Some of the men began quietly to leave the country. Others consulted together in secluded places and plotted to " kill Bill McDonald." Sympathizing citizens encouraged this movement, and anonymous warnings—always the first resort of frightened criminals—began to arrive in the Ranger camp. Captain Bill paid no attention to such communications; he was used to them. He went on gathering and solidifying his evidence, preparatory to the arrest of Ogle and such of his associates as the proofs would warrant. Ogle, the " tiger " of the society, as he was considered, McDonald had not yet seen, for the reason that the tiger did not live in the town, and for some cause had lately avoided those precincts. He arrived, however, in due season. Perhaps the brotherhood let him know that it was time he was taking a hand in the game.

Captain McDonald, one hot afternoon, was talking to an acquaintance on the streets of San Saba, when he noticed a stout surly-looking man, with the village constable, not far away. Now and then they looked and nodded in his direction and presently an uncomplimentary name drifted to his ear.

" Who is that fellow talking to that sorry constable? " he asked.

His companion lowered his voice to a discreet
whisper.

" That is Bill Ogle," he said, " the worst man of
the murder mob."

Captain Bill looked pleased.

" Good-by," he nodded, " I want to see Bill Ogle."

He stepped briskly in the direction of the two men
who, seeing him approach, separated and loafed off
in different directions. Captain Bill overhauled the
constable.

" See here," he said composedly, " I heard you
call me a name a while ago when you were talking
to that murderer, Bill Ogle, who is going down the
street yonder. Now, an officer that throws in with
a murder mob, ain't worth what it would cost to try,
and hang, and if I hear any more names out of you
I'll save this country the expense of one rope,
anyway."

The constable attempted to mutter some denial.
Captain Bill left him abruptly with only a parting
word of advice and set off down the street after
Ogle. Ogle had crossed the street and passed
through the court-house to a hardware store on the
other side—where a number of his friends had collected.

" Don't go over there, Captain," cautioned his
friend, " you'll be killed, sure."

" Well, I'll go over and see," Captain Bill replied

quaintly, continuing straight toward the mob store.

As he entered there was a little stir, then silence. Evidently those present had not expected that he would walk straight among them. Here he was—they could kill him and put an end to all this trouble in short order. But somehow they didn't do it. There seemed no good moment to begin. Captain Bill walked over and faced Ogle.

"Come outside," he said quietly, "I want to talk to you."

Ogle hesitated.

"What do you want to say?" he asked sullenly.

Captain Bill laid his hand on Ogle's shoulder.

"I want to say some things that you might not want your friends to hear," he said—and a quaver in his voice then would have been death—"Come outside!"

He applied a firm pressure to Ogle's shoulder and steered him for the door. The others, as silent as death, made no move. They did not offer to interfere—they did not attempt to shoot. They simply looked on, wondering.

Outside, Captain Bill led Ogle to the middle of the street. It was blazing hot and the sand burned through his boots, but he could talk to Ogle out there and keep an eye on the others, too.

"Now, Bill Ogle," he said, in his deliberate calm way—"I know all about you. I know how you and your outfit murdered Jim Brown—just how you planned it, and how you did it. I've got all the

proof and I'm going to hang you if there is any law
in this country to hang a man for a foul murder like
that. That's what I'm here for, and I am not afraid
of you, nor of any of the men over there in that store
that helped you do your killing. You are all a lot
of cowardly murderers that only shoot defenseless
men from ambush, and I'm going to stay here until
I break up your gang if I have to put you every one
on the gallows or behind the bars, and I'm going to
begin with you.''

As Captain Bill talked the sweat began to pour off
of Ogle and his knees seemed to weaken. Presently
they could no longer support his stout body and he
sat heavily down in the hot sand, trying weakly to
make some defense.

'' Get up,'' said Captain Bill, '' haven't you got
your gun? ''

'' No, sir, Captain, I haven't.''

'' Well, you'd better get one if you're going to go
hunting for me. And there's the men over there
who helped you kill Jim Brown, and your Greaser-
lookin' constable and your sorry sheriff. Get your
whole crowd together, and get ready and then I'll
gather in the whole bunch. Go on, now, and see what
you can do.''

'' Yes, sir, Captain.''

Ogle made several attempts to get on his feet,
finally succeeded, and went back to his friends. Captain Bill immediately set about getting out a warrant for his arrest, but after some delay, found he

could not get the papers until next morning. Ogle, meantime, had been to his friend, the District Judge, who now appeared before the Ranger Captain with the statement that Ogle, whom he believed to be a square man, had said he wanted to leave the country for fear McDonald would kill him; McDonald, he said, having the reputation of being a killer and a bad man generally.

" Yes, Judge," said Captain Bill, " that's the proper reputation to give me, so that some of your crowd of murderers can assassinate me and your court can deliver a verdict that I was a bad citizen and ought to have been killed sooner, the way you've done about all the rest of the forty-three that have been murdered and no one tried for it in this section. Now, I intend to see that he don't leave this country, unless he leaves it in shackles. He committed this murder, and I can prove it. I've got one of the members of the mob as a witness."

" You will stir up old trouble and get things in worse shape than ever," protested the judge.

" If I can't get things in better shape, I'll lay down my hand," said McDonald.

A little later, on the street, Captain Bill saw Ogle approaching. He was armed this time—with a big watermelon. He approached humbly.

" Captain," he said, " you've done me a great wrong, and I want you to accept this watermelon."

Captain Bill did not know whether to laugh or to swear. Presently he said:

"You scoundrel! I suppose that thing is poisoned. I believe I'll make you eat it, rind and all."

Ogle backed away with his melon and presently set out for home. Fearing now that he would escape before the warrant could be issued, Captain McDonald instructed Rangers McCauley, Barker, Neil and Bell, members of his camp, to keep watch, and if Ogle attempted to leave the county to hold him until he (McDonald) could arrive with the proper papers. These were obtained next morning, about ten o'clock, and Captain Bill starting out with them, met his Rangers with Ogle, who had, in fact, attempted to escape. He was taken to jail and a strong guard was set.

Consternation now prevailed among the society and its friends; in the cowboy term they were "milling." Members of the mob were to turn State's evidence; one Josh McCormick, who had been made a member by compulsion—having run into one of their meetings—had been brought from an adjoining county and would testify; a grand jury composed of exemplary citizens had been secured.

And that was not all. Captain Bill one day went to the District Judge, ostensibly for advice.

"Judge," he said, "I want some legal information."

The judge was attentive, and took him to a quiet place.

"Now, Judge," said Captain Bill, "you know that the Buzzard Water Hole mob holds its meetings over there once a month, and the monthly meeting is about due. You know that they meet there to decide to kill somebody or to run him out of the country and take his property, and that they've already done such deviltry as that here for years."

The judge assented uneasily.

" Well, then," continued the Ranger Captain, " I want to know if it will be all right for me to charge in there on that meeting with my Rangers and kill any of them that might make any resistance, and round up the rest and drive them into town and put them in jail—just drive them afoot like a lot of cattle and let their horses be sent for, later; would that be all right, Judge? "

The District Judge was a good deal disturbed.

" No, Captain," he said, " I don't think you'd better undertake that, I should advise against such a move."

" Well, Judge," said Captain Bill, " that's exactly what I propose to do. I'll take chances on the results and I'll bring in the prettiest bunch of murderers you'll find anywhere. Good-day, Judge, and thank you for the advice."

However, this program was not carried out—not in full. There was no material with which to make it complete. Within a brief time from his talk with the District Judge, Captain Bill's purpose was known to every member of the mob. It was a time to take to tall timber and high trees. The society adjourned *sine die*.

The Rangers did, however, visit the Buzzard's Water Hole at the time when the mob meeting was due. Not a soul was to be found anywhere. Then knowing certain members of the gang, and having learned the society signals, Captain Bill and his men went riding over the country from house to house, halting outside to call " Hello!———Hello! Hello! " which was a signal call between members of the society. In reply to each such call a door opened and a man came out quickly, only to find the Rangers, who inquired if he were going to attend the meeting at Buzzard's Water Hole; whereupon, as Captain Bill put it later, " they like to died," and vigorously pretended ignorance of the meaning of the " Hello " signal. Next morning the Rangers were back in San Saba, and when the news came in that they had been around calling on mob members there was not only anxiety, but mystery, for some of these members of the society lived a distance of twenty-five miles away. But a fifty or seventy-five mile ride in a night on an errand of that kind was merely a little diversion, to a Ranger.

The grand jury's work was difficult. It found indictments against many of the assassins, but the district judge made an effort to annul most of these actions on one ground and another, and to trump up charges against the Rangers. McDonald finally gave this official a lecture which he probably remembers yet, if he is alive. About the same time one of the gang leveled a Winchester at Ranger Barker, who with his revolver shot him five times before he could pull the trigger, and was promptly cleared— all of which had a wholesome effect on the community as a whole.

With the arrest of Ogle, the anonymous letters became very terrible indeed. Captain Bill had brought his wife to the San Saba camp for the winter, and one morning appeared before her with one of these letters in his hand.

" Well, I've got to leave San Saba," he said.

" Why," she asked. " Has the Governor ordered you away? "

" No, the Governor hasn't, but read this."

He handed her the letter which informed him that if he did not leave San Saba in two days he would be filled so full of lead that it would require a freight train to haul him to the graveyard. Rhoda Mc- Donald read the communication through. Then she said:

" Bill Jess, if you leave here on account of a thing like that, *I'll* leave *you*."

" Well," said Captain Bill, sorrowfully, " I seem to be in a mighty bad fix. If I stay, I'll be filled with bullets, and if I go, I'll lose my wife. I s'pose I'll have to stay."

The examining trial of Bill Ogle was an event in San Saba. Josh McCormick was chief witness for the State, and was a badly scared man, in spite of the fact that the Rangers had taken him to their camp and guaranteed him protection from the members of the Buzzard's Water Hole crowd. Other witnesses on both sides were frightened enough, for nobody knew what might happen before this thing ended. It was the program of the mob forces, of which Ogle and his lawyers were the acting principals, to impeach the State's witnesses and thus break down their evidence before the court, as was their custom. Unfortunately for them they selected as one of their perjurers old Jeff McCarthy, father of Brown's wife, himself accessory to the crime for which Ogle was being tried. Captain Bill knew of McCarthy's relation to the affair, though the evidence had not been sufficient for his indictment. Furthermore, Captain Bill believed that the old man, like McCormick, whose uncle he was, had been forced into the band, and had acted under compulsion throughout.

McCormick was placed on the stand, and told what he knew about the society and its crimes in general, and about the killing of Jim Brown in particular. His absolute knowledge did not extend to the connection of the two McCarthy's with the killing, and they were not mentioned in his evidence. When he left the stand, a number of nervous witnesses were called by the other side to swear that they would not believe him on oath. Finally old Jeff McCarthy was reached. He was frightened and trembling and in a wretched state altogether. Captain Bill watched him closely while he was making his statement concerning the worthless character of his nephew, McCormick, and the old man shifted and twisted to evade those eyes that were piercing his very soul. Now and then the Ranger Captain leaned toward him and lifted his finger like the index of fate, prompting the District Attorney meantime as to what questions to put to the witness. The old man became more and more confused and miserable, and when at last he was excused he tottered from the stand. He lingered about the place, however, seemingly unable to leave, and by and by, when court adjourned for the day, McDonald found him just outside the door, with others of his kind.

"Jeff," Captain Bill said in his calm drawl, "you did not tell the truth on the stand; you know every word you said was a lie."

Old Jeff McCarthy gasped, tried to get his words, gasped again and failed.

"I don't blame you so much," Captain Bill went on, "for you were afraid this mob would kill you if you didn't testify according to orders—now, wasn't you?"

Again the wretched old man made an effort to reply, but he was past speech.

Captain Bill's finger was pinning him fast.

"They frightened you and made you join their gang, didn't they? And now you would like to get out, but you don't know how—ain't that so?"

The old man was on the verge of utter collapse. He backed off and slunk away. After that Old Jeff haunted the Ranger Camp and finally when he could stand it no longer made full confession to Captain Bill of his connection with the mob, revealing the mob's secrets, its signs and passwords, the names of its members and its gruesome oath.

" They will kill me," he said, " but I don't care. I'm happier now than I've been for years! "

" I don't reckon they'll try that," said Captain Bill. " That thing's about over, around here."

They formed a guard, and escorted the old man home, for he was full of fear.

When the court of examination adjourned, Ogle was held without bail. Through the efforts of District Attorney Lynden it was decided to transfer Ogle's case to Llano County for final trial, Lynden making his fight for this change on the grounds that no fair trial could be obtained in the San Saba court.

In Llano County, Ogle's case was fairly tried, and he received a life sentence. Two accessories to the killing of Brown, were arrested, but just then war was declared with Spain; the Rangers were hastily ordered off to protect the Rio Grande frontier, where a Mexican incursion was expected, and without Captain Bill to keep up the vigorous action, and a sharp oversight on the witness stand, convictions were not obtainable.

However, the San Saba campaign was a success. The society that murdered men for spite, or gain, or pastime, no longer existed. When the next election of county officials came around the old lot was wiped out clean, and men of character and probity

came into power. The roads that led to the Bad
Lands were kept dusty with the emigration of men
who had formerly gathered at Buzzard's Water
Hole, and in their stead came those who would give
to San Saba nobler enterprise and worthier fame.
Eight Rangers were among the new blood that came
to rehabilitate San Saba County. That long winter
of '97-98 had not been altogether spent in chasing
criminals. These eight had found wives, or rumors
of wives; in due time they were all married, and with
eight established resident Rangers, how could any
county help becoming as serene and safe as a Sun-
day-school? Ranger Edgar Neil was elected sheriff;
Ollie Perry was chosen constable; Dud Barker, Ed.
Donnelly, Forest Edwards and Bob McClure also
settled in San Saba, and caused Company B to go
recruiting for Rangers.

Bill Ogle is still in the Penitentiary at Huntsville,
Texas. As late as May, 1908, he wrote to Captain
McDonald as follows:

" Huntsville, Texas, 5/21/08.
" Capt. W. J. McDonald,
" Austin, Texas.
" Dear Sir:
" It has come to my ears from some of my friends,
who have recently visited Austin in my behalf, that
you are bitterly opposed to my being released from
the Penitentiary. I regret very much that you are
taking this stand against me. My friends also told
me that one of your reasons of being in opposition
to my release was, that you had fears of your own
life, should I be pardoned.

" Capt. McDonald, I want to assure you that I have no feeling of bitterness against you, and you may rest assured, that I would never harm you in the least or try to injure you in any way, should I regain my liberty. I feel that in doing what you did, you were doing your duty as an officer.

" My conduct in the Penitentiary ought to be a guarantee to you of my intention to lead a correct life, when I get out, and I feel, that if you will investigate my standing here, and find out what the officers here think about me, you will be convinced of this.

" I trust that you will reconsider this matter, and soften your heart in my case, and you may rest assured, that I will appreciate anything you will do for me as long as life shall last.

" I would be pleased to hear from you, and I hope that you will give me some little encouragement.

" Thanking you in advance for anything you may say or do for me, I am,

" Yours respectfully,
" WILL OGLE."

Captain McDonald's reply to Ogle's letter was, in part, as follows:

" Austin, Texas, June 4, 1908.

" Mr. Bill Ogle,
    " Huntsville, Penitentiary.
" Dear Sir:
    " Your letter of the 21st inst. received, and contents duly and carefully noted.

" I note what you say in regard to what your friends say about my opposing your pardon, claiming that in case of your release I had fears of my own life. Now, Bill, . . . my advice to you is to make a clear truthful statement, giving all the facts connected with numerous murders committed by this mob, and thereby secure your liberty.

" You know I'm not in the Ranger service now, and it makes no difference to me who is released, and I so notified the Board of Pardons.

" You say you have no feeling of bitterness against me, and that you would not attempt to harm me. You can rest assured that I have no fears in that line. I only did my duty as an officer, as you say I did, and I have no animosity against you; and would not have gone before the Board of Pardons, had I not been sent for.

" I understand your conduct has been all right while in jail, and in the Penitentiary, and I am sorry that your conduct wasn't better before you got into that mob, because you know that was an awful thing. Now, don't you?

" You asked me to consider this matter, and that you will appreciate it as long as life shall last. I certainly will not utter any protest, unless the Governor asks me what I know about it, and I'll then tell the truth about it.

" Very respectfully,
W. J. McDonald."

What Captain Bill had said before the Board of Pardons was:

" I don't know the gentleman that is presenting this petition and making this talk to you, but I do know the names of a good many of those signers, and I know Bill Ogle is guilty of this murder, and I know that a good many of these other fellows ought to be where Bill is now."

XXX

Quieting a Texas Feud

As the old century drew near its end, a wave of
disorder and crime that amounted to an inundation
swept over the eastern and south-eastern portion of
Texas. Murders, lynchings, 'mobs and rumors of
mobs, were reported daily. The Pan-handle, even
in its palmiest days, had been a Young Men's Chris-
tian Association as compared with the older, more
thickly settled portions of the State. In the Pan-
handle, crime was likely to be of a primitive, elemental kind—the sort of crime that flourished in the
old, old days when the Patriarchs pastured their
flocks on a hundred hills and protected them with a
club.

In the long-settled districts to the eastward, crime
had ripened, as it were, and manifested itself in
more finished forms. Feuds had developed, and
race prejudice. Communities had been established
which found it necessary to hang their only respectable citizens in order to preserve peace. In other
places old ladies, supposed to have a few hundred
dollars, were murdered by relatives who could not
wait for them to die. These are the things that come

only with long settlement, and where certain human impulses have been carefully bred and nourished.

The Reece-Townsend feud in Colorado County gave the State no end of trouble. The Reece and Townsend families killed one another in the regulation way, when good opportunities offered. They had a fashion of gathering in the streets of Columbus, the county seat, for their demonstrations, and sometimes on a field-day like that they killed members of other families, by mistake. But errors of this sort were not allowed to interfere with the central idea of the feud; they apologized and went on killing one another, just the same.

It was when a boy who belonged to neither faction was shot and killed, at one of these reunions, that Captain Bill McDonald and his Rangers were ordered to Columbus to put down what seemed about to become a general war.

Captain Bill failed to receive the order in time to get his men the same day, but did not wait. He wired two to follow him on first train and set out for Columbus alone. Arriving on the streets of Columbus he saw detachments of armed men gathered here and there—the streets being otherwise deserted. He set out at once for the home of District Judge Kennon to whom he had been ordered to report. After the exchange of greetings, McDonald said:

" We haven't much time, Judge, from appearances. I saw a lot of armed men as I came along, and it looks like we're going to have war.''

'' You are right,'' Judge Kennon said, '' we are expecting it any minute. Where are your men, and how many have you? ''

'' None, Judge. I came alone, but I expect two in the morning.''

'' In the morning! Why, man, by that time the fight will be over! And what can you do with two men here? Nothing less than twenty-five or thirty will help this case.''

'' Judge,'' said Captain Bill, in his deliberate way, '' I believe I can stop this thing if you will come down to the court-house with me. Anyhow, it's my duty to try; and we'd better be getting over there, now, Judge, for this ain't going to wait long. If we can't stop it we can see a mighty good fight, anyhow.''

They set out together. The court-house in Columbus stands in the middle of a big square, with a street on each of its four sides. On one corner of the square, was gathered the Reece faction, and near another corner the Townsend crowd had assembled. Both were fully armed. They were making no active demonstrations as yet, but were evidently organizing for business. It was a still, sunny summer day, and both crowds were in easy calling distance of the court-house.

'' Now, Judge,'' said Captain Bill, when they had

arrived at the court-house, " who is your sheriff, and where is he."

" His name is Burford, J. C. Burford, and he's over there with the Townsend crowd. He belongs to that faction."

Captain Bill stepped to the window and called in the strong official manner of a witness summons: " J. C. Burford," repeated three times.

There was a movement in the Townsend crowd and a man crossed over and ascended the court-house stair. McDonald introduced himself, as the sheriff entered, and added:

" Now, Mr. Burford, why don't you stop this row? Looks as if we're going to have a killing match here, right away."

" Captain, I can't. I'm powerless to do anything with these men. If I undertake to disarm them, it will start a fight that nobody can stop."

" Well, Burford, if you'll do as I tell you, I'll stop it in thirty minutes or I'll resign my job as Ranger."

" All right, Captain, I'll do whatever you say," assented Burford.

" Then call your crowd over here. I want to talk to them."

Sheriff Burford stepped to the window and signed to the Townsend faction. They trooped over and ascended the court-house stair, carrying their guns.

" Mr. Burford," said McDonald, " which are your regular deputies here? "

The sheriff indicated his three deputy officers.

Captain Bill motioned them to stand apart from the others.

" Now, Sheriff," he said, " disarm the rest of these men."

The officer looked a little bewildered.

" I don't know about that," he began.

" Didn't you agree to do what I ordered? " Then, to Kennon—" Didn't he, Judge? "

The judge nodded. The sheriff still hesitated.

" Never mind," said McDonald, " I'll do it myself. Here, boys," he went on in his mild friendly drawl, " come in here and stack your guns in this wardrobe. It's a good safe place for them. They won't be likely to go off and hurt anybody, in there."

What was it about the manner of the man that made men obey? Those aroused, bloodthirsty Texans, full of an old deep hatred and the spirit of revenge, marched in and put away their guns at his direction, with scarcely a word of dissent.

" I don't blame you-all for having your guns until now," Captain Bill went on, as he locked the wardrobe and took the key. " But we want to stop this war if we can. It ain't good for the population. Now, I'll just go over and look after the other crowd."

He went out of the court-house, and crossed the street to where the Reece crowd was gathered. He carried his Winchester and the faction watched him curiously as he approached.

" I guess you boys are going to war, ain't you? "
he said cheerfully as he came nearer.

Nobody replied, and Captain Bill came up close.

" Boys," he said, " your guns are all right, up till
now, but the Governor has sent me down here to stop
this trouble, and I want you-all to help me."

" How can we help you? " asked one of the Reece
faction.

" Like them boys did over yonder, just now—by
giving up your guns. Then by going quietly home."

There was a little murmur of dissent and one big
husky fellow said:

" Well, you'll play hell getting my gun! "

In less than an instant, a Winchester was under
his nose and Captain Bill was crisply saying:

" I will, hey? Well I'll just put you in jail, anyway, to show you how easy it is to do *that*."

The big fellow gave a great jump and nearly fell
over with surprise and fright. His gun dropped as
if it had been hot. The leader of the Reece faction
spoke up quickly.

" Boys, he is right," he said. " The Governor
sent him here, and he's obeying orders. He has no
interest in one side or the other."

McDonald marched the Reeces over to a store,
nearby, where they laid down their guns, and the
clerk was ordered to take charge of them. The big
man under arrest promised all manner of things if
Captain Bill would let him go. He was set free, with
a warning. Peace now seemed to be restored, and

in the general gratitude of the community, refreshments and invitations were tendered to Captain Bill from both sides. He decided, however, to remain on duty during the rest of the day and night. His two men arrived next morning, but everything was still quiet, and there appeared no sign of a renewal of hostilities. The Reece-Townsend trouble, for the time, at least, was over.*

* Report of Adjutant-General Thomas Scurry of Texas (1899):

"During the month of March, 1899, Captain McDonald and two men were ordered to Columbus, Colorado County, for the purpose of preventing trouble between the Townsend and Reece factions. Captain McDonald went alone, his men not being able to reach him in time, and his courage and cool behavior prevented a conflict between the two factions." For fuller official details of this and other work of that period, see Appendix B.

XXXI

The Trans-cedar Mystery

Captain McDonald was still at Columbus when he received a telegram ordering him to report at once to Assistant Attorney General Morris and the local officials at Athens, Henderson County, Texas, for the purpose of investigating the lynching of three respectable citizens—a father and two sons, named Humphrey—in a timbered tract between Trinity River and Cedar Creek, known as the Trans-cedar Bottoms.

Henderson County is in East Texas, and the Trans-cedar Bottoms constitute just the locality and neighborhood for a murder of the Humphrey kind. Shut-in, thickly timbered and lonely—it is a place for low morals to become lower with each generation —for scant intellect to become scantier—for darkened minds to become darker and more impervious to pity, indeed to any human impulse except crime.

The Humphreys had not fitted an environment like that. They were honest, sturdy men—fearless and open in their dealings. They were a menace to a gang who made moonshine whisky, stole whatever they could lay hands on and would swear a man's life away for a lean hog. It was necessary for the welfare of the neighborhood that the Humphreys be disposed of, and they were taken by a mob one night and hanged—three of them to one tree—they having been placed upon horses and the horses driven from under them. Then, when the ropes had proven too long, and the feet of the three Humphreys had touched the ground, the mob had bent back the legs of the victims at the knee and tied the feet upward to the hands, so that the Humphreys might swing clear.

Bill McDonald knew something of the Transcedar country, and the character of its settlement, for, as we have seen in a former chapter, he had passed his youth and his early manhood at Henderson and at Mineola, both within seventy-five miles of that very district. He set out alone by first train, and arriving at Athens, learned the details of the ghastly crime which already, through the telegraphed reports, had stirred the entire State. He learned that the lynching had taken place about twenty-five miles from Athens, near a little postoffice named Aley, and he hurried to that place, without delay, taking with him one Guy Green, an Athens lawyer, familiar with the neighborhood. With Green, the Ranger went straight to the scene of the murder and made an examination of the tracks and various clues that remained. Two days had passed since the crime, and many of the signs had been obliterated. Still there were enough for a man with the faculties of Captain Bill. He identified no less than four trails—one, as he decided, made by five horses; another by three; a third by two, and a fourth the track of a single horse. The trails wound in and out, crossed and recrossed, and were evidently made with the idea of balking pursuit. Captain McDonald did not consider them especially difficult, and having satisfied himself that they could be followed, he went on to Aley, for it was near night-fall.

At Aley he joined Assistant Attorney General Ned Morris; District Attorney Jerry Crook; Tom Bell, sheriff of Bell County, and Ben. E. Cabell, sheriff of Dallas County, who had come over to aid the investigation. He was assured that the work was going to be hard—that the greater portion of the inhabitants were either in sympathy with the lynchers or were so much in terror of them that it would be almost impossible to get direct evidence. Captain Bill looked thoughtful as he listened.

" Well," he said, " I'm going to stay here till I get it, and I'm going after it just like I was going for a doctor. You can give it out that I mean business and that nobody need to be afraid to testify. I'll take care of them."

He discussed the case with the officials and learned that one Joe Wilkerson was suspected as having been connected with the murder—it being well-known that Wilkerson had pursued the Humphreys

and bemeaned them; finally accusing them of stealing hogs, and swearing to some meat which the
Humphreys had earned by digging wells. In the
evidence it had developed that the Wilkerson hogs,
though mortgaged by him, had in reality been sold,
and that he had thus attempted to evade the consequences of this illegal act by saddling the Humphreys with a still heavier crime. The Humphreys
had not been convicted, but Wilkerson had never
ceased to vilify them. Later, one of the Humphrey
boys, George, had been set upon by some of the Wilkerson crowd and in defending himself had killed,
with a knife, one of his assailants. The courts—
there were honest courts in Athens—had cleared
him, but in the Trans-cedar tribunal he had been
doomed. These facts constituted about all the foun-
dation of known motive upon which McDonald would
have to build his evidence. It was while he was discussing these things with the attorneys on the night
of his arrival that a man rode up to the gate just
outside and called his name. Captain Bill rose, but
the others protested, declaring that it might be a plot
to shoot him in the dark. However, he went, six-
shooter in hand, and sticking it in the face of the
caller, demanded his business. The man protested
that he meant no harm, but had come from one Buck
Holley, who lived two miles down the road and said
he knew Captain McDonald and wanted to see him.
The Ranger Captain reflected a minute.

"I don't know any Buck Holley," he said. "I

knew a scoundrel by the name of Bill Holley some years ago up in the Pan-handle, and if that is who it is I don't want to see him. I judge you fellows have got a gang down the road there to shoot me from ambush. Who are you, anyway? ''

The man said his name was Monasco; that he was staying at Holley's and that he had a brother named Bill Monasco, in Amarillo.

'' I know Bill Monasco,'' McDonald said, '' and he has a brother that was sent to the penitentiary. Is that you? ''

The visitor acknowledged that he was the man— that he had been recently released.

'' Well,'' said McDonald, '' that's about the kind of a crowd that I would expect to find Bill Holley running with, and you can tell this *Buck* Holley, as you call him, that I suspect him of being connected with this mob, and that I used to make him stand hitched in the Pan-handle, and that I'm going to do the same here.''

Monasco said '' good-night,'' and Captain McDonald never saw him again. Somewhat later, when he met Bill Holley on the streets of Athens, he said:

'' Look here, Bill, I'm afraid your partner, Monasco, didn't tell you the message I sent the night I came. I said I didn't know Buck Holley, but that I knew a sorry bulldozing scoundrel by the name of Bill Holley, and that I supposed he was down the road there to take a shot at me from ambush. You weren't in this lynching mob, I reckon, but they're your friends, and you'd help 'em if you could. Now, Bill, you've been courting a funeral a good while, and if you try any of your nonsense here, you'll win out.''

He searched Holley for weapons and relieved him of a big pocket-knife, the bully protesting that he was no longer a bad man. Captain Bill learned, however, that he had recently whipped his wife, taken her clothes and driven her away from home, and later had attempted to kill her father for 'interfering in her behalf.

The Ranger Captain was out early the morning after his arrival in Aley, and on the trail. The tracks of the five horses were followed to the houses of Joe Wilkerson and his tenant, and to the homes of John and Arthur Greenhaw. In Wilkerson's lot the officers found part of a well-rope, the remainder of which had been cut away. It matched precisely with the rope used to hang the Humphreys—the freshly cut ends being the same on both. The Wilkersons and one of the Greenhaws were taken into custody forthwith, and other arrests followed, as the criminals were tracked home.

But it was hard to get evidence. A few who were anxious to testify, hesitated through fear. Others, subpœnaed and examined, were evidently in sympathy with the mob and withheld their knowledge accordingly. Captain Bill had been reinforced by Private Olds from Company C, and now began systematic investigation. He established his court of inquiry under a brush arbor—a framework of poles, with brush a-top to keep out the sun—and there for two months held high inquisition. It was a curious, exclusive court. The Ranger Captain gave it out that he would invite such attendance as he needed, and that mere spectators would kindly remain away. His wishes were heeded.

Little by little evidence collected. Men willing to testify gained confidence from Captain Bill's assurance of protection and told what they knew. Men unwilling to testify found themselves unable to hide their facts where they could not be reached by the keen persuasive probing of the man with those ferret eyes, that quiet voice and those alert extended ears. The testimony brought out the facts the Humphreys had known of an illicit still run by two men—one Polk Weeks and a man named Johns. Also that they had known of John Greenhaw stealing cattle and hogs, and that John Greenhaw had once drawn a gun on the elder Humphrey, who had taken it away from him, unloaded and returned it, instead of killing him with it and rendering the community a service. These things, added to the other provocations already named, had made the Humphreys sufficiently unpopular in a neighborhood like the Trans-cedar bottoms to warrant their being hung to a limb, trussed up to swing clear of the ground.

In the course of time, practically every resident of that district had been before the brush-arbor court of inquiry, and if a shorthand report had been taken of that testimony it would have furnished material for many a character study and tale of fiction.

Guilty knowledge of the crime actually killed a man named Eli Sparks, whose conscience tortured him day and night to the point of giving testimony, yet whose fears upon the witness stand caused him to withhold the truth. He was a large red-faced man, evidently greatly excited when questioned, and concealing more than he told. Soon after his first examination he met Captain McDonald and offered to testify again, saying that he had been too frightened to tell the truth, the first time, but thought he could do better, now. The Ranger Captain scrutinized him keenly and made the prophecy that Eli Sparks would not live thirty days, unless he got rid of the load on his conscience. He died in just half that time; not, however, until he had fully confessed a complete knowledge of the details of preparation for the crime, and how once he had gone with the mob when they had intended hanging the Humphreys, but for some reason had postponed the event. The poor wretch did not go the second time, but his guilt nevertheless dragged him to the grave.

Another who came to the brush-arbor inquiry was a banker who testified that the Humphreys had received their just deserts for the reason that they were thieves and should have been hung long before.

" How did *you* come to escape, then? " asked Mc-

Donald. " I understand that you were once indicted
for cattle-stealing yourself, and that you actually
got the cattle. Is that so? "

Under severe pressure the witness admitted that
there had been such a charge and that the cattle had
by some means got into his possession. He got
away at last and disappeared out of the case entirely, though he had been active up to that point.

The efforts of the men believed to be concerned
as principals in the crime, to establish their innocence, were sometimes wary, sometimes crudely
absurd, and always fruitless. The mesh of fact that
was weaving and linking itself about them became
daily more tightly woven, more impossible to tear
away. Knowing themselves closely watched, they
dared not attempt flight. To do so would be to confess guilt, and capture would be well-nigh certain.
Like Ahab, having compassed the death of a neighbor, they " lay in sackcloth and went softly."
Finally it came to pass that three of these " children of Belial " turned State's evidence—that is,
they confessed fully, sacrificing their comrades,
under the law, to save themselves. Eleven men, including these three, were brought to trial.

Yet, conviction was not easy, in spite of the direct
character of the evidence. The accused men employed lawyers who were ready to balk at no methods
that would save their clients, and there were plenty
of witnesses willing to testify as instructed. Efforts
were also made to influence and coerce the State's

witnesses, and McDonald found it necessary to threaten certain counsel for the defense with subornation proceedings, before he could get the way clear for action. Even then it was thought advisable to transfer the cases to Palestine, in the adjoining county, for trial—sentiment in the neighborhood of Athens being regarded as too favorable to the accused. In the final trial John and Arthur Greenhaw and Polk Weeks, who were not only murderers, but cowardly traitors, were given their freedom in exchange for their evidence that sent their eight associates to the Penitentiary for life.

Polk Weeks, in giving his evidence, appeared much disturbed, but confessed how he had climbed the tree and tied the ropes, and tied them too long, making it necessary for the legs of the Humphreys to be bent upwards, to clear the ground. John Greenhaw corroborated this, but grinned as he told it, remembering how amusing it had been. He did not live to enjoy his freedom, for he was shot soon after his discharge by a son of one of the murdered Humphreys—young Willie Humphrey, who was never punished for that righteous act.*

* Extract from a letter relating to the Humphrey case, written by Assistant Attorney General N. B. Morris to Adjutant-General Thos. Scurry; included in the latter's Annual Report for 1899–1900.

" You will remember that at the request of the sheriff, county attorney, and other local authorities of that county, Captain McDonald and Private Old were sent to assist them and myself in the investigation of that horrible murder which was then enshrouded in a mystery that it seemed almost impossible to uncover. Before the Rangers reached us the people in the neighborhood seemed afraid to talk. They said they

XXXII

Other Mobs and Riots

RANGERS AT ORANGE AND AT PORT ARTHUR. FIVE AGAINST FOUR HUNDRED

A RIOT at Orange, Texas, followed the Trans-cedar episode. Orange is a lumber town on the Sabine River in the extreme south-east portion of Texas, and many negroes are employed in the saw-mills. A white mob composed of the tougher element in and about the city had organized, with the purpose of driving the negroes away. The negroes received anonymous warnings, and as they did not go immediately, were assaulted. Some twenty or more of the mob, one dark night, surrounded a house where a number of the colored men were assembled and opened fire, killing one man and wounding several others. Ranger Captain Rogers of Company E, with his men, was ordered to Orange, but soon

---

would be murdered, too, if they took a hand in working up the case. About the first thing that Captain McDonald did was to assure the people that he and his associates had come to stay until every murderer was arrested and convicted, and that those who assisted him would be protected. They believed him, and in consequence thereof, soon began to talk and feel that the law would be vindicated, and I am glad to say that it was. The work of the Rangers in this one case is worth more to the State, in my opinion, than your department will cost during your administration. In fact such service cannot be valued in dollars and cents." *

* For further official details of this and other work of that period, see Appendix B.

after his arrival, while making an arrest among desperate characters, was disabled through injury to an old wound. Captain McDonald then came down from Athens with Rangers Fuller, Jones, Old, McCauley, Saxon and Bell. They lost no time in taking a firm grip on the situation and landed twenty-one of the offenders in jail, with evidence sufficient to convict. But it was a hard profitless work. Whatever the citizens might want, Orange officially did not care for law and order. A gang controlled the law of the community, and the order took care of itself. Private Fuller found it necessary to kill one man who interfered with an arrest and attempted to use a knife. Later, Fuller was summoned to Orange, ostensibly to answer to the charge of illegal arrest, but in reality for purposes of revenge. Captain McDonald protested to the Governor that it was simply an excuse to get Fuller over there to kill him.

It turned out accordingly: Fuller was washing his face in a barber shop when the dead man's brother slipped up behind and shot him through the head with a Winchester, killing him instantly. The assassin was made chief deputy sheriff, as a reward, and in due time was himself killed by the city marshal, who, in turn, was killed by the dead man's family; which process of extermination has probably continued to this day, and perhaps Orange has improved accordingly. There was room for improvement. The cases against the twenty-one men arrested by Captain Bill and his Rangers were all dismissed, as soon as the Rangers got out of town.*

Port Arthur, also on the Sabine River, below Orange, is a city of oil refineries, and is a port of entry, as its name implies, its outlet being through Sabine Pass. In March, 1902, trouble broke out there between the longshoremen and the operators of the refineries. As a result the longshoremen struck, and when the operators introduced Mexican laborers, the strikers, numbering about four hundred, drove them away and issued a manifesto, declaring that no more Mexicans need apply.

It was at this stage of the proceedings that Captain Bill was ordered by Adjutant-General Scurry to take several men and be on hand when the next Mexicans arrived. He took four—Privates Grude Brittain, Jim Keeton, John Blanton and Blaze Delling—picked men—and arrived on the ground a day in advance of the next hundred Mexicans, then on the way.

The Rangers proceeded immediately to the refineries, which are located several miles from the city, and saw nothing of the longshoremen that day. It was likely they would be on hand next morning when the Mexicans would arrive. Threats had been made that these Mexicans would not be allowed to leave the train for the refineries, and that if any such attempt was made, blood would flow.

* For official particulars concerning this incident and other work of that period, see Appendix B.

When the train pulled in next morning Captain Bill and his men were on hand, fully expecting trouble. Everything was quiet, and the Mexicans were marched by the Rangers to the refineries and went immediately to work. Then, there still being no sign of interference, Captain Bill said:

"Well, boys, let's go down in town now and see what's become of the mob."

The mob was not hard to find. It had assembled on the street and was a good deal excited. Men were talking, and gesticulating, and denouncing, in words noisy and violent. As Captain Bill and his men drew up, a voice loud enough for them to hear said:

"There are them damned Rangers, now."

The little company of five continued to advance until within easy talking distance; then McDonald said:

"What are you men doing here, gathered in a crowd this way, on the street?"

A longshoreman asked:

"Are you the Rangers?"

"That's what we are," said Captain Bill.

"Come down to protect the Mexicans, I guess."

"That's what the Adjutant-General sent us for," returned Captain Bill pleasantly.

"Well, we're not going to let them work."

"They're already working," smiled Captain Bill.

"How many men did you bring with you?" asked the leader of the rioters.

" Enough to whip this crowd, if a fight is what you're looking for," Captain Bill answered—still pleasant.

" Where are they? "

" Here," said Captain Bill, indicating his brigade of four—five with himself.

" Hell! " said the leader of the longshoremen, " there are four hundred of us."

" Well, that makes it just about even," drawled Captain Bill, more pleasant than ever, " if you think you want to fight, get at it! "

The leader of the strikers looked at the little army thoughtfully. Then he turned to the others.

" Boys," he said, " I think these Rangers are all right. Let's all have a drink! "

The Rangers politely declined this invitation, but continued on friendly terms with the strikers. There was no further trouble, and a few days later Captain McDonald and one of his men left Port Arthur. The remainder of his force stayed a few weeks longer, but the war was over.

XXXIII

Other Work in East Texas

IT was only a short distance—as distances go in
Texas (only a hundred miles or so, in a south-
easterly direction)—from the Trans-cedar country,
made celebrated by the Humphrey lynching, to certain sections of Walker, Houston, Madison and
Trinity counties, where similar social conditions
have developed.

In Kittrell's Cut-off, for instance, and around
Groveton, there has developed a special talent for
assassination. Men walking along the road in daylight are sometimes shot from behind. When it is
night-fall the assassin may lie in wait by the roadside. If he gets the wrong man by mistake, it is no
difference—it keeps him in practice. Sometimes the
victim is called to his door at night and shot down
from the dark. These are a few of the methods for
removing individuals not favorably regarded by the
active set, and many other forms of murder are
adopted or invented for particular cases. Even
Captain Bill McDonald found these districts hopeless as fields for reform, he said.

" If a whole community has no use for law and order it's not worth while to try to enforce such things. You've got to stand over a place like that with a gun to make it behave, and when you catch a man, no matter what the evidence is against him, they'll turn him loose. In Groveton, for instance, when I was there they had only two law-respecting officers—the district clerk and the county attorney, and the county attorney they killed. Good citizens were so completely in the minority that they were helpless. Kittrell's Cut-off was probably one of the most lawless places you could find anywhere, though it was named after a judge. It's a strip cut off of Houston and Trinity counties and added to Walker, and its name is the only thing about it that ever had anything to do with the law. Many murders have been committed there and no one ever convicted for them, so far as I know."

Captain Bill was ordered to investigate a Kittrell's Cut-off murder during December, 1903. A man had been assassinated from ambush, in the fashion of that section, and such attempts as had been made by the local authorities to uncover the murderers had been without result. But such murders had become so common there that the few respectable citizens of the locality had decided to appeal to Governor Lanham for aid, and their plea asked especially for Captain McDonald.

McDonald went down; looked over the ground and sent for one of his men, Blaze Delling, to assist in handling the situation—the community being simply infested with men of low, desperate natures. Already the Ranger Captain had taken up the trail and had arrested three men, and these were brought for trial.

What was the use? Before the final trial, the three principal witnesses suddenly sickened and died; the District Attorney found himself without a case; the prisoners were discharged.

It was about this time that County Attorney H. L. Robb (himself a victim later), asked that Captain McDonald be sent to Groveton in Trinity County to unravel the mystery surrounding the murder of an old lady, committed about a year before. Captain Bill went reluctantly, for he was tired of that section and cared not much for a " cold " trail at best.

On arrival at Groveton, he learned the facts so far as known. A feeble old lady named Touchstone, living alone, had been murdered for a stocking full of money supposed to be hidden somewhere on the premises. She had only a life interest in the money, anyway, but the heirs to her trifling hoard of probably not more than a few hundred dollars, had been impatient and had frequently demanded their shares. They were a devilish brood, but the old lady did not seem to fear them and carried a stout stick for defense. She had been found murdered, one afternoon, her throat cut, and her body left lying in the dooryard, where it had been mangled by hogs. Naturally the relatives were suspected, but thus far no evidence had been found against them.

There was evidence enough, however, for a man who had eyes trained to follow clues and to distinguish signs. In a comparatively brief time, Captain McDonald felt warranted in causing the arrest of one Ab Angle, and several others. Angle had married a granddaughter of the murdered woman and all were relatives. In the course of time, Angle's heart failed him and he confessed the crime in full. In his sworn statement, he said:

"We all talked the matter over about going and robbing Mary Jane (Mrs. Touchstone) and Hill Hutto said: 'Let's have an understanding.' George Angle, Wash and Joe Tullis, Hill Hutto and Mrs. Tullis and myself (all relatives) were to meet over at Mary Jane's to see where she kept the money, and to get it. That was our intention—to get the money on Saturday night. Hill Hutto was to be there when we got there. It was just dark when we got started, and we went through the fields in an easterly direction, in a trail through the woods.

"The understanding was that Joe Tullis and I were to do the watching, and Joe was on one end of the gallery and I was on the other end—he being told to watch the east end of the road, and I to watch the west end. Hill Hutto was to be there, talking to Mary Jane, while George Angle and Mrs. Tullis were to go in at the front, and Wash was to go in at the back of the house. She (Mrs. Touchstone) had some meal spread out on the floor to dry. She was sitting down—I do not know on what—talking to Hill.

" Mrs. Tullis said, ' Mary Jane, we have come to see whether you have that money yet, or not.' Mary Jane started to get up, but Hill Hutto, George Angle, Wash Tullis and Mrs. Tullis grabbed her and carried her out on the gallery and told me and Joe to watch the road, good, and we told her (Mrs. Tullis) we would, as far as we could see. She (Mrs. Touchstone) started to holler, but Wash put a handkerchief over her mouth. He had a white handkerchief in his right coat-pocket. . . ."

The confession then relates how they put out the fire (fearing its light) by throwing a bucket of water on it and how they jerked off a bonnet which the old lady had on. It proceeds:

" They (her precious relatives) carried her to the edge of the gallery and asked her to say where the money was, and she said she did not have any, and they pushed her off, and as they pushed her off, Hill Hutto struck her with a stick."

It was at this point probably that they cut their victim's throat—a detail which Angle's confession does not mention—through delicacy, perhaps. He says:

" They went out and examined her, going through her clothes carefully, in search for her possessions. Hill Hutto, Wash Tullis, George Angle and Mrs. Tullis did the examining, and they got one-half and one-quarter of a dollar. George Angle and Wash Tullis spent the money. Hill Hutto, Wash Tullis, George Angle and Mrs. Tullis looked over the house and went through the trunks and the bed. If they got any money, I do not know of it. They came out of the house and looked under the house to see if they could find any dirt dug up, or any fresh signs, but they could not find any, and we went out at the west end of the gallery, and climbed over the fence and took the trail through the fields and Hill went the back way. . . ."

Many half-burnt matches were found under the house by Rangers McDonald and Delling to confirm this statement. The confession proceeds:

" The stick and the bucket were thrown out near where she was. The stick was her walking-stick and the bucket the one Wash put the fire out with. Hill threw the stick out, and Wash threw out the bucket. Hill said he would leave the bucket out there and the people would think she just went out to slop the hogs and fell out. It was understood that night by all six of us that Wash and George would come back and get the hogs in there, and that they would dig a hole on the left of the gate as you go in."

He details how Wash Tullis and George Angle changed their shirts before breakfast—for the removal of ghastly evidence, of course—and how *after breakfast* they changed their trousers. He relates how the hogs were to be " tolled into the yard," and adds:

" The understanding was that we were to find her by the buzzards, but Jim Ray found her before the time."

Now, it would be natural to suppose that a confession like that would hang the confessor and his

confederates as high as Haman. It did nothing of
the sort. Angle's relatives prevailed upon him to
retract his confession, and under the law, as administered in that district, they were all discharged
except Angle himself who was sentenced for three
years for having *committed perjury by swearing to
a confession which he subsequently declared a lie!*

It is hardly to be wondered at that men like Bill
McDonald should lose interest in a neighborhood
where conditions like these exist. What use is it
to track and bring home criminals only to see them
go free, perhaps vowing vengeance against their
captors. A detective was assassinated in Groveton,
and Ranger Dunaway, on invitation of Attorney
Robb, went over to look into the matter. On their
way to the court-house both Robb and Dunaway
were fired upon from the window of a law office.
Dunaway was severely wounded, and Robb, fatally
injured, lived but a short time.

It would be monotonous to detail the instances of
crime and of the captures made in the neighborhood
of Groveton, Madisonville and neighboring communities; to record the careful and brave work of
Captain McDonald and his Rangers which led only
to failure in the end, through the lack of public and
official co-operation. When the men who administer
the law, and a controlling number of the citizens,
do not want justice, then perhaps it is just as well
that law abiding citizens should move away and let
the rest murder one another to their hearts' content.

A father and son waylaid and killed an old man named Tummins in Madison County, and were arrested single-handed by Captain Bill. The two were discharged on the plea of self defense.

A young man by the name of Hunter Gibbs was entrapped and assassinated near Madisonville, and his murderers were traced home and arrested by McDonald and his Rangers. They were eventually discharged.

A man named Wright Terry (this was in Groveton) after killing an officer and a doctor and nearly killing a drummer, was brought to book by Captain Bill, and might have gone free like the others if he hadn't good-naturedly agreed to plead guilty and take a life sentence rather than discommode his friends. But enough, let us turn to pleasanter things.*

* For certain details of the Touchstone episode and other work of this period, see Captain McDonald's report for two years ending August 31, 1904, Appendix C.

XXXIV

A Wolf-hunt with the President

CAPTAIN BILL SEES THE PRESIDENT THROUGH TEXAS AND
ACCOMPANIES HIM ON THE "BEST TIME OF HIS
LIFE." QUANAH PARKER TELLS STORIES
TO THE HUNTERS

It was early in April, 1905, that Governor Lanham summoned Captain McDonald and informed him that a wolf-hunt had been arranged for President Roosevelt, by these two big ranchmen, Tom Waggoner and Burke Burnett, somewhere in their pastures up in Comanche County, Oklahoma, and that he, McDonald, was to accompany the President as a special body-guard, particularly through the State of Texas.

Captain Bill looked unhappy.

" Governor," he said, " you know I'm a hell-roarin' democrat, and don't care much for republican presidents in general and this one in particular. I'd rather you picked another man for the job."

" All the same, Captain, we've picked you, and you'll have to serve," said Lanham.

Captain Bill saluted.

" Just as you say, Governor," he said, " only if

I'd done the picking I'd picked a man that wanted the job. There's enough of 'em.''

Captain Bill proceeded to Fort Worth to join the President's party. Col. Cecil Lyon introduced the Ranger Captain to President Roosevelt, and Burke Burnett, also present, said:

'' Now, Captain, you've got a very precious charge —the President of the United States. He's in your hands, don't let anything happen; don't let anybody assassinate him.''

Captain Bill smiled, in his quaint fashion.

'' Burke,'' he said, pleasantly, '' if anybody gets killed on this trip I'll be the man charged with it, and the President of the United States won't be the victim, either.''

Without delay the President and party took the Fort Worth and Denver train toward the Panhandle. Once inside, out of the throng and under way President Roosevelt with his accustomed good-nature and friendly fellowship promptly struck up a conversation with his Master of Affairs.

'' Look here,'' he said, '' you were introduced to me as Captain McDonald: you're not Captain Bill McDonald of the Rangers, are you? ''

Captain Bill nodded.

'' That's my name, Mr. President,'' he said, '' I've been captain of a company of Rangers for a long time.''

'' Is it possible? Well, I've heard a good deal about you.''

Theodore Roosevelt has been accused of a good many things, but no one ever accused him of not being able to make friends, or to keep them.

Captain Bill smiled, as who wouldn't.

"Why, Mr. President," he said, "I didn't think you'd ever heard about the Rangers."

The President's teeth shone in an expansive appreciation.

"Yes, indeed I have, and I've heard all about you. I remember very well when you captured Kid Lewis and his partner, Crawford, up here at Wichita Falls, and kept the crowd from lynching them as long as you stayed there."

After that, conversation was easy, and Captain Bill's opinion of his distinguished guest improved steadily. They discussed hunting, marksmanship, the Rough Riders, the capture of bad men and all the subjects of the strenuous life of the frontier.

With the President had come a body-guard of four secret-service men, whose chief duty at this time was to protect him from the crowds who pressed upon him here and there when the train halted and he went out, as he did when there was time, to greet the people and perhaps make a brief address. Captain Bill noticed that the secret-service men did not seem quite equal to these occasions. Perhaps they were not accustomed to handling the range-bred enthusiasm of that elemental region. When the presidential party pulled into Wichita Falls the platform was thronged. The crowds made a rush as the train came to a standstill—trying to climb over one another, it would seem—to get near the President. The secret-service men were helpless—they pushed and protested, but accomplished little. Captain Bill stepped out on the platform. Hardly a man in that crowd but recognized that lean weather-beaten face, and that white hat. A good many remembered that picture from a night and a morning nine years before when, at their jail, a lone Ranger Captain had risen up in wrath and ruled the mob. Some there remembered Bill McDonald a good deal longer than that—for twenty years or more, when he had found that place a lawless settlement on an untamed frontier and brought order out of human chaos and put a governor on the wheels of law. When he spoke, now, they listened.

" Get out of the way, boys! Stay down there, you fellows; don't crowd up here! " he said, and a sudden impulse of order was the result.

Now and then he added a word of caution, but it was hardly needed. Captain Bill knew his crowd, and the crowd knew Captain Bill. The President observed and marveled. At Vernon there was another crowd—rollicking and noisy—and again the Ranger Captain held the disorder in hand. When the train started once more President Roosevelt said to his body-guard of four:

" Boys, you ought to take a few pointers from Captain McDonald in handling a crowd," and the " Boys " agreed to do it, knowing all the time, as everybody there knew, that it would need Captain Bill's twenty years' special acquaintance with that crowd to achieve his results.

At Vernon they took a train for Frederick—a little station in Comanche County, from which place they would ride a distance of twenty-five miles to the camping place, located on a creek called the Deep Red. At Frederick the President relieved his special guard of four, and sent them back to Fort Worth to wait his return.

It was on April 8th that they arrived at Frederick where a good share of the hunting party, and an enthusiastic crowd had gathered to welcome them. The hunting party set out immediately for the camp, arriving about nightfall.

Whoever chose the camping place made a good selection. The Deep Red—a branch of Red River— is a fine running stream, with plenty of timber and good grass. From all about the howling of their game—the small gray wolves, or coyotes, which infest that country. The surroundings were ideal.

There were about fifteen in the hunting party, which included their hosts, Tom Waggoner and Burke Burnett; also young Tom Burnett, who was in charge of the horses—himself a daring horseman —Lieut.-General S. M. B. Young (known to the Indians as " War Bonnet ") ; Lieutenant Fortescue (formerly of the Rough Riders) ; Dr. Alexander Lambert of New York; Col. Cecil Lyon of Texas; Sloan Simpson, Postmaster of Dallas; John R. Abernethy of Tesca, Oklahoma (later, by the President's appointment, United States Marshal); certain ranch-men and cowboys—by no means forgetting Chief Quanah Parker, of whom we have heard before in these chapters, now specially invited by the President's request. Chief Quanah was then about sixty —tall, straight as an arrow and a fine rider.

It was a pretty extensive camp, altogether. There were a hundred horses and a " chuck " wagon— a regular " cow outfit ";—a buggy for Burke Bur-nett and General Young; two hacks, one of which belonged to Chief Quanah, and other vehicles. Then there was a pack of forty greyhounds, some stag-hounds, and about a half-dozen long-eared deer or fox-hounds, for special work.

The excitement and joy of the tents and blazing campfires, and the howling of the wolves, made everybody eager for morning and an early start. So when supper was over and the guard set for the night, the Great National Hunter and his friends and protectors lay down to rest, the campfires still throwing a wide circle of light, on the fading edges of which the coyotes gathered and looking up howled their anguish to the stars.

It was a little more than daylight, next morning, a bright cool morning, when the hunting party was up and away. The hunters were mounted, all except General Young and Burke Burnett, who were in the habit of following the chase in their buggy. The dogs to be used for the morning run mingled with

the riders, the others being confined in the chuck
wagon in a large cage, to be kept fresh, and used in
the afternoon, when the first detachment should be
run down. At the head of the party rode Tom Burnett and " Bony " Moore and behind these came
President Roosevelt of the United States, and Captain Bill McDonald of Texas.

It was no trouble to find a wolf in that locality.
One was soon started up and the hounds were away,
with the party of horsemen and Burke Burnett's
buggy following pell-mell in a general helter-skelter,
for which the President set the pace. As the Ranger
Captain saw the Chief Executive of the nation go
careering over ditches and washouts and through
prairie-dog cities, his admiration grew literally by
leaps and bounds. He wished, however, he hadn't
promised to bring the President home intact. Bill
McDonald was considered something of a rider, himself, but he was not entirely happy in this Tam
O'Shanter performance. Still he stayed in the
game.

" It looked mighty scary to me," he said afterward, " but I wouldn't quit. The others followed,
but some of them would go slower."

It was great excitement, great sport and great
fun—a wild race across the prairie—a final bringing
of the wolf to bay with the " worry " and " death "
by the dogs, and general rejoicing by all.

But when the next wolf—or it may have been the
third one—was cornered there was a genuine ex-

hibition. It was not killed by the dogs, it was taken alive, by one man. John Abernethy was that man, and he took that wolf with his hands. This was the manner of it. Whenever the dogs ran upon the wolf, the wolf would turn and snap savagely, and if those teeth of his happened to touch any part of the dog they left their mark, and sometimes that part of the dog remained with the wolf. This made the dogs careful—and shy.

But Abernethy was not careful—at least he was not shy. He ran up close to that cornered wolf and fell upon him, and when the wolf snapped at him, just as he had snapped at those dogs, Abernethy by a quick movement of his hand caught the wolf by the lower jaw and held him fast, and in such a way, that jerk and writhe and twist as he might he could not get free. Then Abernethy, who was about thirty years old and a muscular man, quick of movement and fearless, holding fast to the wolf's jaw, carried that wolf to his horse, mounted and rode away, still carrying his captive, alive.

Well, of course, President Roosevelt admired that beyond any feature of the expedition. He had Abernethy do it again and again, and Abernethy never made a failure. Sometimes he tied the wolf's jaws together with a handkerchief; just held him and tied him in a deft workman-like way and made off with him hanging on his saddle. It looked easy enough, to see Abernethy seize the wolf, and presently a young fellow in the group of hunters decided that it *was* easy. But when he tried it, he only got a knife-like slit across his hand and abandoned the contract. Then the President wanted to try it, himself, as of course he would, but there are some things which even a President cannot be permitted to attempt.

However, he was not to be kept altogether out of danger, and in the characteristic incident which follows, those who will, may, perhaps, find some allegorical significance.

As the party rode along—this was during a quiet recess between wolves—they came upon a big rattlesnake, about five feet long, and thicker than a man's wrist, coiled up, on a prairie-dog hill. When the President saw it, he got down from his horse and taking his quirt (a small rawhide ridingwhip about two feet long) he went up to the big rattler and struck him. The snake was coiled, and sprang, but Roosevelt stepped aside and quickly struck him again and again, then stamped his head into the earth. There were plenty of rattlesnakes around there, for the country was one great prairie-dog colony, and when they came upon another, the President, like Abernethy, repeated his special performance. The others did not like it—it looked too risky—and that night when the President was not in the vicinity, Cecil Lyon and Captain McDonald quietly removed the quirt which had been left hanging on the Presidential saddle, and said nothing of the matter at all. But the President was a good deal disturbed when he wanted to use the quirt next day, and wondered and grumbled about it, until finally Captain Bill confessed the fact and reasons of its disappearance.

"We were afraid you'd get snake-bit, Mr. President," he said, "and we're having too much fun to have it stopped by an accident like that."

Theodore Roosevelt saw the joke and laughed. Then he led them away on a race that if not as dangerous as coquetting with rattlesnakes was at least more boisterously exciting.

They got four or five wolves that first day and the next, most of them also taken alive by Abernethy, and these they carried to camp and lariated out. It was a good start for a menagerie, and they added to it daily.

It was on the second day that Chief Quanah's family arrived—his favorite wife, Too-nicey, and the two others whose names are not remembered, but may have been Some-nicey and Quite-nice-enough, together with a small boy and a papoose; and these in their hack followed the hunt with the others. It was a genuine jubilee when a coyote was started up and was followed by that boisterous company; the buggy of "War Bonnet," and Burnett hitting only the high places; Too-nicey and her matrimonial alliance bouncing along in the hack, with the dog-wagon, wildly excited—a regular canine explosion—bringing up the rear. Then, what excitement when the wolf was finally run down and killed or captured; what rejoicing by everybody—

IN CAMP WITH THEODORE ROOSEVELT.
" They gathered about the big fire, cowboy fashion."

including Too-nicey, Quite-nicey, and Pretty-nicey, or whatever their names might be.

But now it developed that the three Nicey's could serve a good purpose on a hunt like that as well as for mere decoration. They had eyes—marvelous eyes—that could see a wolf far across the prairie when the eyes of white men could not distinguish even a sign. There was no need of a glass when the wives of Quanah sat in their hack and scanned the horizon. Certainly that was an unusual hunting party, and very likely a unique experience, for all concerned.

But perhaps the best part of the hunting was the evening, after all. Then it was that they gathered about the big fire, cowboy fashion, with Chief Quanah Parker in their midst, talking to them— repeating the traditions of his father and his tribe —the tale of his mother's capture, the story of his own life and battles—his views and his religion of later years.

In a former chapter we have told of the massacre of Fort Parker and the capture of the little girl, Cynthia Ann Parker, who was adopted by the tribe, married a chief, and in time became Chief Quanah's mother. Gathered about the campfire on Deep Red Creek, in a wide circle of loneliness, with " Tom " Burnett, who understands the Indian language " better than the Indians themselves," acting as interpreter and the President of the United States listening, the son of that little captured girl told that story, now, and he supplemented it with the story of his father—a sequel that will not be out of place here.

The tribe had loved the little captive white girl, the story runs, and the little girl had learned to love her captors. She had learned their speech and forgot her own; then, by and by when she was no longer a little girl, a great chief named Nacona had wooed her and made her his wife. Nacona was a mighty warrior and made frequent raids on the white settlements and carried off much property— cattle and horses.

But finally his last raid came. Captain Sul. Ross (later Governor Ross), stationed at Fort Griffin with a troup of Rangers—sixty trained Indian fighters—was watching for an opportunity to fall upon Nacona, unawares. The opportunity came when Nacona, with his braves and many of their squaws and children, were camped one day at the mouth of Talking John Creek in Hardeman County. There was good hunting on Talking John Creek, and Nacona and his braves, fresh from a raid on the white settlements below, had stopped there for a few days to rest and recuperate before taking up the final homeward march. They felt secure and had no thought that Rangers were anywhere in the vicinity.

Then suddenly there was a clatter of horses' feet, a crack of carbines, and Captain Ross with his sixty fighting devils were upon them. There was no time for preparation. Most of the Indians fled wildly, leaving their squaws and their captured plunder. Nacona's wife, who had been the little captured Parker girl, was in the camp with him; also their two children, Quanah, and his little sister, Prairie Flower.

With the first charge of the Rangers, Nacona seized his rifle, leaped upon his horse and rushed after his braves, in the hope of gathering them for battle. That his wife and children would not be harmed by the white men he knew. He knew also, that the case was desperate, and he realized this more fully when he found that his braves were hopelessly scattered, and in full flight.

Nacona prepared to meet his death. The mounted Rangers were already close upon him and he would die like the great chief that he was. Beneath a large mesquite tree he dismounted and seating himself began chanting the death song. Captain Ross and a detachment of Rangers rode up. Nacona still chanted on. Then suddenly it may have occurred to him that they meant to take him alive. They would imprison him, perhaps hang him. He would die fighting.

Rousing as from a dream, he ceased his chant and throwing his rifle to his shoulder, fired. The bullet missed, but it brought a quick answering shot from a Ranger at Captain Ross's side, and the chief dropped forward, his face in the grass.

So died Nacona, bravely, as a chief should die,

and was buried where he fell. In time his grave became a landmark. And Nacona's wife, who had been Cynthia Ann Parker—no longer of the white race, but an Indian in language and habits and affiliations—was brought by her new captors, once more to dwell among her own kind, bringing with her the boy Quanah, and his little sister, Prairie Flower. The mother was never satisfied with civilization and always longed to return to the tribe. Little Prairie Flower—homesick and delicate—pined away and soon followed Nacona to the Spirit Land. The boy Quanah was sent back to his father's people, for he was a chief in his own right. In time he became a great leader of the Comanche Tribe, and, unlike his father, a friend of his mother's race. He surrounded himself with the comforts and many of the luxuries of white men; his home to-day is truly a white man's home, with handsome furnishings, a piano and pictures; his voice has been heard in the white man's councils, and a white man's city was named in his honor. But the language of white men he has never learned.*

Altogether that wolf hunt was a great success. Seventeen wolves completed the result of the five days of hunting, most of them taken alive and lariated out around the camp—a lively and musical collection that delighted all parties concerned, except

* The story as told by Chief Quanah not having been preserved, most of the details here given are drawn from an article by Fred. Harvey.

possibly the wolves themselves. As for President Roosevelt he enjoyed this vigorous isolated vacation continuously. But it was not easy to preserve the isolation of that camp. Every day visitors came riding or driving across the country, from somewhere, to seek an audience with the nation's Chief Executive. There were men who wanted office for themselves; men who wanted office for other people; men who wanted every sort of Presidential assistance under the sun; men who came merely out of curiosity and for the purpose of relating how they had visited " Teddy " in his hunting camp and taken a hand in the sport. A guard of soldiers from Fort Sill was supposed to picket the reservation, but would-be visitors eluded the men and somehow got through the lines. They did not get past Captain Bill, who met them and serenely but surely turned them back. If they had business, Washington was the place to transact it, he said. The President was here only for pleasure. Some went willingly enough —others protested, but all went. The President's days in the field, and those rare evenings about the campfire were not to be marred by business or any mere social diversions.

And when it was all over Theodore Roosevelt, in his enthusiasm pronounced it all " Bully! " and repeated it, and said he had never had a better time in his life, which was probably a correct statement.

And when they all rode back to Frederick he led the way again, and they set out with a whoop and a run and yell, regular cowboy style, and as they came into town where there was a great crowd waiting, the people went fairly wild, as of course they would. Then the President had to talk to the crowd again—he had said a few words on his arrival—and tell them what a good time he had had, and what a great country this was in general, and that part in particular, and how much he thanked them for letting him come there, and how he was going on to Colorado for a bear hunt, but how he never expected to have any better time than he had had right there in Comanche, on the Deep Red wolf-hunt with Tom Waggoner and Burke Burnett, and Bill McDonald and John Abernethy, and Quanah Parker and Too-nicey, Some-nicey and Plenty-nice-enough—

No, he didn't say all that either, but he said the right thing for the occasion, just as he always does, and especially on an occasion like that, where he is happy and full of life and the wild freedom of the open. And every man within sound of his voice was his friend forever, from that moment, regardless of his politics, and no man of all there, was a warmer admirer and friend than Captain Bill McDonald of Texas, who was a " hell-roaring " democrat and hadn't wanted to go.

He did not accompany the President to Colorado, though the arrangement would have just suited both sides. But after all, he was a Ranger, and there was other kind of game—game on which it is always open season—waiting to be brought home. He accompanied the President's party a distance on their journey; then he said:

" Well, Mr. President, I'm getting out of my jurisdiction. I guess I'll leave you, now."

" But Captain, you are coming to see me in Washington, some day," said the President as he grasped his hand.

" I don't know, Mr. President. I don't know how to put on a plug hat and one of these spike-tailed coats, and pigeon-toed shoes."

" Well, don't try. Come exactly as you are, and there are a few of those spike-tailed fellows around the Capitol that I'll let you take a shot at. Now remember, you're coming—just as you are! "

XXXV

The Conditt Murder Mystery

A TERRIBLE CRIME AT EDNA, TEXAS. MONK GIBSON'S
ARREST AND ESCAPE. THE GREATEST
MAN-HUNT IN HISTORY

It was during the latter part of 1905 and the
spring of 1906 that Ranger Captain McDonald was
engaged in unraveling a mystery which gave opportunity for the employment of his natural talent for
detective work, combined with the skill and experience acquired during a long period of following
criminals and uncovering crime.

On September 28th, 1905, two miles from the little
town of Edna, Jackson County, Texas, during the
temporary absence of J. F. Conditt—employed in
rice harvest, seven miles distant—his wife and four
young children, ranging in ages from a baby boy
of three to a little girl of twelve, were murdered in
broad daylight—their bodies left as they had fallen
in and about the premises. The murders were committed in the most brutal and bloody way, with
knife, adz, and such household tool and implement
as came to hand. Three of the murdered children
were boys. The little girl of twelve had been violated. Only an infant of a few months had been left

alive. The story of that ghastly crime—its motive; its commission; its detection and the punishment of its perpetrators—can only be epitomized here, for its details would fill a volume and belong only in the official records; neither are they yet complete. We shall attempt, therefore, no more than the outlines, with such particulars as will show the scope and the importance of Captain McDonald's work in solving a mystery and fixing the guilt, not only without the assistance of those most interested, but in the face of their bitter opposition.

The Conditt family had but recently moved to Edna. They were working people, respectable but poor, and had taken a house formerly occupied by negroes. This in itself was an offense to their immediate neighborhood—a negro settlement—and when Mr. Conditt repaired his fences and thereby shut off from public use a windmill where the negroes had been accustomed to go for water, his offense in their eyes became a crime. They did not want him there and resolved to get rid of him. How many or how few were concerned, directly and indirectly, in the conspiracy to drive out or destroy the white family that had settled among them, will perhaps never be known. That negroes seldom betray one another, and that a negro conspiracy is the most difficult of all plots to illuminate, are facts only too well established by our recently recorded history. The Conditt murder plot furnishes an unusual example of this peculiar African phase.

The negroes were sullen, at first, in their manner toward the Conditts. Then one of them—a certain Felix Powell—spoke insultingly to Mildred Conditt, the little girl of twelve. Then came September 28th —nine o'clock in the morning—the day and hour of destruction.

It was one o'clock in the afternoon before the crime became known. Monk Gibson, a colored boy of sixteen who had been plowing for Mr. Conditt in a field about two hundred yards from the house, carried the news. He ran to the house of a white man named John Gibson, some distance away, and reported that he had just seen Mrs. Conditt being chased around the house by two men. John Gibson went on a run to the Conditt premises; found no trace of the two men, but did find the murdered family, a house like a slaughter pen, and in the midst of this horror, a wailing infant. Gibson, the white man, hurried the colored boy off to bring Mr. Conditt from the rice field, and set out to spread the alarm. In a brief time the country was aflame. Monk Gibson, returning with Mr. Conditt, was put under arrest, and it was now found that he was smeared and splashed with blood. He explained the stains by saying that his nose had bled and that he had hurt himself creeping through a wire fence, but there were no indications of his nose having bled, and he could show only the merest scratch of a wound. That he was concerned in the crime was never doubted, but only the unreasoning then believed

he had committed it alone. Questioned, he told conflicting stories, finally stating that men whom he did
not know had dragged him to the house, compelled
him to view their work, splashed him with blood and
set him free.

Of course these statements were not believed.
The whole country round about Edna, now terribly
aroused, was determined to have the truth. If Monk
Gibson was alone in the crime, and there were many
who soon reached this conclusion, his punishment
would not wait the slow process of the law. If he
were one of several, he must reveal the names of his
associates. He was put through the severest ordeal
of examination, but he would utter nothing more
than the confused contradictory stories already told.
Every method was tried to extort information, yet
he only repeated his conflicting stories and refused
to tell names.

It was now pretty generally assumed that he had
nothing to tell and that he alone had committed the
crime. A lynching mob was forming, and a report
came from Bay City that two hundred men had
chartered a special train for Edna and were coming
to destroy the boy murderer that night. Sheriff Egg
of Edna and his deputies resolved to remove the
prisoner to a place of safety, and quietly arranged
their plan. As soon as it was dark they had
swift horses taken to the back of the jail, one for
Gibson and others for the officers who would accompany him. Then quietly they got him out

through a back window; mounted him, unfettered, between two officers, and slipped away toward Hallettsville, where it was believed he would be safe.

They never reached Hallettsville. While galloping at full speed along an open road they came to a curve. The officers had no thought that Gibson would try to escape, and he was riding free. But at the curve, Gibson did not turn. He kept straight on, drove his animal over a fence and disappeared in the thick darkness. When the officers recovered themselves and made their way into the field, they found the horse he had been riding, but their prisoner had vanished. They came back to Edna crestfallen and discredited. The people at first declared that the deputies had put Gibson in hiding. Then, only half convinced, and fiercely angry, they joined in what was, perhaps, the greatest man hunt ever known in Texas. Every available horse and gun was secured—every available man was presently in the saddle.

But this was only a beginning. Within a brief time fresh car-loads of horses were shipped to Edna; ranchmen sent their cowboys; every pack of bloodhounds in south Texas was mustered into the service; commissary camps were established; leaders were appointed for the various bands; business was suspended, the country became one vast encampment and all for the purpose of running down a single boy of sixteen who had slipped

away from the deputies and was believed to be
hiding in the swamps.   In the midst of all this,
Governor Lanham ordered Adjutant-General Hulen
with four companies of State troops to invest the
place; whereupon Edna became a military camp in
fact.

Captain McDonald was working in another part
of the State when he first saw the reports of the
Conditt murder.   His headquarters being now at
Alice, the scene of the crime was in his territory, and
before many days he was notified by General Hulen
to report at Edna with men and blood-hounds to
join in the search.   Arriving at the front he found
such a turmoil of excitement and animosity and
trouble of many kinds as is not often gathered in
any one place.   Men and groups of men, each more
distracted than the other, were rushing hither and
yon on a hundred fruitless and mainly imaginary
errands.   Nobody was really doing anything; everybody was blaming everybody else; everybody was
mad at the soldiers, mad at the arriving Rangers,
mad at each other; and meantime Monk Gibson was
still at large.

Captain McDonald looked over the ground, as
quietly as they would let him, and gave it out as his
conclusion that no one man could have committed
all that crime in open daylight, let alone a boy of
sixteen.   The sentiment was almost wholly the other
way by this time, and the Ranger Captain's opinion
was bitterly opposed from the start.   What the

people wanted was a victim. If they could capture
Monk Gibson they would have a victim, and they
did not want any complication that would interfere
with this elementary proposition and the summary
idea of justice which lay behind it. The presence
of military and especially of Rangers was a menace, and for Bill McDonald to try to confuse matters with his detective theories, which might result in Gibson going clear, even if captured, would
not be lightly borne. He was given to understand
that the people of Edna knew what they wanted,
and when they wanted Rangers they would invite
them.

Captain Bill, however, followed his own ideas.
He felt sure that Gibson was only one of several
that had perpetrated the crime, and was doubtless
a tool of older men. Moreover there were bloody
hand-prints, left by one or more of the Conditt murderers, and these he could not believe had been made
by the hand of a boy of sixteen, small for his years
as Monk Gibson was declared to be. He further
believed that Gibson was somewhere in hiding near
his home, for by long experience he had learned
that the hunted negro will always go home, regardless of risk.

Meantime, Monk Gibson's parents were in jail,
and their premises had been searched more than
once. Other negroes had been arrested on suspicion,
only to be discharged for lack of any tangible evidence. Captain McDonald went his own way, hold-

ing to the theory that the negro boy would be found in the neighborhood of his own home. His two blood-hounds, Trouble and Rock, he took there repeatedly to try to pick up the trail, yet always without success. He believed the boy would come home for food, and to the nearby windmill for water. The barn near his father's house was searched daily, and while for some reason Captain Bill did not attend to this detail himself he was assured each time that the search had been thorough.

Yet Monk Gibson was hiding in that barn all the time. There were some unthreshed oats in the barn, and he had found a place where he could work himself under the straw, leaving no trace on the outside. Sometimes at night he had crept out to a pig-pen for water, and had picked some ears of corn in a nearby patch. One morning when he could stand it no longer he came out and called to a negro named Warren Powell, whose brother, Felix Powell, already mentioned, was to play an important part in this tragic drama. Warren Powell immediately took charge of the boy, Monk, tied him and notified the officers. General Hulen, Captain McDonald, Sheriff Egg and others responded quickly, and putting the boy in a buggy made a wild gallop for the jail, by a circuitous route, to avoid the crowds. He was landed safely inside, tossed from man to man between a line of bayonets, and when the infuriated populace gathered they were driven back by a cordon of armed officials.

Captain McDonald now got himself disliked in more ways than one. For one thing he persisted in his theory that Monk Gibson alone could not have committed the crime; for another, he urged that Gibson be taken to a safer, quieter place for protection. Furthermore he would not permit them to obtain testimony from the prisoner by torture. Approaching the jail one night he heard screams of agony. Entering, he found an assembly of examiners in Monk Gibson's cell, with Gibson tied up by the thumbs, the boy screaming, but refusing to tell anything more than the conflicting incoherent stories told at first.

"Take that boy down," said Captain Bill. "Don't you know that anything you get out of a witness by torture is not evidence enough for a mob, let alone a court of law?"

Meantime, the Ranger Captain had been picking up threads of evidence of his own. For one thing he had observed that two negroes—Felix Powell, already mentioned, and one Henry Howard—had taken a curiously intense interest in all the investigations—seemingly fascinated by every movement of the officers, especially of the Rangers. He noticed, too, that certain other negroes of the settlement were acting in a manner which to one with a special knowledge of their characteristics, appeared suspicious. He made carefully guarded inquiries, and learned that while Powell and Howard claimed to have been working for a man named John Young all day on the day of the murder, they had in reality worked for Young only during the afternoon. When he spoke to them about it their answers were contradictory. Finally Powell acknowledged that he had not worked for Young during the forenoon, and could give no satisfactory account of his whereabouts for the morning. It was generally believed, at first, that the murder had been committed about one o'clock—the time of the alarm by Monk Gibson—but the condition of the bodies when found made it evident that the crime had occurred much earlier—Captain McDonald believed as early as nine o'clock. McDonald finally questioned Powell directly, and believed he detected guilt in his every look and word. Powell denied knowing Monk Gibson at all, though the two had been raised in the same neighborhood. Gibson on the other hand had already acknowledged that he knew Powell, and had always known him. Finally Captain Bill said:

" Well, Felix, I think I will put you in jail awhile to refresh your memory."

The suspected man nearly collapsed at this and protested his innocence. Searched, a knife was found on him, which had a rusty, inoffensive look on the outside and according to its owner was very dull and used only for cutting tobacco. But when this knife was opened it was found to be of razor-like sharpness, and when a match was passed through the jaws and blade recesses, the end of

the match brought up blood! Two of the Conditt children had died of ghastly knife wounds.
Captain McDonald believed that this knife had
made them.

Evidently he was alone in that belief. The arrest
of Powell was condemned generally as a diversion,
to aid in clearing Gibson—it being widely declared
that such was the Ranger Captain's purpose. To
this, however, he paid not much attention—his one
desire being to get as much evidence as possible and
bring the guilty to justice. He did not feel warranted in arresting Howard and the others at this
time, though fully believing them concerned as accessories, if not as principals, in the plot to kill. That
Monk Gibson had not been alone in the crime he
was quite positive. The prints of the bloody hand-
mark sawed out of the Conditt house could not be
made to fit Gibson's hand by any stretch or adjustment of that member. Neither did it look as if it
would fit Powell's hand, though the actual fitting
was not then tried, for Powell was wary, and must
be entrapped into a test that would require such
nicety of adjustment. But there had been one
more suspicious circumstance. A shirt had been
found tucked away under a bridge over a creek
where it had been washed, though it still bore
evidence of blood stains. Captain McDonald approached Powell with the shirt in a small bundle
under his arm. " That is not my shirt! " declared

Powell quickly, before a word had been said, and before it was possible to tell what the folded garment was.

Yet the grand jury then in session refused to listen to McDonald's evidence, or to indict any one but Gibson, who was charged by that body with the entire crime.

By this time the soldiers had gone back to Austin and only the Rangers and local officers were in charge of the jail. When the indictment was found, Captain McDonald demanded that the prisoner be removed to San Antonio for safety and the District Judge consented to the removal. Threats that such a removal would not be permitted were plenty enough, but the Rangers, without announcement or manifestation of any sort, made ready, and when the train was about due quietly and swiftly hurried him to the station and put him aboard. He landed in San Antonio safely and for the time the Conditt case was quiescent. Felix Powell was turned out of jail as soon as the Rangers were gone, evidently as an affront to McDonald, and to show the community's disbelief in his theories as well as their general disapproval of his efforts. McDonald with plenty of other work crying to be done was not eager to continue a thankless task, though it was work of a kind he loved. That winter, when Gibson's trial was coming on in San Antonio, he urged the prosecutors to try him as one of several and not as the one alone, who had committed the crime. They would not listen to him, and they would not let him testify, declaring that his theories and so-called evidence would spoil their case. They tried Monk Gibson for the entire killing and a rational jury naturally failed to convict, though Felix Powell and Henry Howard were brought from Edna as witnesses and did their best to aid the prosecution. The jury was divided and Monk was taken back to jail.

It was not until the spring of 1906 that Captain McDonald was again actively concerned in the Conditt case. Early in the season, while attending the Stockmen's Convention at Dallas, he met prominent men from the South Texas districts and reviewed with them the story of the crime and the progress that had been made, or rather had not been made, in convicting the guilty. He stated freely his theories concerning Powell, Howard and other negroes and went over the details of his evidence.

The stockmen began by opposing Captain Bill's theories and ended by joining in a movement to have the State continue the investigation at Edna under his direction. They employed a young lawyer named Crawford to bring the matter before the Governor, who agreed to reopen the investigation, but suggested that it be done by another man than McDonald for the reason that the citizens of Edna were prejudiced against the Ranger. The stockmen's answer to this was, that unless McDonald could be sent they would have nothing further to do with the matter.

The Governor agreed, then, and Captain Bill made ready to go to Edna and remain there until he should succeed in establishing his theory or be ready to acknowledge himself baffled.

XXXVI

The Death of Rhoda McDonald

THE END OF A NOBLE WOMAN'S LIFE. HER LETTER OF GOOD-BY

It is at this point that we must pause to record a circumstance which seems totally out of place in the midst of an episode of this kind, but which, because of its association with events, cannot be elsewhere set down. Yet, after all, why should not the end of a noble life be written here, when that life had been always a part of the active service of him whose career we have been following—the life of an unfaltering hero of the home who never said " stay " but " go," no matter what the danger; who even at the very end sent him back to his duty, and died alone.

Rhoda McDonald had not been a robust woman for a number of years. Those early frontier days on Wanderer's Creek had been hard, and must have told on her in the long run, as well as all the anxious nights and days that had filled up the years of a Ranger's wife.

At Alice, though manifestly in poor health, she still maintained a home, doing such light housekeeping as her strength permitted. Her interest in her husband's work was as active as ever; she knew every detail of the situation at Edna as reported by the press, and when in May, 1906, he was ordered there for further investigation, she bade him go, despite reluctance on his part, for she believed that he alone could bring to punishment the perpetrators of that terrible crime. They arranged that in his absence she should go to a sanatorium in San Antonio, and try to regain strength; and in accordance with this plan she closed the little household at Alice, and at San Antonio went under a doctor's care. When Captain McDonald had been in Edna a short time, he was notified that an operation would be necessary to save her life. He hurried to San Antonio and found her cheerful, though evidently aware of her danger. Her talk, however, was all of his work and the prospects of his further progress. When the ordeal was over and the physicians declared that her chances for recovery were very good, she would not let him stay to verify this opinion, but hurried him back to his work.

" I want you to find the men that murdered that poor woman and those little innocent children," she said, " and you must not waste your time here with me."

So he went back, and for a few days encouraging letters came from doctors and attendants. Then came a telegram which said: " Conditions not so favorable; come."

She was dead when he got there, but she had left

a letter of good-by. That letter is a classic. As an epitome of a simple, noble, unselfish life—calm and fearless in the face of the supreme mystery—it seems without a flaw.

" My Dear Husband:

" When your eyes look on these lines I will have crossed the Great Divide, and these wishes of mine I am sure you will fulfil. Enclosed is a note from Lee (my brother), which matures next spring. I managed to save it from my means, or some of it, two years ago, and Lee has been so good to keep it at interest, which I have added to the original amount, until it has reached the amount of the note.

" Please send Sister, your sister, $25.00 and give Ruth $25.00. She has to work very hard. Allow Lee this year's interest for his kindness and trouble. I want Eula (your niece) to have the brooch you gave me; Dot (your niece) my fur and the small diamond ear-bob. Give Mollie (my sister) the other diamond ear-bob. Give Jim my books, which are at Quanah, and my cameo ring. I want Ruth to have my watch and the breast pin that was our mother's. Give Helen White my engagement ring —the little one with the small diamonds. In the little bag is $15.00 that belongs to the Lord. Be sure to give it to the ' Salvation Army People,' to feed the poor and hungry.

" My clothes, turn over to Mollie and Ruth and what they don't want tell them to give to the poor. Of course, the diamond ring will be yours.

" I want you to keep my Bible and read it, because you will derive more comfort from it than all else besides. My prayers for you have always been mingled with those for myself, and I hope they have not been in vain.

"Please see that my grave has plenty of trees, so that the birds may build their nests in them. Give Ruth my black silk dress, which is at Wichita Falls. Get Ruth or Mollie to help you find the things.

" I am sorry for every cross word or look that I ever gave you, but feel sure you will not hold them against me.

" With lots of love—Good-by.

" Rhoda."

He took her to Greenville, Texas, for burial, for they had no settled home, while in Greenville there were relatives. Then he returned to Edna to carry out the mission which in her last spoken words to him she had bade him fulfil.

XXXVII

THE CONDITT MYSTERY SOLVED

CAPTAIN BILL AS A " SLEUTH." THE TELL-TALE HAND-
PRINT. A RANGER CAPTAIN'S THEORIES
ESTABLISHED

CAPTAIN MCDONALD realized that his task in Edna
was to be a hard one—made harder by the fact that
the citizens of Edna still bitterly opposed his investigation; still believed that his chief purpose was
to cheat them of Monk Gibson's life. There was
one important exception to this opposition. Sheriff
Egg of Edna, though with little faith in the Ranger
Captain's theories, volunteered to help test them and
his assistance was valuable.

Another favorable condition for his work was,
that certain of the suspected negroes had fallen out
among themselves, and he presently discovered that
there were strange insinuations and implied charges
drifting about the settlement which might mean
much, or nothing at all. Felix Powell had been arrested for knocking down his sister-in-law, Warren
Powell's wife, and was working out his time on the
road when Captain McDonald returned to Edna.
The Ranger Captain gave the disturbed elements a
little judicious stirring and they fomented.

"If I told all I know about that nigger, he'd hang for murder," Irene Powell blurted out. Detective McDonald smiled quietly, but did not use undue haste. He had Felix Powell removed from the public highways and once more put in jail. Then quietly he went to the negroes and made it easy and even enticing for them to talk. He knew the negro character very well—its weaknesses and its animosities, and these he played on—gently, very gently, at first, but effectively. Little by little he learned that Felix had already been accused of the crime by those of his own color—some of whom were said to know the facts. He learned that Felix had been greatly exercised over the arrival of the first blood-hounds.

"They'll trail a man to town," he had said, "but they can't follow a man that has oil on his shoes."

All night he had lain awake, listening for the bay of the hounds. Once he had sat bolt upright in bed.

"Here they come!" he had exclaimed to a man who was staying with him. Soon after, he said: "I could put my hand on the man that committed that murder." And again: "There's one woman knows, and she may tell. As for Monk, he's told so many lies, the white people won't believe him, anyway."

Two little children named Reed, looking at the bleeding legs of some tied chickens, said to each other that the bloody string reminded them of the clothes their mother had washed for Felix Powell.

This was repeated and whispered, and one of Powell's acquaintances charged him with the crime.

" They'll hang you for it, Felix," he said.

" When they do, a lot of white folks will go to hell with me," was the reply.

All these things came in due course to Captain Bill, and by and by an affidavit for murder was prepared and Powell was formally accused of the crime. When he knew of this he became furious and attacked McDonald in his cell and had to be overpowered and chained. Later, in a fit of rage, he snapped these chains and tore the shackles from his limbs. Then a heavier chain was put on him and he was padlocked to the floor.

Besides Felix Powell, charges were brought against Henry Howard and four women believed to be concerned in the killing—directly or as accessories to it, either before or after the fact. One of these—Augusta Diggs—on the second day of the examining trial, confessed her knowledge of the crime. She confirmed Captain Bill's belief that the murder of the Conditts had taken place in the morning and declared that Powell had come to her with the story of how he and Monk Gibson had killed the Conditts, bringing his bloody clothes for her to wash. She had refused and he had taken them elsewhere— to Bethel Reed. Other witnesses, willingly or unwillingly, gave further damaging evidence. Listeners began to wonder if there wasn't something in all these accusations besides a mere negro feud—to suspect that perhaps Bill McDonald might be able to establish his theories, after all.

But it is likely they would still have doubted and the case would have come to naught, had there not been one more link in Captain Bill's chain of circumstance. He had been closely observing Felix Powell's right hand when he could do so without attracting the prisoner's attention, and mentally comparing it with the bloody print sawed from the Conditt house. The print was a peculiar one; it showed an oblong spot for the thumb; a longer one for the forefinger; then two somewhat shorter ones for the middle and third finger, with a mere dot for the little finger. It was as if the hand had been maimed by accident, and the fingers cut away. Captain Bill at first had made a sketch of the print, which he could surreptitiously compare with the hand of Powell, when opportunity offered. The comparison puzzled him. Powell's little finger might make the dot, for it had been deformed by a bone felon and had a crooked bone at the end. But his other fingers were normal, and it was hard to imagine they had made that bloody impress. Still, the Ranger detective did not give up. He wanted to see the hand and the print together, or to see actual prints of the hand, by the side of tell-tale evidence left on the Conditt walls. Finally, one day, he got Felix Powell, whose diversions were few enough, interested in an experiment of camphor-smoked paper upon which almost photographic reproductions of any yielding object could be made. The negro was attracted by the results and willingly enough made the impress of his open hand. Captain Bill felt a qualm of disappointment. Only the dot for the stub of a little finger compared at all with the print left by the murderer. Then suddenly he had an inspiration. He put an object the size of a closed knife into Felix's hand, and told him to make a print with his fingers closed. The shadow of the gallows stretched out toward Felix Powell in that instant, but he did not know it. He pressed his hand to the paper, and as he lifted it Bill McDonald's heart gave a fierce bound of triumph. The likeness to the print of blood was exact. As Captain Bill said afterward, '' I saw that Felix Powell's hand with a knife in it, would fit the print left on the Conditt walls, to a gnat's heel.'' Something of what was in his captor's mind must have filtered into the skull of Felix Powell, then, for he became wary and frightened, and when Captain Bill urged him to make other prints he moved his hand each time and blurred them. He was anxious, too, to know what use was going to be made of the ones already taken. When later he learned what had been done with them, and that his hand was identical with a bloody print found on the Conditt premises, he broke out in a rage.

'' Aren't there any other hand like that in the world? '' he cried.

There could be none. The tests of measurement

and the similarity of line had been applied. They tallied exactly. They convinced Sheriff Egg completely—they convinced the most skeptical in Edna. When that examining trial ended, Captain Bill McDonald, Ranger and detective, from being a man whose presence was resented and whose theories were despised, became suddenly to the people of Edna a mighty criminal sleuth; a veritable Sherlock Holmes; a hero whose name was on every tongue. Outside of Edna, Texas had suspected this before, but now Edna took the lead in singing his praises, and every paper in the State joined in the chorus.

It is not within the purpose of this book to follow here the case of the Conditt murderers through the courts. The evidence as finally accumulated was voluminous and damning so far as Felix Powell and Monk Gibson were concerned. That Monk Gibson was a tool of Powell (and perhaps of others) was most likely, for it was proven that Powell had been seen walking around and around the field with him as he plowed, early on the morning of the murder, and the big track and the smaller one had been found there, side by side. That Powell had enticed the negro boy to join in the crime, we may easily believe, and that Monk Gibson *had* joined in that fearful tragedy cannot be doubted, and he had plowed on until one o'clock with those dead bodies lying there close by, thus giving his confederate, or confederates, a chance to establish an alibi, probably in accordance with a preconcerted plan.

Both Powell and Gibson paid the extreme penalty of their crime. Powell went to the gallows at Victoria, Texas, on the 2d of April, 1907. Monk Gibson was hanged at Cuero, Texas, a year later, in June. Neither made any confession that was of legal value, though Gibson, a few minutes before his execution, gave to Captain McDonald a rambling statement in which he involved others besides Powell.

The cases of Henry Howard and of the women arrested as accessories to the plot and its execution, had not been disposed of when this was written. Howard was then under indictment as principal and accessory on evidence supplied by McDonald. Whether that evidence is found sufficient to convict will only be decided by the juries of the future.

XXXVIII

The Brownsville Episode

AN EVENT OF NATIONAL IMPORTANCE. THE TWENTY-FIFTH INFANTRY'S MIDNIGHT RAID

The year 1906 was Captain Bill McDonald's last and most important year in the Ranger service. He was still concerned in the work at Edna when there occurred not far away an event in which certain negro characteristics were even more strikingly manifested—an event which was presently to grow into an episode of national importance.

On the night of August 13, 1906, armed men, in number from ten to twenty, believed to be colored soldiers of the Twenty-fifth Infantry, quartered at Brownsville, Texas, appeared about midnight upon the streets and "shot up the town," firing recklessly into many buildings, killing one man, severely wounding another and endangering the lives of many citizens. Official investigation failed to identify the offenders, and three months later, President Roosevelt assuming that the offense was nevertheless committed by certain members of the Twenty-fifth Infantry, with guilty knowledge on the part of their comrades, dismissed the entire command, "without honor," on the ground that the three companies, numbering one hundred and seventy men, had banded in a " conspiracy of silence for the purpose of shielding those who took part in the original conspiracy of murder."

Captain William J. McDonald, then of the State Rangers, was prominently identified with the early investigation of this unusual episode, and the story of his court of inquiry, with its revelations, and of his remarkable experiences following the same, has become history.

Brownsville, Texas, is a city of less than ten thousand population, situated on the north bank of the Rio Grande, in the extreme southern portion of the State. It has long been a military point—its garrison, Fort Brown, being situated but a little way from the business center. Opposite Brownsville, on the Mexican side of the river, lies Matamoras.

Late in the summer of 1906, three negro companies—B, C, and D, of the Twenty-fifth Infantry, Major C. W. Penrose commanding, were ordered to Brownsville, and quartered at Fort Brown. They arrived July 28th, in bad humor. There was a military encampment of State troops at Austin, and they had not been permitted to participate in the maneuvers—drills, sham battles and the like—in progress there. They had been told that the Texas boys did not care to drill with them—that if they went to Austin and took part in the sham battles, blank cartridges might be discarded for real ones by the white troops. Of course this was idle talk, but they repeated it and nursed their resentment, becoming noisy and braggart, as ignorant men, whether white or negro, will. On the way they had torn down the signs, "For Negroes," placed by law, in the South, in the cars intended for colored passengers, and had boasted to the conductor that "all women in Brownsville would look alike to them, whether white, negro or Mexican."

They were not long in beginning their demonstrations. They set in drinking immediately upon their arrival, and their anger grew when they found they were not permitted to drink at the bar with white men, increasing still further in violence when one or more of the saloons set up a separate bar for their accommodation. They became loud and insolent on the street; crowded white women from the walks, and made themselves generally offensive and hateful.

Brownsville as a community did not openly resent these indignities, but individuals did. A Mr. Tate, an inspector of customs, whose wife was run over and rudely jostled by a negro soldier, administered summary correction with the butt of his revolver. In another case an ex-ranger named Bates applied like treatment for similar offense. A third instance is recorded of a negro soldier who, returning drunk from Matamoras—a favorite excursion point—was ordered to move on by a Mr. Baker, another inspector of customs, and upon becoming more obnoxious was eventually pushed into the mud. But public feeling reached the boiling-point when a Mrs.

Evans—a lady of refinement—upon dismounting
from her horse was seized by the hair and dragged
violently to the ground by a tall negro soldier. She
clung to the bridle of the frightened animal, that
reared and plunged and finally tore her free from
her assailant, who then ran away. As a result of
this assault, patrols were put on and soldiers' passes
canceled. This doubtless added to the ire of the
negroes, and whatever purpose of retaliation they
may have had would appear to have assumed
definite form. The catastrophe was not delayed.

Monday, August 13, was a rather quiet day, owing
to the new restrictions, and a majority of the citizens perhaps believed that their troubles with the
military were over. But there were others who
claimed to have heard muttered threats, and these,
as evening drew on, were anxious and watchful. It
was about midnight that a bar-keeper named Natus
was serving a final round of drinks to a few belated
customers, white men, in a saloon where a bar had
been erected for the accommodation of negro
soldiers. The men lingering about the bar were
talking quietly, and it is certain that they had been
discussing the possibility of an outbreak from the
garrison. Suddenly they were startled by a succession of shots, loud voices and general commotion
from the direction of the fort. One of the group
cried out:

" That must be the niggers coming, now! "

A fusillade followed, coming nearer. The bar-

keeper, Natus, sprang to the front doors, flung them
shut, and fastened them. An instant later, he ran
into the back yard to prevent entrance in that quarter. He was not in time. Before he could close the
gate, he received a volley, and dropped dead.

The mob of murderers passed on, pouring their
fire into houses where men, women and little children
were asleep. Their course was up an alley, leading
from the fort through the town. Already, before
killing Natus, they had fired on a house in which
were two women and five children—one of the shots
putting out a lamp. Ten shots had passed through
this house, all aimed about four and a half feet above
the floor, evidently intended to kill. They had next
met the chief of the police, fired upon him, killing his
horse and shattering his arm. Next came the Miller
Hotel, where they fired at guests in the windows,
breaking the glass and filling the casements with bullets. They shot at whatever they saw moving, and
wherever they saw a light. In a house where a woman and two children were asleep, two bullets passed
through the mosquito bar that covered their bed.
For two blocks and a half the assault on the defenseless street continued, then suddenly the assassins
disappeared in the direction of the fort—the midnight raid was over. In ten minutes had been written a unique chapter in the history of the American
Army—a chapter that would be told, and retold, and
debated and deformed until its volumes would fill a
library.

And now from the garrison came shouts and the sound of bugle—a general call to arms. The town, already in a turmoil, fell into a panic of fear and disorder. A renewal of the attack was expected at any moment. It was believed that a general massacre would take place. Men armed themselves with whatever they could lay hands on; women and children hid themselves and waited in terror and trembling.

Morning came without further assault. Daylight showed the shattered glass, the bullet holes in the weather-boards and window casings, and, on the street, empty shells, cartridges and clips—of government rifles. At one place in the mud lay a soldier cap. The night had been too dark and the town too poorly lighted to identify the individuals of the mob, but the evidence as to its origin seemed unmistakable.

A citizen committee to deal with the situation was quickly formed. Telegraphic reports of the outbreak, with urgent demands for immediate action and for the removal of the negro troops, were sent to Governor Lanham, General Hulen, Senators Bailey and Culberson and to the President of the United States. No immediate relief seemed forthcoming from any source. Governor Lanham waited for Washington, Washington waited for an investigation. The public at large took but a small interest in the whole affair—the metropolitan dailies according it but the barest mention in obscure corners. It would be a big matter to them some day. It was a big matter to Brownsville already.

" We cannot convince our women and children that another outbreak may not occur at any time. Their condition is deplorable. They will scarcely venture out of their homes and only feel secure there by our maintaining a heavy guard and patrol of armed citizens every night. We know the accidental discharge of a fire-arm, any overt act of an excited citizen—and our citizens are fearfully excited—would precipitate upon us the whole negro force at Fort Brown." . . . This from a telegram sent to President Roosevelt on August 18, five days after the raid. Brownsville was in a sad plight indeed.

Three days more brought no relief from any source. At the fort, the soldiers were kept under arms, perhaps fearing a general attack from the citizens, while on their part the citizens expected a general outbreak of the troops, at any moment. The officers in command were supposed to be conducting an investigation, and when it was given out that the midnight attack could not have come from the garrison, but had probably been made by a gang of Mexicans from across the river; when it was further stated that the garrison had been attacked, and the shots said to have been fired from there during the raid, had been fired in defense; such statements only meant, to the citizens of Brownsville, that Major Penrose and his officers were going to protect

their troops, or had been intimidated by them.
Rumors of another outbreak continued. Women
barely slept. Men began to move their families
away. Two rangers of Captain McDonald's command—Blaze Delling and Sam McKenzie—came
over from a subordinate ranger camp at Harlingen,
twenty-five miles distant, and these undertook to
collect evidence, and aided in patroling the town.
Other appeals for help had brought no result. Telegrams for relief were answered non-committally, or
not at all. When Captain McDonald himself, with
the other two members of his little company—
Sergeant W. J. McCauley and C. T. Ryan—arrived
on the evening of the twenty-first, Brownsville,
resentful and despairing, hailed the veteran regulator with open arms.

XXXIX

Captain Bill on the Scene

THE SITUATION AT BROWNSVILLE. RANGERS MC DONALD AND MC CAULEY DEFY THE U. S. ARMY. CAPTAIN BILL HOLDS A COURT OF INQUIRY

Captain McDonald had been serving as Sergeant-at-Arms for the Democratic State Convention at Dallas when the Brownsville attack occurred. Brownsville was in his district and he had expected to be ordered there at once, but was counseled by Governor Lanham to remain in Dallas until Adjutant-General Hulen, of the State troops, then maneuvering at Austin, should be advised to act. On the morning after the outbreak, General Hulen had been implored by the mayor and citizens of Brownsville to come to their relief, and Captain McDonald supposed that Hulen would promptly respond, with troops from the Austin encampment. A few days later, when the convention ended, the Ranger Captain hurried to Austin and found that no action of any kind was in progress, or contemplated. The State troops were still at Camp Mabry, maneuvering, and firing blank cartridges. Captain Bill went out there.

"Give me some of the men that are over there bombarding the hills, and I'll go down and settle that Brownsville business," he said.

General Hulen replied that he had no authority to investigate any action of Federal troops; to do so would be to invite a charge to treason.

"Treason!" said Captain Bill, "Why, them hellions have violated the laws of the State, shooting into people's houses and committing murder. I don't care what else they are, they're criminals. It's my sworn duty to investigate such business as that, and I'm going to do it, if I have to go there alone!" And Captain Bill might have added, "If this be treason, make the most of it."

Certainly he did not consider that he needed other authority to hunt down criminals than that invested in him as Captain of Company B, Ranger Force. The Commonwealth of Texas and its laws had been for a quarter of a century—first, last and all the time—his chief consideration. To him, Texas was the biggest thing under the sky. Without further discussion, now, he proceeded immediately to his headquarters at Alice, picked up McCauley and Ryan, and hurried to Brownsville. At Corpus Christi, District Judge Stanley Welch, who had an office at Brownsville, boarded the train. He greeted Captain McDonald and his Rangers with enthusiasm, and spoke feelingly of the fact that nothing had been done by either State or Federal authorities. He assured the Rangers that they had full power to take such steps and to use such means as were necessary to identify and punish the offenders.

It was about six o'clock in the evening of Tuesday, August 21, that Captain Bill and his little force of two reached Brownsville. The Captain immediately paid a visit to Mayor Combe, and to Chairman of the Citizens' Committee Kelley. He learned that a Major Blocksom, under orders from Washington, had arrived at the fort, to join Major Penrose in his investigations, but that neither these officers nor the Citizens' Committee had made any progress toward the identification of the criminals. Members of the committee further informed the Captain that in spite of some existing prejudice among the townspeople, Major Penrose was an estimable gentleman, doing all in his power to bring the offenders to justice. He had stated, they said, that he would get to the bottom of the mystery if it took him ten years to do it.

" Ten years! " said Captain Bill. " What does he need all that time for? He could do it in ten minutes, if he wanted to and tried. He knows his men, and he could find out who was absent during the shooting. And he knows just about who would be likely to get into a gang like that. I'll find them out, myself, and I won't be ten years about it—nor ten days, neither."

They applauded Captain Bill, then, and added him to the Citizens' Committee. They knew the sort of thing he had done, time and again, and that he was not given to vain boastings. Also, they denounced their chief State officials and the country generally for indifference and inaction.

Captain McDonald now looked up his two men, Delling and McKenzie, to learn what they had done. They had done a good deal in a quiet way. They had discovered Mexicans living near the post who claimed to have seen shots fired from there, before and during the raid, and to have followed the track of the raiders by the flash of their guns. Further, the Rangers had learned that a squad of soldiers, with Captain Lyon of Company C, had visited the jail immediately after the shooting-up of the town, claiming that citizens had fired on the post, and making a demand for Captain Macklin (white) and Corporal Miller (colored), of Company B. Captain Lyon had not explained why he expected to find these officers in jail, perhaps leaving it to be assumed that they had taken refuge there during the attack mentioned. Delling and McKenzie also had located two ex-soldiers (negroes) supposed to have been out with the mob—at least, it seemed certain that they had inside knowledge of the matter. One of these ex-soldiers kept a saloon a distance from the center of the town, and the Rangers had ascertained that on the evening of the raid this saloon had closed earlier than usual, a suspicious circumstance. McDonald and his men worked most of the night, continuing these investigations. They located one of the ex-soldiers and lodged him in jail, where

Captain Bill put him through a sort of "third degree" examination. Later he looked up the prisoner's wife and questioned her. By morning he had learned enough to warrant him in beginning an investigation in the fort itself.

With his sergeant, W. J. McCauley, "one of the bravest and best," he was on his way to the fort next morning, when he was stopped by members of the Citizens' Committee.

"You can never go into that fort and come out alive," they said.

"Why not?"

"Because those men are all under arms, and excited. Unless you can show an order from Major Penrose they will shoot you down, sure."

"Well, I'm sorry, but I'm not going to get any order from Penrose. Them niggers have violated the laws of the State, and it's my duty to investigate the crime. I never yet had to have an order to go any place my duty called me. I'm going into that fort, and the only pass I want I've got right here."

The Captain carried an automatic shot-gun that would go off about half a dozen times a second, and his sergeant bore a Winchester repeating rifle, also automatic in its action. These lay in position for easy and immediate use. The two men had been together in many conflicts, and had faced death too often to waver now. McKenzie, Delling and Ryan had been left behind so that in event of a fight at the entrance, and another outbreak, the town would not be without protection. The committee stepped aside, and McDonald and McCauley proceeded to the garrison. At the entrance they were suddenly confronted by a file of about twenty soldiers, with rifles leveled.

" Halt ! "

Captain Bill and his sergeant never even hesitated. With their own arms in position for instant action they marched steadily into the muzzles of those leveled guns—the Captain, meantime, admonishing the men behind them.

" You niggers, hold up there! You've already got into trouble with them old guns of yours. I'm Captain McDonald, of the State Rangers, and I'm down here to investigate a foul murder you scoundrels have committed. I'll show you niggers something you've never been use' to. *Put up them guns!* "

And the guns went up, with the quick, concerted movement of a drill. There was something in that total disregard of danger—in that tone and manner and in those eyes, now gray and hard and penetrating—that inspired awe and obedience. Captain Bill gave them no time to reflect.

" Now, where's Major Penrose? " he said.

The negroes became respectful, even deferential. One of them said: " Yes, suh, cap'n—yes, suh. Major Penrose is right over in his house—second building, suh."

" One of you niggers come and show him to me."

Captain Bill, it may be remembered, does not mince his words. A white man who has committed a crime is, to him, always a " scoundrel," or worse, openly. A black offender, to him, is not a negro, or a colored man, but a " nigger," usually with pictorial adjectives.

One of the men now hastily escorted the Ranger Captain and his sergeant to Major Penrose's headquarters. Major Blocksom, who already, perhaps, had seen enough to warrant his subsequent characterization of Captain Bill's willingness to " charge hell with a bucket of water," was on hand; also, District Attorney Kleiber. As the Captain entered, he said:

" I am Captain McDonald, of the State Rangers. I am here to investigate a very foul murder, which these men of yours have committed."

Major Penrose, rising, said:

" Come into my office."

They went in, followed by the others. Captain McDonald seated himself at the end of the table, with Sergeant McCauley at his left and Major Penrose at his right. Attorney Kleiber and Major Blocksom sat below, on either side. The court of inquiry was open. There were no preliminaries.

" Major Penrose," Captain Bill began, " I have come here to see what you can tell me about this murder that has been committed in Brownsville."

Penrose replied readily, and with apparent frankness:

" I can tell you absolutely nothing. I cannot find out a thing from my men."

Captain Bill faced him steadily.

" Well, it seems very strange to me," he said, " that you cannot find out anything about your own men. I've been in charge of men for twenty years, and I've never had any that I couldn't find out anything I wanted to know from, if they knew it."

Major Penrose looked a trifle depressed.

" Here in a little camp of less than two hundred men," Captain Bill went on, " fifteen or twenty of them break out and shoot into people's houses and commit murder and then come back to quarters. And yet you can't detect any of the criminals. How about the officer of the day and the guard in charge of the guns and ammunition? Don't they know anything? "

Major Penrose shifted a little.

" The colored officers probably know whatever there is to know about this matter," he said, " but I have no way of getting it out of them."

" Well then, I have," declared Captain Bill.

" Very well," assented Penrose, " I wish you would do it."

The Ranger Captain became suddenly a fox—his ears alert, his nose sharp, his eyes needle-pointed.

" What niggers were out that night? " he asked.

" Only two were out that night, and all answered to roll-call, at eight and eleven o'clock."

" You are sure only two were out that night? "

" Perfectly sure."

" How about Corporal Miller and Sergeant Jackson? "

" Corporal Miller was here, I know, because I saw him. Captain Macklin also saw him and talked with him."

" Where was Captain Macklin, at the time? "

" He was officer of the day, and in charge that evening."

" Send and get Captain Macklin; I want to talk to him."

Captain Macklin of Company B arrived, wearing a sort of uneasy bravado, which did not improve under Captain Bill's keen scrutiny.

" How many of your men, Captain Macklin, had passes on the evening of August 13th? " was the first question.

" Only two," replied Macklin, giving two names not down on Captain McDonald's list of suspects.

" Where were the others? "

" They were all in the barracks and answered to eight o'clock and eleven o'clock roll-call."

" What happened after that time? "

" I don't know. I went to my quarters soon after eleven o'clock and turned in a little before twelve. I was asleep when I heard somebody knock on my door. I got up and found it was about ten minutes after midnight. I didn't know what the knock was for, so I smoked a couple of pipes and drank a bottle of beer and went back to bed. I got up again at three o'clock, when everything was in commotion."

" Now, Macklin, your quarters are just back of Company B's barracks; it was a hot night and the windows were open, and according to your own story you were awake just when all this shooting and racket and the call to arms came off. How does it come you didn't hear it? "

Captain Macklin looked rather discomposed.

" Well, I was only awake a little while, and of course I was pretty sleepy."

" You were awake enough to smoke two pipes and drink a bottle of beer? "

" Yes."

" And you couldn't have done it in a minute."

" Well, no."

" And yet you say you didn't hear a thing of what was going on outside? "

" Well, of course, I suppose I did hear noises, but I didn't think them anything unusual."

" Nothing unusual about shooting and bugle blowing and a general call to arms? "

" I didn't say that I heard those. Of course I didn't hear them."

" How did it happen, Macklin, that Captain Lyon and some men, after the raid that night, went to the jail to find you? "

" They didn't do it. I never heard of it, at all."

" Where was Corporal Miller that night? "

Captain Macklin was clearly relieved to get away from the story of his own personal movements on the night of that fateful 13th.

" Corporal Miller was in the barracks. He was present at both roll-calls."

" Very well, send for Corporal Miller. Send and get that Miller nigger and let me talk to him."

Corporal Miller came promptly. He carried his gun and wore the air of a major general. His manner was distinctly defiant and insolent. Nobody said anything for a moment, but Captain Bill's X-ray eyes were boring him through. Miller grew uneasy, shifted his feet and seemed to be shriveling. Major Blocksom said:

" Corporal, Captain McDonald wants to ask you some questions. Set your gun down over there."

Miller obeyed rather sullenly, and came to attention.

" Miller," said Captain Bill, " where were you on the night this murder was committed? "

The tone and directness of the question dazed the man. He did not immediately find words. The Captain repeated:

" I want you to tell me, Miller, where you were when this murder was committed, on the night of August the 13th."

If Corporal Miller had any other story to tell, he had forgotten it.

" I was down town," he said.

" How long had you been down there? "

" All the evening, ever since dark."

" Where were you before that? "

" I was over in Matamoras. I came back to Mack

Hamilton's house (Hamilton was the ex-soldier already in jail), and sat talking to his wife. Then I went up town. When the shooting happened, I was down the other side the beef market, at a saloon.''

Captain Bill's eyes gleamed a little. All of this was in direct contradiction to the testimony of Major Penrose and Captain Macklin.

'' Now, Miller,'' he said, '' you couldn't have been anywhere you say, because you were here at eight o'clock and eleven o'clock, and answered to roll-call.''

It was impossible for the man to reason, just then. He only realized that his statement was being contradicted, and that he was on the defensive.

'' I reckon I know where I was! '' he said sullenly.

Captain Bill was seemingly aroused.

'' You scoundrel, don't you give me any of your back talk! You answer my questions, sir! ''

At this point Major Penrose interposed a query as to the whereabouts of Miller at some previous time—during a shooting affair that had occurred ten years before. Captain Bill promptly checked this diversion. He said:

'' Hold on there, Penrose, we don't care for that now. I'm investigating what happened last week. You-all failed to find out anything. I'm finding out something. When I get through with Miller you can ask him about ninety-six or seventy-six, if you want to.'' Then, to Miller: '' What did you do after the shooting? ''

The man's reply became a mixture of incongruities. He had stayed at the saloon, he said, until all was quiet, about one o'clock. Then he had come up to the Post, to defend it, having heard that it had been attacked by citizens. Captain Lyon had a squad of forty-five men out looking for Captain Macklin at the jail. He, Miller, had taken a gun from a gunrack that had been broken open, and joined the search. He didn't know why Captain Lyon had expected to find Captain Macklin in jail.

Corporal Miller was excused and other negroes summoned and examined. Their stories were confused, contradictory and full of guilt. Finally a soldier appeared, whose name, C. W. Askew, corresponded with the initials written in the cap, found in the street the morning after the raid.

Askew came in with the usual " sassy " look, faced Captain Bill, wilted, and lost his memory. He had previously lost his hearing, it would seem, for like Captain Macklin, he had heard nothing of the shooting, or the confusion, until the call to arms, when he had hurried to a rack that was broken open and got the first gun he came to.

" Let me see your cap," said Captain McDonald.

Askew handed it over.

The cap was a new one. Inside were the initials, " C. W. A." freshly written and corresponding exactly with those in the cap found on the street.

Captain Bill handed it back.

" Where is your old one? " he said.

" I've got two or three old ones."

" I want to see them; get them and bring them here."

Askew started for his caps and Captain Macklin went with him. They returned, presently, with two old caps, in size 7¼ and 7⅜, respectively. Askew's new cap and the one found in the mud were both number 7's. Captain Bill look them over, then turned to Askew.

" Don't you generally write your name in your caps? " he asked.

" Yes, sir, most generally. Anyhow, I do sometimes."

" Did you write your initials in this new cap? Is the handwriting yours? "

" Yes, sir."

" That will do. You can go, now."

C. W. Askew of Company B, Twenty-seventh Infantry, withdrew, and Captain Bill was alone with his board of inquiry. For some moments he regarded the two officers with silent scorn. Then, to Major Penrose, he said:

" When I came here you told me you couldn't find out anything. I've been here a half an hour and I've found out enough, with what I got last night, to warrant me in charging a bunch of your men with murder. How do you explain that? "

Major Penrose's face showed that he was unhappy. He said:

" You have had more experience in such matters, and understand better how to go at it than I do."

" Yes, I have only asked for the facts—that's all. I didn't try to get anybody to tell me a lie. I've found that a whole bunch of these niggers was out that you and your captain said was in. You-all are trying to cover up this matter, and it makes you just as sorry and guilty as these niggers, making you accessories to the crime."

In employing the word " sorry " here, Captain Bill meant " mean " and " paltry," but any one could see that the word applied equally well in its other uses.

" You are sorrier than these niggers," he went on, " because you, as their officers, and as men of the United States Army, ought to be first to hunt out the guilty ones, instead of trying to hide them. As for Macklin there I think he was out with the niggers, and when he didn't come home with them— he having got scared and hid out, I reckon—they thought he'd got caught and put in jail." *

Captain Bill turned to District Attorney Kleiber.

---

* "Captain Lyon claimed he could not find Captain Macklin anywhere and went to the jail and other places looking for him. . . . Some of Lyon's men after leaving the jail met five white gentlemen and threatened to shoot hell out of them and called them 'd—d white s— o—b—.' I have their names (meaning the names of the gentlemen), and some of them claim they could identify the soldiers that used this epithet. . . . Lyon and his crowd then went to where the murder was committed and found a policeman with a gun, and one of them said: 'There is a s— of a b— now with a gun.' The whole crowd of forty-five men cocked their guns on him and would have taken his gun, but he was one that was not afraid of them and talked back to the black devils, and of course they let him alone."

From Captain McDonald's report to Governor Lanham and Adjutant-General Hulen.

" I want to make a complaint," he said, " against
these men here for being accessories to this murder
by trying to cover it up. If this kind of thing is
going on in the army, it's time the country found it
out."

Neither Major Penrose nor Captain Macklin
made any coherent defense to these charges, and
Captain McDonald, with his sergeant, left the Post.
The Rangers spent the rest of the day in completing
the evidence against the thirteen suspects—one ex-
soldier and twelve privates of Company B. It did
not appear that members of the other two companies had taken part in the raid, though there was
plenty of evidence to show that many of them had
full knowledge of the affair and of the parties concerned. District Judge Welch issued the warrants,
declaring the evidence amply sufficient, and heartily
approving Captain McDonald's action throughout
—District Attorney Kleiber assenting. They agreed
that the statutes clearly gave the Ranger Captain
the right to arrest and hold any offender against
the State law, whether in federal or civil employ.
The cases of Officers Penrose and Macklin, however,
they decided to leave to military tribunals.

On the following morning, Thursday, August 23d,
armed with the warrants, Captain McDonald and
Sergeant McCauley again appeared at the entrance
of Fort Brown. Evidently the garrison had recovered its poise a little over-night, and was again
defiant, for once more a file of men with guns stood

there to bar admission. Among this guard were Corporal Miller, Sergeant Jackson and most of the other suspects. As the Rangers approached, the U. S. rifles once more came to a level accompanied, as before by the peremptory word,

" Halt! "

Captain Bill, looking along the barrel of his automatic shot-gun, was inclined to be almost polite.

" What do you damned niggers want, this time? " he said.

" You must get an order from Major Penrose to come in here to-day," was the answer.

" You niggers put up them guns! You've already committed one murder! " was Captain Bill's single comment as with Sergeant McCauley he pushed straight ahead. Both Rangers entered with their own guns leveled, and would have opened fire instantly had there been the slightest movement on the part of the guard. But whatever their orders, the negroes gave way and made no further resistance.

The Rangers presently found Major Penrose and showed him a warrant for twelve of his men. The officer appeared to have cheered up a bit. He ran down the list with quite a business-like air.

" You've got six or eight of the right men," he said, " but the others were not in it."

" Oh, then you do know that some of your men are guilty—and who they are," commented Captain Bill. " Well, pick 'em out. Which ones are they? "

Penrose hesitated.

" I mean that you have six or eight of the right kind of men," he qualified.

" All right, then pick out the ones that are not the right kind of men."

But the major would not or could not undertake to do this. McDonald then said:

" Now, I'll tell you what I want you to do with these men. I don't want to put them in the jail; the sheriff is no good, and it would take too many of my men to guard them. I want you to put them in the guard-house here and hold them on this warrant until I get through investigating. Will you do that much? "

Penrose first refused, but Major Blocksom, who was present, said that this was a fair proposition, and the major agreed to do it. The men were placed under guard and there seemed a reasonable chance that the whole matter would be sifted by the courts and that the guilty would be punished. The Rangers left the garrison to continue their inquiries about town, in the pursuit of further evidence, well satisfied with their progress thus far, and greeted everywhere with the congratulations of thankful citizens.

XL

What Finally Happened at Brownsville

HOW STATE OFFICERS FAILED TO SUPPORT THE MEN WHO QUIETED DISORDER AND LOCATED CRIME

But, meantime, something was going on. Telegrams were racing to and fro between Fort Brown and Washington, and in the course of the day Captain McDonald noticed that Major Penrose and his officers were paying visits to prominent Brownsville attorneys. A whisper came to him that the three companies were to be moved—the prisoners with the others. Noticing that the major and his companions went into the office of James B. Wells—a prominent lawyer, formerly judge of the district— the Ranger Captain and one of his men followed them. Immediately upon the entrance of the Rangers, the conference, such as it was broke up. Evidently something was on foot, but Captain McDonald, strong in his faith in the law as expounded to him by Judge Welch and Attorney Kleiber; also, in the co-operation of these officials, expected nothing more serious than the removal of the remainder of the troops. An order for such removal was, in fact, received on that day—August 23d.

It was on Friday, the 24th, that matters reached a climax. Early that morning Judge Wells— "Jim" Wells, as he was familiarly called—met Captain McDonald with some news. (The two were of old acquaintance.) Wells said:

"They are going to take your prisoners away, Bill, and you can't help yourself."

"The hell I can't! I'd like to see them take my niggers away from me, and me with warrants for them, issued on the authority of the judge and attorney of this district. Where'd you get your information?"

Wells replied that it had come through the telegraph operator, and that the order was to move the prisoners with the balance of the troops. Captain Bill did not fully credit this news, but he set out at once for the office of Judge Welch, who had issued the warrants. In front of the clerk's office he met Welch; also, District Attorney Kleiber and Major Blocksom. Captain Bill suspected that Major Blocksom was in league with Penrose to get the prisoners away, and he did not much like the appearance of the three there together. With his usual frankness he stated what was in his mind, adding the information just received from Judge Wells. He was assured by Judge Welch that no movement looking to the removal of the prisoners was in progress, and by Major Blocksom that Major Penrose's agreement to hold the prisoners subject to his (McDonald's) orders would be carried out.

Still, the captain was not entirely satisfied. For some reason there appeared to be a change in the official atmosphere of Brownsville since his arrival. When the city was in despair, he had been welcomed with open arms and accorded all authority. Now that he had entered the dreaded stronghold, in defiance of loaded muskets, and placed the very criminals behind them under arrest; now that nobody was any longer afraid of an outbreak, and women and children could sleep at night, there seemed a disposition to ignore his work and his authority. He could not believe that in their anxiety to be rid of the negro troops, the citizens of Brownsville would willingly surrender men who had committed murder in the streets, and trust to the meager chance of the offenders getting justice in a military investigation, a sample of which the city had already seen. It was his purpose not to allow the accused men to leave the jurisdiction of the county until a complete investigation could be made. He was satisfied that Major Penrose and his associates were fighting that investigation, and he suspected that they had by some means obtained the co-operation of the local authorities.

While considering what to do next, Captain Bill became aware that a company of negro troops had already left the Fort and were marching to the railway station. Promptly mustering his Rangers he accompanied the soldiers, making sure, meantime, that they had none of his prisoners among them.

As a precaution against being taken unawares, he then notified the railway officials that the special train made up for the removal of the troops would not be permitted to leave Brownsville until he was satisfied that it had none of his prisoners aboard. It did not occur to Captain Bill that there was any suggestion of humor in the fact that he was ranging himself, with his little company, against what is usually regarded as a strong combination—a railroad company backed by the United States Army; the latter represented by three companies of armed and unruly negroes. It may be added that in the performance of his duty he would without a moment's hesitation have opened fire on all three companies. Captain Bill has almost no sense of humor, sometimes.

Returning from the station he saw another company of soldiers leaving Fort Brown. Seeing the approach of the Rangers, this company halted, hesitated, wheeled and once more entered the fort. The Rangers now arrayed themselves in front of the entrance, and stood guard. Presently the company that had marched to the station also returned and entered the enclosure. Nothing further happened. Nobody else attempted to leave the Fort. By and by, the Ranger Captain left his men on guard and went over to the office of District Judge Welch. As he entered, he noticed that Major Penrose and one of his officers, Captain Lyon, were in close conversation with Welch, and he heard Welch say:

" Well, that will be all right! "

Captain did not hesitate.

" Judge," he said earnestly, " you are not compromising with these people? "

" No, Captain, but the Major here has some orders about these men. I've agreed to send them out of the State, after we get through with them, so they won't be bothered," and to Penrose he added: " This is the man who will have to escort them out."

Captain Bill regarded him sternly. He believed this to be a subterfuge.

" Judge," he said, " those niggers are not going to be moved from here. They are my prisoners, and I'm going to hold them. I'm going to wire to the Governor for assistance to help me hold them."

" And I am going to move them away," said Penrose, " for I have an order from the President to do it."

Captain Bill looked interested.

" I should like to see something from President Roosevelt," he said. " I was on a wolf hunt with him once, and I know him very well. I should like to see something from the President."

Major Penrose replied:

" This is confidential. I have shown it to the judge, here; he can tell you."

" If it is confidential, how in the devil can you show it to the judge, and not to me, when they're my prisoners, and I'm here representing the State? "

Penrose qualified:

" It isn't exactly from the President; it's from the Secretary of War."

" Well, I should like to see that."

" I'm sorry, but I can't show it to you. I'm going to move those men, however, at all hazards."

" And I'm going to hold them at all hazards, until I get orders from Governor Lanham to the contrary. I'm going now to wire for instructions and assistance, and with my four men I can hold them niggers, and your whole command, if necessary, until the Governor says to let them go."

Captain McDonald wired Governor Lanham immediately, as follows:

" To Gov. S. W. T. Lanham and Gen. John A. Hulen, Austin, Texas.

" The military authorities are trying to take our prisoners from here for the purpose of defending them and defeating justice, and will attempt to do so at once, over my protest. Please send assistance to prevent this outrage. The officers are trying to cover up the diabolical crime that I am about to uncover, and it will be a shame to allow this to be done. I turned warrants over to them in due form, with the promise that they would hold the prisoners in the guard-house, and turn them over to me when called for. Everything is quiet, but I propose to do my duty. " Signed, W. J. McDonald,

" Capt. Co B, Ranger Force.

No reply came from the Governor after a reasonable wait, and without further delay Captain Mc-

Donald sent to the fort a formal demand for his prisoners, reviewing fully the nature of their offence. Major Penrose replied that he had been directed by higher authority to assure the safety of the said prisoners, and added that when such safety was assured they would be delivered to the civil authorities for trial. He added further,

" After a most careful investigation I am unable to find anyone, or party, in any way connected with the crime of which you speak."

The cat was out of the bag, and in full view, now. Major Penrose, regardless of the revelations made in his office, two days before (or, perhaps, because of them); regardless also of his own confession that Captain McDonald had got at least six of the right men, had determined now to make a general and complete denial. He had consulted legal advice—the best in Brownsville—and the result was a plea of " not guilty " for the entire command.

The captain immediately repeated the demand for his prisoners, closing his note by requesting Major Penrose, politely enough, to wait until he (McDonald) had received instructions from his superior officers (the governor and adjutant general), before attempting to move the men.

Major Penrose made no reply to this, and the eventful day wore on. Toward evening it was noticed that a group of officials was gathering in the office of Judge Wells. Captain Bill took one of his men and went over there, each carrying an automatic gun across his arm, as usual. They entered unnoticed, and found a group which included Judge Welch, Attorney Kleiber, Mayor Combe, Congress-man Garner, State Senator Willacy and others. Some very earnest talk was in progress in this group, concerning a row and bloodshed which Bill McDonald was likely to bring down upon the com-munity, when, as a matter of fact, the Rangers had brought to the community the only sense of security it had known since the raid. Judge Welch, who had been first to welcome the Ranger Captain and to accord him authority, was now strenuously con-demning that very authority and advocating its re-moval. Just then he happened to catch sight of Captain Bill and his Ranger, standing close by, their guns across their arms. He came near falling over in his surprise and there followed a moment of gen-eral embarrassment for the " Anti-Ranger " party. Judge " Jim " Wells was the first to address the captain.

" Bill," he said, " you won't listen to us. You're going against the law and you're going to start a row here that can't be stopped without terrible sacrifice. Those nigger soldiers won't go away and leave those prisoners behind without breaking out again, and next time it will be a good deal worse. They think those prisoners will be lynched, if they're left here. They'll look after them all right, and turn them over to the proper authorities. Don't, for God's sake, get us into another row, Bill."

The Ranger Captain looked from one to another.

"There was a row here before I came," he said. "There's been none since. I come here when the town couldn't get anybody else to come, and you fellows was all scared to death. As for the law, I didn't go into that post until Judge Welch here and the district attorney told me it was all right, and I arrested them niggers on warrants that Judge Welch issued. It's a strange thing to me that the law ain't all right to-day, when it was all right yesterday and day before. As for the rest of the niggers leaving, they'll go fast enough when they get a chance, and I'm going to keep my prisoners here till I get orders from Governor Lanham to turn 'em loose. Furthermore, I don't believe the people of Brownsville want them taken away from here, and I'll tell you right now, that so long as I and my men are here, them niggers are in no danger, nor the people neither."

Judge Welch spoke up. He said:

"You haven't any sense, McDonald. You're running up against the local authorities as well as the United States. I'll settle this thing, right here. I want those warrants."

"Judge," said Captain Bill, "those warrants are not returnable until the third day of September, and this is the Twenty-fourth of August. I'm going to hold that bunch of niggers with those warrants until I hear from Governor Lanham. I've wired the governor for assistance, and I'm waiting now to hear from him."

Congressman Garner spoke up at this point.

" That is a very reasonable request of Captain McDonald's," he said, " that the prisoners be held until he can hear from the governor."

Captain Bill parleyed no further, but leaving the group, crossed over to the Miller Hotel—the same that had been fired on by the mob.

Still no word from the governor and adjutant general. That they were being bombarded with telegrams and protests, and that every influence was being brought to bear, the Captain did not doubt. Yet he did not wholly lose faith. He believed that in the end the governor would stand by what had been done and support him in the position he had taken. He left a part of his force to keep watch on the entrance of the fort, and went in to supper. When he had finished, he came outside to take his turn at standing guard. Presently he saw a body of armed men approaching. There appeared to be forty or fifty of them, most of them dressed in khaki, and in the dusk he at first took them to be soldiers. Then as they drew nearer, he discovered that they were led by Judge Welch, District Attorney Kleiber, and the Mexican sheriff, who for the first time was taking an active part in the Brownsville drama—having previously been safely locked up in his own jail. Viewed at this distance of time and space, how silly it seems that those officials, knowing Bill McDonald, as all Texas knew him, could have hoped to frighten him with a nondescript muster like that. They drew their posse—Mexican riff-raff—up in front of the hotel. Judge Welch asked:

"Where's Captain McDonald?"

Captain Bill himself came forward.

"What's the trouble, now, judge?" he said. "Looks like you're going to war, with all these armed men."

"I've come for those warrants," said Welch. "I've got an order for them."

"All right, Judge; you don't need an army, if you've got an order from the proper authorities. Come in here by the light, where I can see it."

So they went in, followed by the Mexican sheriff and his khaki muster, and all the other crowd that could get in—all the citizens and guests of the hotel; the drummers and ranchmen and tourists—they all pushed and elbowed in until the hotel lobby was full and the balcony around the court was crowded (and there were ladies on the balcony), a fine audience indeed for this, the closing scene. Everybody was inside that could get in, now, and the room grew quiet. In the center of the lobby, in a little group, were the chief actors. The Ranger Captain and his sergeant stood together, their automatic guns, as usual, in position for quick and easy service. They made a picturesque pair, with their typical Texas hats, and arms, and dress, and their determined faces. Judge Welch facing them, fumbled a little and produced his order.

Captain Bill held it to the light. It ran as follows:

" To Captain William J. McDonald, Company B,
Ranger Force, Brownsville, Texas.

" You are hereby directed and required to immediately turn over the warrants for the twelve
soldiers and one ex-soldier, delivered to you for the
arrest of these men, without any further attempt
at execution of the same.

" Signed, Stanley Welch, Dist. Judge,
" 39th Dist. State of Tex."

Captain Bill finished reading and regarded the
judge steadily.

" This is your own order, Judge," he said.
" What is the meaning of it? "

Judge Welch started in to repeat some of the argu-
ments of the afternoon.

" You won't take the advice of your best friends,"
he said, " and are bound to start something here
that will cause the blood to flow in these streets."

Captain Bill looked at him and let his gun rest a
little more easily on his arm.

" If that is what you brought this gang here for,
we'll start it now," he said.

There was a spontaneous round of applause, from
both the lobby and the balcony. The ladies in the
latter strained forward to get a view of the man
who had defied a command of soldiers and who now,
before their very eyes, was facing a sheriff's armed
posse, undismayed.

" I'll tell you, Judge," Captain Bill went on. " You-all look like fifteen cents in Mexican money, to me, when I'm doing my duty, you and your ki-ki militia here, and your Mexican sheriff that you told me yourself was no good, and had done nothing, and was locked up in his own jail for protection when I come here."

There was more applause at this point—also, laughter, the latter rather nervous, on the part of the ladies. Captain Bill proceeded:

" Now, you bring him and his gang down here to arrest me for contempt of court, I suppose—you, and your district attorney, after you both told me that I had a full right to enter the post and use such means as was necessary to bring those criminals to justice. Looks like as soon as I get things started and some of the guilty men locked up, the law is all changed and you come here demanding my warrants, and expect to put me in jail if I don't give them up—is that it? "

Judge Welch assumed an air of superior virtue.

" I'm not afraid to do my duty," he blustered.

" Nor I," said Captain Bill, " so fly at it! "

There was more applause then, of course. It was the moment of the dramatic climax—the instant for a telegram from the governor, upholding the position of Captain Bill and putting his enemies to rout. The stage machinery was perfect, too, for a telegram did indeed come at that moment, only, instead of sustaining the chief actor in the drama, it cut the ground from under his feet. Captain Bill took the yellow envelope from the messenger, opened it and read the contents. There were just two sentences. The first was equivocal and meant nothing. The last meant surrender and humiliation.

" Austin, Texas, August 24, 1906.

" To Captain W. J. McDonald, Brownsville, Texas.

" Have requested Gen. McCaskey to prevent removal of soldiers charged with recent murder. Consult district judge and sheriff and act under and through them.

" Signed,

" S. W. T. LANHAM, Governor."

After all, it requires defeat to reveal true greatness. Few they are who with the eyes of the multitude upon them can stand with calm eye and steady nerve, unmoved and unfaltering, when the last support is snatched away. It was all at an end, now; all his effort had gone for little or nothing— his final hope had failed. But those watching him could not have told that the crushing blow had fallen. He folded the telegram with a hand that betrayed not the slightest tremor, and with a voice that was entirely steady, and even pleasant, he said:

" Well, Judge, if nothing else will do you, I am ready, now, to give you my warrant for those prisoners. Major Penrose has the other copy and is holding them with it. I can get along, I guess, without a warrant. The train won't leave until tomorrow morning, for the men in charge are instructed not to leave until I say so, and I don't intend to say so, to-night.''

The crowd that had been still and breathless during the last few moments, gave a great round of applause at this, and the drama was over.

Captain McDonald still had a very small hope that affairs might take a turn before morning, and all night, with his little army, he patroled the entrance of the fort to see that the prisoners were not moved. That a battle would have followed any such attempt there is not the least doubt. He withdrew all interference next morning, and the train carrying the troops, including the prisoners, left about six o'clock, for San Antonio. The prisoners were taken to Fort Sam Houston, the remainder of the command to Fort Rena, Oklahoma. When the final investigations took place, the man who, according to Major Blocksom, had been willing to '' charge hell with a bucket of water,'' in the cause of justice and duty, was lying ill—the result of his old wounds combined with the misery of unfair treatment. Sergeant McCauley, who was ready with all the evidence, was invited to testify, and did so, but not a single indictment was found by officials, civil or military. The '' conspiracy of silence was complete.'' *

But, perhaps, after all, the efforts of Captain Bill

* Austin, Texas, Sept. 5, 1906.

To Whom it May Concern:

This is to certify that I did on yesterday examine Captain W. J. McDonald and found him suffering from chronic bronchitis of both had not been wholly without result; for he made a report of the matter to Washington, and President Roosevelt, doubtless recalling that wolf-hunt and knowing the integrity and courage of the writer, viewed that report in the light of evidence. When the official verdict, " Not guilty," was reached, he dismissed, " without honor," the entire command of the Twenty-fifth Infantry.

The Brownsville episode had become national history; a curious chapter—the end of which would not soon be written." *

---

lungs, but worse on the left side, having been shot and these organs having been injured.

He is now suffering a great deal and very much debilitated. I advised him to suspend his active life for a short while and to go to some water-place for a few weeks of rest. I think it may take three or four weeks for him to recuperate.　　　　　Respectfully,

L. L. LACEY, M.D.

That Sergeant McCauley was on hand and turned over the cap marked C. W. A. to the grand jury is shown by the following receipt:

BROWNSVILLE, TEXAS, Sept. 12, 1906.

Received from William J. McCauley, Sergeant Company B, State Rangers, one United States soldier's cap, marked on sweat-band with name of C. W. Askew.

WILLIAM VOLZ,
Foreman of Grand Jury.

* During 1908 a secret investigation was being conducted by the War Department, with the result that President Roosevelt recommended the reinstatement of such men as could establish their innocence and were willing to help bring the guilty to justice. A partial report of this investigation will be found in Appendix D, at the end of this volume.

JUDGE'S WELCH'S CHARGE TO THE GRAND JURY.

However much we may be inclined to criticise Judge Welch's attitude during Capt. McDonald's stay in Brownsville, his charge to the Grand

XLI

The Battle on the Rio Grande

WITHIN three months from the night of the Brownsville raid, there occurred another tragedy in the banks of the Rio Grande. In the hours of earliest morning of Tuesday, November 6th—Election Day—while asleep in his office room at Rio Grande City, District Judge Stanley Welch, prominently connected with the Brownsville episode, was shot dead in his bed by some unknown assassin;

Jury that somewhat later took up the investigation, leaves little to be desired. He said:

"And now, gentlemen of the Grand Jury, among the other responsible duties of your position is that of making a full, thorough, and complete investigation of the unprovoked, murderous, midnight assault committed by the negro soldiers of the Twenty-fifth United States Infantry upon the citizens and homes of Brownsville on the night of the 13th of August. An inoffensive citizen was shot down and killed by them while closing his gate. An unwarranted and cowardly assault was made on the Lieutenant of Police of Brownsville, and his arm shattered by their bullets, requiring its amputation.

"Fiendish malice and hate, showing blacker than their skins, was evidenced by their firing of volley after volley from deadly rifles into and through the doors and windows of family residences, clearly with the brutish hope on their part of killing women and children, and thus make memorable their hatred for the white race. Hard words these, but strictly true and warranted by uncontested facts.

"It was my province to come among your patient people even while their terrible fears and horror of another outbreak were upon them, and this cowardly killing being doubtless the harvest of factional discord, widely sown and carefully tended in that hotbed of political corruption and violence along the Mexican border.

Rio Grande City lies up the river from Brownsville a distance of about one hundred miles. It is the county seat of Starr County, and has no railroad nearer than Sam Fordyce, the terminus of the St. L. B. & M., some twenty miles away. There are no railroads at all in Starr County—a big county, full of cactus, hard, spiny mesquite grass, Mexicans, and hot burning sand. Riot and plot would flourish naturally, in a place like that, as they do in all Latin-American territory.

Starr County, in fact, is rather more Mexican than Mexico herself, using the word to convey the less fortunate characteristics of that hybrid race. It

---

God spare me in my life the sorrow of ever again witnessing the faces of agonized women and fear-stricken children, tensioned with days and nights of suffering and waiting for relief, with none coming from either Nation or State to give them assurance that greater and unspeakable outrages were not to follow.

"Tardy relief did come. At the eleventh hour the fiends, who disgraced the uniforms they were permitted to wear and shamed a nation, were removed. That all of the three companies were blamable must be conceded, for they knew who were guilty and they shielded and sheltered them, and failed to give them up. Hence it is that it has been left to the civil authorities of the State, and especially to this District Court, to apprehend, if possible, those directly guilty of murder, assault to murder, and the ruffianly conspiracies to that end, as the authorities of the United States, in charge, have declared their inability to discover who were the uniformed thugs and murders that committed the outrages.

"The lengthy investigation of a committee of your leading citizens, made while these outrages were fresh, is at your service. I also present is not the better class of citizens that leave Mexico, or Italy, or China, and the United States has suffered accordingly. The border counties of Texas, because of their situation have been peculiarly unfortunate in this regard. In Starr County the elective offices are held almost entirely by Mexicans, and the struggle for place is very fierce and bitter. Affairs generally are conducted by Mexicans, and even the schools are in Mexican hands. From a statement concerning the school trustees and teachers, in Starr County, it appears that out of twenty-four trustees only seven could speak and write the English language, and out of thirty-nine teachers nineteen of them had no knowledge whatever of our national tongue. Commenting on this report, D. C. Rankin of Dallas, in an article in the Corpus Christi Crony, says:

---

to you three affidavits made before me by W. J. McDonald, Captain of Company B of the ranger force of Texas, against twelve of the negro soldiers and one civilian, a negro ex-soldier. All these parties are under arrest, and within the jurisdiction of the civil authorities of the State, and to await the action of our courts. Hence it is that if it has ever been known by committee, Sheriff, State Ranger or other officer or individual who, if any of these men are guilty, that knowledge should come to you as the grand inquisitorial body that represents, not only the County of Cameron, but the State of Texas.

"I have no hesitation in saying that I share in the universal belief that among those under arrest are many of the murderers, but something more than mere belief and opinion are required to vindicate the law. Evidence must be had upon which to predicate an indictment, and warrant a trial. If you indict on mere suspicion or opinion and without evidence, you leave our people and community open to the charge of injustice and the proceedings will resolve themselves into mere delay, for in the end an indictment unsustained by evidence must be dismissed."

" The male teachers are political heelers for the party in power, and the lady teachers are backed by workers in the ring. . . . No wonder that law and order amount to nothing in that rotten section, and no wonder that District Judge, Stanley Welch, was assassinated while asleep in his bed. No wonder that when Rangers were sent there to preserve the peace and protect the citizenship from the ravages of the so-called Americanized Mexicans, that they were ambushed and fired upon by a lot of these desperadoes."

It is this story of crime and ambush that we shall undertake to tell in this chapter. When the assassination occurred, District Attorney Kleiber, who also may be remembered as having figured in the Brownsville story, was asleep in the room adjoining the one occupied by Judge Welch—the two inhabiting a small one-story brick building not far from the court-house. They had retired about the same time and Kleiber slept soundly until next morning at seven. Hearing no movement in Judge Welch's room, he called, but received no answer. Thinking the judge had overslept, Kleiber then rose, and opening the door between, called again. The judge did not stir, and going nearer the district attorney saw blood coming from his left side. Judge Welch was lying on that side; the window behind him was up—the shutter closed. He had been shot in the back, from without, through a broken slat in the blind. Attorney Kleiber recalled having been partially roused from his sleep by some sudden noise, and now supposed it to have been the fatal shot.

Mr. Kleiber at once notified the authorities, and by eight o'clock news of the murder was on the street. It was Election Day, as already stated, and excitement followed the report, with demoralization among the better element—the party to which Judge Welch belonged. It should be explained here that the two parties in that section are the " Reds " and the " Blues "—nominally Democrats and Republicans, though the distinction would seem one of patronage rather than of politics. In Rio Grande City the party of Judge Welch, called the Reds (Democrats)—is in the minority.

On this Tuesday, November 6th, 1906, its franchise was even more restricted than usual. When the fact of the murder became known about fifty mounted men, " Blues," went through the crowds, demanding that the polls be instantly opened. Local officers were either unwilling or unable to deal with this mob, and open warfare between the Blues and the Reds was imminent. To avoid bloodshed, Chairman Seabury of the Reds assembled the best men among the leaders of the Blues and persuaded them to agree with him that no armed men should approach the court-house, where the voting place had been established; also that one man of each party should be appointed as special peace officer at the polls, and that a Blue and a

Red should vote alternately as long as there existed material for such an arrangement.

The agreement was kept two hours, after which the Blues took possession of the court-house; entered the door, and held the same, backed by armed men on foot and on horseback, terrorizing and keeping out most of the opposition voters. When the polls closed at 6:30 p.m., about one hundred and twenty-five electors had not cast their votes.* There had been plenty of intimidation and some personal violence, but no loss of life. The elements for riot and bloodshed, however, were all there, and it needed only a little brisk stirring to precipitate a general killing.

Meantime, news of the murder of Judge Welch, with a report of the general situation at Rio Grande City, and a request for Rangers, had traveled overland to Sam Fordyce and by telegraph to Austin, not arriving in time for action that day. Captain McDonald's territory included Starr County—his headquarters having been removed to Alice in 1903,† and on Wednesday morning of November 7th, 1906, he was called by telephone from the governor's office at Austin. Governor Lanham himself was at the Austin end and conveyed the news of the assassination, which McDonald had just learned from another source.

* For further details of the condition at Rio Grande City at this time, see Appendix E.

† Company B had been transferred from Amarillo to Fort Hancock in 1902 for a comparatively brief period.

" How many men have you at Alice? " inquired the governor.

" Two, including myself. My sergeant, W. J. McCauley, is here. One of my men is on a scout below Corpus Christi, and the other (his force had by this time been reduced to three) is guarding two murderers at Edna."

" Captain," was the governor's next question, " would the fact that you have not been favorably disposed toward Judge Welch since the Brownsville affair make any difference in your undertaking this matter, now? "

" If you think so, Governor, you ought to get another Ranger Captain for this company; a Ranger that would let a thing like that make any difference in a case of this kind would be no good for any purpose that I know of."

" Well, then, Captain, take whatever force you have, and proceed as soon as possible to Rio Grande City, and I will send additional men there, as quickly as possible. I will wire the authorities that you are on the way with one Ranger and that more will follow at once."

" All right, Governor, I'll start first train, and do the best I can."

" And Captain " (The governor had suddenly remembered Brownsville)."

" Yes, sir."

" Be conservative, Captain. Investigate, and try to quiet matters, but be conservative, quite conservative, Captain."

"Yes, sir, Governor, all right. I'll be conservative—as conservative as the circumstances will permit."

"Now, do that, Captain. Just quiet matters, and I'll send you reinforcements at once. Only be as conservative as possible till they come."

Captain Bill wasted no time in his preparation. The train would leave in half and hour, and he didn't stop to pack a dress suit. He notified Mc-Cauley, and gathered up a young fellow named Marsden, who had Ranger ambitions, and started with such clothes and guns as he had on.

It is a slow, roundabout way from Alice to Rio Grande City. You have to go from Alice over to Corpus Christi and there wait for a train that takes you down to Harlingen. Then at Harlingen you must wait for another train to take you to Sam Fordyce, and at Sam Fordyce you can hire a hack that will carry you to Rio Grande City, unless you are waylaid and murdered along that lonely road which follows the river and winds between a thick growth of cactus, mesquite and all the thorny rank vegetation of that sandy semi-tropical land. Starting from Alice in the forenoon, one with good luck may reach Rio Grande City by ten o'clock at night, though it will be safer to wait at Sam Fordyce until next morning. Those who travel from Sam Fordyce to Rio Grande City after nightfall, go armed, and need to.

Captain Bill had good luck on the way down.

While waiting for the Harlingen train at Corpus Christi he fell in with Sam McKenzie, his ranger, who had been on a scout in that section, and at Harlingen he found Blaze Delling, who had resigned from Company B to become U. S. River Guard. He brought both men along, and with a force like that he felt able to cope with a mob of whatever size or nationality. Of course, nothing was known at Rio Grande City of the increase in the Ranger army. It had been given out there that Captain McDonald and one man had been ordered down, and that reinforcements would follow, accordingly as Governor Lanham had wired.

The day was well along when the little army finally reached Sam Fordyce and secured a conveyance for the final stage of their journey. An old frontiersman by the name of Inman, who owned a hack and pair of small mules, agreed to undertake the journey. It was late in the afternoon when they started.

Night fell, clear and starlight, but there was no moon, and the narrow winding southern road hedged thickly with mesquite and yucca and cactus growth was dark enough, except here and there where it opened to the river or to a hacienda (Mexican ranch), with its half dozen thatched huts, or hackles, surrounded by brush fences.

The Rangers drove along quietly, speaking in low voices when they spoke at all, peering into the darkness ahead, for they had no knowledge of what conditions were awaiting them, or what they were likely to meet along the way. Besides, it is the Ranger practice to go warily on dark nights and not traverse an unknown road with festivity and boisterous mirth.

It was about 8:30 o'clock and they had covered a little more than half the distance to Rio Grande City, when they heard the noise of approaching wheels and vaguely distinguished the outlines of some vehicle in the darkness ahead. They were at the time about opposite Casita Ranch—a poor place with the usual brush fences. Mr. Inman slackened down his mules and pulled the Ranger hack a little to one side of the road, supposing it to be only one of the traveling coaches that make daily trips between Rio Grande City and the railway terminus. But when the approaching vehicle was about thirty paces away, there was a sudden flash in the dark, a report, and a bullet went singing over the heads of the Rangers.

The Rangers were instantly in battle front, guns up and ready. They did not fire at once, however, for there might be some mistake.

" Hold up there! " called McDonald. " We are Texas Rangers! Stop that shooting! " and this admonition Private McKenzie quickly repeated in the Mexican tongue.

There was no chance for mistake, after that. The hacks had been moving right along and were now not more than twelve feet apart. Then the ap-

CAPTAIN BILL'S LAST BATTLE.

"As pretty a fight as ever took place on the banks of the Rio Grande."

proaching hack stopped and three figures with guns were seen to leap to the ground. Captain Bill, who was standing up in the hack with his Winchester leveled on them, thought at first that they were getting out to surrender their arms, and three of his Rangers, McCauley, McKenzie and Delling quickly jumped down, facing them. But at that instant the epithets " Cavarones! " and " Gringoes! " came from the Mexicans, and then " Tetterly! Tetterly! " (Shoot! Shoot!) with which signal the Mexicans, both on the ground and in the hack, let go at the Rangers, point blank, while from behind the brush fence two guns in ambush opened an enfilading fire.

Then for the thirty seconds or so that it lasted, there was as pretty a fight as ever took place on the banks of the Rio Grande. With seven Mexican and five Ranger rapid-fire guns going—a round dozen in all—there was one continuous explosion, and an unceasing glare.

" From where I stood in the hack, I could see the whites of their eyes," Captain Bill said afterward, " and I felt as if I could pick the buttons off their coats. I let go as fast as I knew how, and at a different Mexican every time."

But though rapid, the Ranger fire was cool and accurate, while the Mexican marksmanship was inexcusably bad.

In less than half a minute it was all over. The seven Mexican guns were silenced, the Mexican force demolished. In the road, a man lay across his gun, dead. Two were limping and staggering away—one with a broken leg, the other to die; two more—the ambushers—were hiding in the weeds (where they were presently captured), while in the Mexican hack, which was now once more moving slowly along, was a freight of yet two more, both dead.

Sergeant McCauley, from his position on the ground, looked up to where Captain McDonald, still standing in the hack, was already reloading.

" Pretty little fight, Uncle Bill," he said, casual like.

" Yes," said Captain Bill, thoughtfully filling the magazine of his Winchester, " but do you reckon the governor will think we've been conservative enough? "

When the dead and wounded and prisoners were gathered and a general observation of the field was taken, it was found, from the empty shells, that each side had fired about an equal number of shots— some sixty, in all.

Marvelous as it may seem, not a Ranger was touched by any of the thirty or more shots fired at them, though Mr. Inman, the driver, got a pretty hot bullet through the very narrow space just under his arm—a bullet that cut his undershirt and scorched his skin, and made him think for the moment that he was wounded. Old veteran that he was, he sat quietly holding his team—a silent observer of the spectacle—only regretting that, being unarmed, he could not have a more active part.

Captain Bill now took Delling and started for Rio Grande City, leaving the remainder of his force in charge of the dead, wounded and prisoners. They kept a sharp lookout for new attacking parties as they drove along, and discussed the recent battle in voices that were jubilant, but modulated.

" Of course, from the governor's telegram, they only expected to meet two men," Captain Bill reflected. " It must have been a surprise when they suddenly found five guns going." And a little later, speaking out of what seemed a troubled conscience, " But I'm afraid the Governor won't think I was conservative."

Then presently they met two more vehicles coming, this time in a hurry. Ready for action, the Rangers waited until they were up close, then stopped them. They, also, had come to meet the Rangers, but this time with a note from the county judge, telling them to hurry, as the town was up in arms, and an outbreak was momentarily expected.

Captain McDonald sent one of the hacks after his men and their prisoners, with orders to get Mexicans from the Casita Ranch to watch the dead men until the inquest, next day. Then with the other hack he pushed on to Rio Grande City. From the tone of the judge's note he expected to find matters in a desperate condition. When he arrived, however, there seemed to be no special excitement.

Everybody was armed and there were groups on the street, but there was little noise or open disturbance. The Ranger Captain looked up the judge and sheriff and made a report of his battle and its results, the news of which was soon both general and effective. When he went out among the crowds and told them to disarm—to go home and put their guns away and quit their foolishness—it was like the dismissal of a State encampment. By the time his men arrived everything was peaceable. It was too late that night to make a report to the governor, but Captain Bill summed up the situation in a telegram next morning. Governor Lanham had protested at the length and cost of a telegraphic report from Brownsville; this time there was no waste of words.

" Rio Grande City, Nov. 8, 1906.

" Gov. S. W. T. Lanham,
" Austin, Texas.

" We were ambushed; four Mexicans dead, one wounded, two captured; preparing to hold inquest. Everybody disarmed; everything quiet.

" W. J. McDonald,
" Capt. Co. B,
" Ranger Force."

That told the story, adequately, cheaply and modestly. The papers over the State made a good deal to-do over it, and reviewed Captain Bill's other exploits—real and imaginary—but to him it was only in the day's work, the work he had been carrying on for a long time, now, nearly a quarter of a century.*

The inquest was held that morning according to program, and the verdict justified the Rangers. After which, the four unlucky Ranger-hunters were buried in a lonely old graveyard near the place where they fell. The names of the four were, Farias, Osuna, Vincia and Perez—all known in Rio Grande City. Their comrade who was wounded, another Osuna, confirmed the Rangers' account of the battle. The original plan had been for all to lie in ambush behind the fence and fire on the Rangers deliberately, at close range. Losing patience, however, in an attempt to clamber over the thick barrier, all but two decided to remain in the hack.

The better element of Rio Grande City, though rejoicing over the results of the ambush, were naturally apprehensive as to what might happen next. Friends of the dead men were numerous, and it was believed that a bloody outbreak with reprisals would follow. Captain McDonald assured the citizens that he had no such fears, and the arrival of State troops and Ranger Company D, Captain Hughes, helped to restore confidence.

Captain Bill did not remain long in Rio Grande

* "The Fort Worth Record," commenting on this report, compared it to Perry's famous "We have met the enemy and they are ours." The Record adds: "Perry and McDonald are made of the same stuff. If McDonald had been in Perry's place he would have been equal to the emergency. If Perry had been in McDonald's place he couldn't have done better."

City. He was still engaged in solving the Conditt problem at Edna and could not undertake to unravel the mystery of Judge Welch's assassination. It remains unraveled to this day. Perhaps time will furnish a clue. Perhaps the secret lies buried in the old graveyard back of the Casita Ranch.

Nothing was ever done with the prisoners taken by the Rangers. That is, nothing was done with the two men caught in ambush. The wounded man was afterward made deputy sheriff, probably as a reward of merit for having engaged in a shooting match with the Rangers and escaped alive.

XLII

The End of Rangering and a New Appointment

STATE REVENUE AGENT OF TEXAS. THE " FULL RENDITION " BILL ENFORCED. A GREAT BATTLE AND A BLOODLESS TRIUMPH

THE Rio Grande affair was Captain Bill's last Ranger service of dramatic importance. He was continuously busy during the two months that elapsed between that episode and his official retirement, but it was only in the usual line of duty, chasing murderers, putting down riot and disarming unruly men—the things he had done so often that to look back on his career now was to gaze down a kaleidoscopic vista of death and disorder—a whirling maze of bad men and guns.

It was in January, 1907, that he went to Bellville as a witness in a murder case, and it was while he was there, January 16th, that Governor T. M. Campbell, who had just succeeded Governor Lanham, appointed him State Revenue Agent of Texas. Captain Bill's first knowledge of the matter came to him through the morning paper at Bellville. When his duties were over there, he set out for Austin to inquire into it. He knew that a State Revenue Agent was appointed to keep a general

supervision over the collection of the State revenues
—taxes, license money and the like—but he had
only a dim idea as to the specific duties of the office.
He was by no means certain that he wanted to exchange the wide free life of Rangering, whatever
might be its drawbacks, for the routine duties of an
office in the Capitol, with a desk, a revolving chair
and a stenographer, whatever might be the comforts
and perquisites of these things. He was no longer
a young man, and he had been shot through from
different directions. Desperate wounds, long hard
vigils, cold and exposure, had left him weather-
beaten and with shoulders and chest no longer as
full and erect as in the old days. Yet his eye was
just as clear, his ear as alert and his nerve as steady
as in the beginning, and if this appointment was
merely a sinecure; a reward for deeds performed—
a sort of official manifest that he was down and out
—he would have none of it. He could *wear* out, and
he might some day stop a conclusive bullet, but he
declined to *rust* out.

Perhaps there was a pretty general belief in
Texas that Captain McDonald's appointment was,
in fact, a sinecure, but if so the idea was transient.
Arriving at the State Capitol, he called on Governor
Campbell, without delay.

'' How about this appointment, Governor? '' he
said. '' What kind of a job is it? ''

'' Well, it's a better job than you've got, Captain.
The pay is better and it's safer, too. You're going

to die, or be killed, someday, going about in all
kinds of weather and getting shot at, from ambush.
We can't afford to lose you, just yet.''

'' Thank you, Governor, I don't want to be lost,
either,'' Captain Bill said in his gentle drawl, '' but
I don't know as I can fill the bill. What do I have
to do as State Revenue Agent, anyway. No chance
to handle a gun, is there? I can do that about as
well as anything.''

Governor Campbell laughed and handed Captain
Bill a copy of the statutes.

'' There's the law, on the subject,'' he said.
'' You'll find all the information you need, right
there.''

Captain Bill took the book and spent several days
reading and re-reading whatever he could find bearing on the matter of tax-paying; also on the duties
of tax-assessors and tax-gatherers in general, and
on those of the State Revenue Agent in particular.
He found that he knew a good deal on the subject,
after all; not in technical detail, perhaps, but funda-
mentally and vitally. In his wide general knowledge of the conditions prevailing in every portion
of the State he knew that the poorest counties—
those least able to bear the burden—carried a dis-
proportionate load of the State expenses. He had
never given the matter much consideration before,
taking it for granted that in a new county, and a
poor county, taxes could not help being high. This
was true, no doubt, but he saw clearly enough, now,

that in such counties, taxes had been by far too high, all along, and that the " Full Rendition " law provided a remedy for just that thing. Captain Bill had but one idea about law, which was that it must be enforced. To enforce that law would be interesting, and righteous. He went back to Governor Campbell.

" Governor," he said, " I think this job will suit me pretty well, if I can run it my way."

" Well, Captain, that was what you were appointed for."

" Governor," Captain Bill proceeded, " there's some of our counties and people paying twice as much tax as they ought to, and some of them, the ones that ought to pay most, and the railroads and corporations, are not paying half enough."

Governor Campbell nodded.

" How would you rectify that, Captain? " he asked.

" Well, you see, the tax rate is the same for all counties, and the poor counties to provide for their own home expenses have to assess on a high valuation in order to make the amount big enough to go around, while the rich counties that are practically out of debt assess on a low valuation, sometimes not more than a fourth the value of the property. That might be all right if it was only the *home* levy that counted, but you see the *State* levy is assessed on the same valuation as the home levy, and the result is that a county that is in debt is paying State taxes on a valuation about twice or three times as big as those big rich counties that have had the most benefit from the State and are best able to pay for it. Why those old rich counties get an allowance of school money from the State that is actually more than all the taxes they turn in. Now the way to fix that is to make all the counties assess exactly alike—on full valuation—and get the State levy down where it belongs and the State expense fairly apportioned. The Full Rendition bill provides clearly for this case, and ought to be enforced.''

Governor Campbell looked thoughtful. He foresaw the storm that a man with the convictions and determination of Bill McDonald could stir up in a State like Texas. Presently he said:

'' Well, Captain, that was what the Full Rendition Bill was passed for, but it's been considered a dead letter, so far.''

'' It won't be a dead letter if I take the job, Governor. It will be the livest letter in the statute book, for a while.''

Campbell smiled grimly. In imagination he already heard the howl that would go up, and the imprecations that would descend upon appointer as well as appointee. After all, perhaps a Ranger Captain in a job like that was not a perfect selection. Then presently he turned to Captain Bill.

'' Well, Captain, you've got your appointment,'' he said.

The State Revenue Agent lost no time in beginning his work. Already many of the annual assessments for 1907 had been made, and if any re-assessments were to be taken there was no time to lose. In 1906 the assessed values of Texas properties had aggregated $1,210,000,000. State Agent McDonald resolved that they should properly be more than double this amount, and he undertook at once the first step in that direction. He did this knowing full well what would result. He knew that a man's purse is his tenderest point, and that to lay a finger on his taxes is to touch a spot already sore. He knew that what he was about to do meant to antagonize practically every corporation in the State, and every rich county as a whole. Also, perhaps, a majority of the press. Papers that had lauded him to the skies for his achievements would be first to belittle him, now, and to cry him down. What he was undertaking was distinctly a minority crusade; a struggle for the pioneer; a fight for the under dog.

Yet I think his chief consideration was the enforcement of the law. That would be likely to be so; the law's enforcement had been his habit so long. If the other things weighed at all, they probably only added zest to his resolve.

He began by issuing a general letter to assessors throughout the State. In part the letter ran:

" Dear Sir:

" As State Revenue Agent with well defined duties imposed upon me, I feel called upon to communicate with Tax Assessors relative to the rendi-

tion and assessment of real and personal property
for Taxation. . . .

" An inspection of the tax rolls of your county
for 1906 and some years prior thereto, discloses the
fact that real and personal property is assessed
at only a certain percentage of its value instead of
" at its value " as required by the Constitution and
laws of the State. I will take occasion during the
year to visit such counties as may be practicable
and examine into the mode of rendition and assessment . . . and I hope to have your assistance."

The letter then called attention to, and quoted
from, the law, setting forth the duties which good
officers and citizens would perform in full, and the
penalties for being, and doing, otherwise. Near the
end of this letter he said:

" This duty is imposed upon you by the law, and
I suppose I am not presumptuous in asking you to
follow it strictly so that there will be no embarrassment when I call for the purpose of making an investigation," etc., etc.

It was a careful dignified letter, entirely justified
by the conditions. It is true the Revenue Agent
did not fully explain in that last clause just what
would be likely to cause the " embarrassment "
when he appeared upon the scene " for the purpose
of making an investigation," and the thoughtful assessor who had followed Bill McDonald's career
and remembered some of his former investigations

may have inferred that it would have something to do with guns.

Certainly that letter made those assessors mad. Also it made the people mad. And the newspapers. Even the people and newspapers of the counties that would benefit by the Full Rendition law—not quite understanding, at first—got mad as a preparation for further enlightenment. Never, since Joseph laid a twenty per cent. levy on the Egyptians, after first taking away all of their land, was there such a general madness over any tax order under the sun. In all the history of Texas there had been no such commotion—such a cyclone of indignation as that which had its storm center in the State Revenue Agent's office at Austin. Newspapers that only a week before had been praising Bill McDonald as the bravest man since Bowie and Travis—a fit successor to those heroes of the Alamo—now denounced him as a bloodthirsty desperado, who proposed to hold up the people of Texas as he had held up bad men—at the point of a six-shooter. They declared that his sole purpose was to fill the State Treasury to bursting with the people's money, so that it might be an easy prey for grafters, already lying in wait with schemes. Then they denounced Governor Campbell for appointing such a man, and prophesied his political ruin and general downfall. Some of them could not, and others would not, see that a full assessment for all was the only fair system, and that, if the values increased, the general rate of levy would lower accordingly. None so blind as those who will not see, and property owners, public and private, in counties where assessments had long been far too low to give them a fair share of the State's burdens, were naturally blinded by that self-interest which was stirred in with Adam's dust.

Indignation meetings prevailed. Assessors elected " by the people," told their constituents that they would " obey the will of the people," and tell any petty Revenue Agent that he could go to, with his bluff—that the " people " of Texas were bigger than any individual in it and knew what they wanted in the way of assessments, regardless of any fool laws to the contrary.

Perhaps the coolest man in the State sat in the State Revenue Agent's office at Austin, and smiled that bland winning smile of his as he greeted the reporters and declined to get mad or to recede from his position, merely referring them to the law as set down; dictating, between times, answers to excited assessors in which he assured them that his first letter was quite genuine and meant what it said, and that furthermore if they had—as some of them stated—already turned in their assessment rolls for 1907, they must go back and do it again, observing the law both in letter and spirit, in order to avoid that little " embarrassment " when he should call somewhat later in the year. And this kicked up the dust worse than ever.

There was, however, a percentage of public sentiment in favor of the law and justice, regardless of
personal interest. There were men in high places
who stood boldly for the new order of assessment,
and there were newspapers, even in the old rich
counties that for a principle were willing to lose
subscribers and pay the additional tax, besides. The
names of those men and of those newspapers Texas
should inscribe on a roll of honor in her State
Capitol, for it was by such as those that some
seventy years ago her independence was won.

Governor Campbell, assailed on every side,
breasted the storm and stood firm. If his political
structure must go down to ruin because of an effort
to secure justice and the enforcement of the statutes
as laid down, then perhaps the ruin would be better
than the edifice. He discussed the matter thoughtfully and earnestly, here and there, when called upon,
and was listened to with respect though with un-
certain approval. Other officials throughout the
State were inclined to be governed by the temper of
their constituents. Yet there were notable exceptions. In February, 1907, at a convention of county
judges, in Dallas, the statement was made that an
attempt to carry out the instructions of the State
Revenue Agent in the matter of the Full Rendition
law would mean the political death of such county
judges or commissioners as engaged in that effort.
This statement, though wide, was not general.
Among others to dissent was Judge Hill of Eastland

County, who declared that if the people of Texas did not want a man in office who would carry out the law he, for one, would be glad to resign. That was a fine brave statement and had its effect. A resolution pledging the members of the association, individually and as a whole, to support and maintain the letter and spirit of the Full Rendition law, to the end that the taxes of the entire State might be equal and uniform, was unanimously adopted. The right word from the right source had been spoken. It began to be echoed in public places.

It was along in March, 1907, that the State Revenue Agent decided that he would not wait to call on the assessors during the year, but that he would gather them in Austin where he could talk to them, all together. A meeting of the State Association of Assessors, near the end of the month, was the result.

The assessors came together in many frames of mind, but mainly belligerent. Some of them had given it out to their constituents before they started that they were going down to tell that old Ranger that he might be able to round-up cattle-thieves and Mexicans, but that a bunch of county assessors would be a different matter. When these officials began to collect around the Capitol there was plenty of talk—not always complimentary. The State Revenue Agent loafed around among them. It was noticeable how the criticism subsided in the various groups as he sauntered in their direction. It was rumored

that, though a civil officer, he still wore a " forty-
five " in a holster and carried an " automatic " in
his hip-pocket. When the members were finally
assembled in general meeting, and " Captain Bill "
rose to address them—they were quite still. He did
not make a long speech, but it was to the point.

" We have been assessing in this go-as-you-please
sort of a fashion a good while," he said, " and now
we are going to do it the other way. We've been
assessing by custom—now we're going to do it by
law. The present tax rate is twenty cents on the
hundred. We want to get it down to five cents on
the hundred and adjust it so that every man will
pay what he should—no more and no less. I don't
want to pay out money any more than the next one,
but I want to pay what is right, and I know you
men want to *do* what is right, with your people, when
you find out what the right thing is. This law is
right, and just because we've been going according
to an old unjust custom, is no reason now, why we
shouldn't go according to an old and just law."

It was in this strain that he talked to them, using
the friendly familiar vernacular which meant sincerity and a genuine interest in their welfare. They
saw that he was in earnest, and he spoke to their
better inclination. Also, he had the strong side of
the argument. A paper commenting on the matter
said:

" Thrice was the Captain armed, for the reason
that he was in the right, and had the laws of the

State to back him "—a statement true in the main, though it leaves the reader to guess in what third way the " Captain " was thought to be armed.

At all events, whatever rebellion may have existed must have been pretty well quieted by the next day, for the following resolution was unanimously adopted:

" *Resolved,* That we, the Assessors of the State of Texas, in convention assembled, will make what improvements we possibly can to increase the renditions of 1907, and promise to fully comply with the law, in the assessments of the future, and we hereby authorize the secretary of this convention to notify all assessors not present to co-operate with us in this matter." *

When that association disbanded, if there was any indignation and resentment existing for the State Revenue Agent it made no outward manifestation. One assessor said:

" As to what my duty was, I very well knew that before I went to Austin. But like most other assessors I followed a custom instead of the law. When a change was demanded I though it would cause a great deal of confusion among the people who had made an inventory of their property. I find it is

* The New York "Sun," commenting on this, said:
"Many of the assessors came to Austin with a feeling of animosity toward Captain McDonald, but he brought them all into line and before the meeting adjourned resolutions were unanimously adopted thanking him for taking up the question of assessments and promising to assess property at its full market value."

not the case. I have very little trouble, and in my judgment I will get forty per cent. raise, for an average.''

And another assessor, writing to the Fort Worth Record, said:

'' Well, I am going to do my duty. I am swearing every man to the value of his property, as well as to the rendering of it, so when brother McDonald comes around, if he ever does, there will be no kick coming my way.''

The result came when the inventories were all gathered and the items footed. Between the figures of 1906 and 1907 there was an actual difference of $414,137,246 in favor of the latter year. A part of this vast increase would come from the natural property growth of the State, but in the main it was due to the revised inventories and valuations. And this was a mere beginning, undertaken under disturbing and adverse conditions. The increase of 1908 over 1907 added another total of $561,297,248 to the property assessment values, aggregating an increase over the year 1906 of $975,434,494. Perhaps Texas will be a three billion dollar State yet, as has been prophesied, and the tax rate in the pioneer counties will be such as to encourage still further settlement and progress.

Not that the system is perfect yet. There are still assessors who shirk their duty, and hence counties who default in their burdens. No great reform can be immediately complete, but if State

Revenue Agent McDonald survives long enough, this one will be so, in time, and already it stands as his greatest monument and victory.*

[Full rendition of property values for the purposes of taxation has always been the law in Texas. The Thirtieth Legislature provided for the reestablishment of an old and dishonored system. For a fuller understanding of the conditions before and after the enforcement of this and other laws the reader may refer to Governor Campbell's Message of Jan., 1909 (Appendix F), and an address by Hon. W. D. Williams (Appendix G), at the end of this volume.]

* In addition to this work, State Revenue Agent McDonald has very largely increased the State income by the systematic and vigorous enforcing of the law, providing for the licensing of various public entertainments and for regulating the sale of liquors. His experience in putting into effect the new "Baskin-McGregor" law somewhat resembled his adventures with the Full Rendition law and ended with as signal a victory.

XLIII

In Conclusion

So now we have arrived at the end of our story—the story of " a man who does things "—who has been making history for twenty-five years, who is still making it, to-day. It is the story of a life so full of incident and episode that we have been able to give only a chapter here and there—to touch the high places as it were; for the tale entire would fill a library, and would involve the chronology of a State, which in that quarter of a century has increased its population nearly five times, its wealth in a like proportion, while its progress in education and morals has been incalculable. It is with the improvement last named that Bill McDonald, and the little army of State Rangers from which he had been selected as an example, have been chiefly concerned, though advancement in other directions has been collateral and dependent on moral growth. Order is not only the first law of Heaven, but of the frontier, and by the sturdy Frontier Battalion has the fight for order been made, and won. For in spite of plague-spots here and there (and in a State of so vast an area, and so recent and motly a settlement, it would be strange indeed if these did not exist), Texas is to-day a splendid empire of beautiful towns and cities—of fair and fruitful farms, and of handsome, hardy law-abiding men and women.

The Pan-handle has become a garden—not a Garden of Eden, exactly, but a garden of agriculture and home-culture—a larger garden than Eden, and happier and more profitable than Eden has ever been, since the fall.

And the best evidence of what the Ranger Force has done for Texas may be found in the steady reduction of its numbers. By the very nature of its achievements it has each year reduced the necessity of its existence. To-day it consists of four little companies, aggregating about thirty men, all told. They are brave, picked men—who face death daily and are not afraid. If from among these Bill Mc-Donald has been marked for special distinction, it is not because he has been more willing to do and dare, or more resolute in its purpose of reform, but because he was at his birth marked by that special genius which, whatever his environment, would make episodic achievement and peculiar distinction his inevitable portion. Long before he became an officer he was a peace-maker. Wherever trouble occurred, McDonald had a genius for being there, separating and disarming the combatants, admonishing them in that convincing manner which few men ever resented. No one ever knew him to flinch at a time like that—perhaps no one ever dreamed that he would be likely to do so.

He was variously gifted. His perceptions were abnormally keen—his deductive conclusions often startling in their exactness. In his detective work, he was sometimes referred to as the Sherlock Holmes of Texas, though his processes would seem to have been more instinctive, and perhaps less intellectual, than those of Dr. Doyle's imaginary hero. For he had the eyes of a fox, the ears of a wolf and he could follow a scent like a hound.

" Cap, you have eyes in the back of your head and can smell a criminal in the dark," was once said to him, and perhaps this statement was not so wide of the mark.

His understanding of character—frontier character—was likewise a gift. Almost every man has a right side, and Bill McDonald always seemed to know how to reach that side. When no right side developed, he knew how to handle the wrong one. He seldom failed to win the confidence and the respect—even the friendship—of his prisoners. Such enemies as he has to-day are not among the men he caused to be punished, but among those who feared —and still fear—capture and punishment. There may be a good many such. Time and again his removal was not only requested, but demanded—sometimes by a whole community—a community which did not want the law's enforcement, and such a demand was likely to be accompanied by the threat of political revolt. But Texas, from the days of Sam Houston, has had good governors—governors to whom such a demand was in the nature of a compliment and the best reason for retaining the " offending " incumbent. Hence Bill McDonald not only remained in service, but was given an ever widening usefulness.

His " suddenness " and determination was a constant amazement to law-breakers. Once when he was in El Paso he received a telegram stating that some of his horses had been stolen from a ranch he then owned on the Oklahoma and Texas line. That ranch was nearly five hundred miles away as the crow flies, but Bill McDonald was on the train bound in that direction while the telegram was still damp. Arriving at his ranch, he struck the trail and set out alone to follow it, without rest, through Greer County, riding hot foot a distance of three hundred miles; overtaking the thieves at last somewhere beyond Norman, Oklahoma. Sid Woodring, a wary old outlaw, was in that gang, also his nephew, Frank Woodring, and a third member whose name is not recalled. It was a genuine surprise when Bill McDonald, whom they thought at the other end of Texas, charged in among them and had them disarmed almost before they realized what was going on. He marched them back to the jail at Norman; had them indicted in Greer County, where court was then in session; got them convicted for terms ranging from five to ten years, and returned with his recovered horses—completing, in the space of a few days, one of the neatest and most spectacular bits of official work on record.

The amount of his work was something enormous. In the two years ending August 31st, 1904, Ranger Company B, which he commanded, traveled 74,537 miles, made 205 scouts and 174 arrests. Thirty-one of the arrests were for murder, and nearly all for desperate crimes. When it is remembered that some of those scouts required days, and some of the arrests were hundreds of miles apart, and the result of long and arduous trailing and persistent detective work, the labor and the result can be better understood. Nor is this an unusual report. It has been selected at random and is by no means of the busiest period—the period of the early nineties— those riotous Pan-handle days.*

There was no show, no fuss and feathers about this work. Riot threatened or broke out here and there—the newspapers carried a line that Captain Bill was on the way to the scene. He arrived—often alone—disarmed a mob; made an arrest or two, perhaps; gave out a few quiet admonitions, and it was all over—next day to be forgotten. With many another man such cases would have meant resistance, bloodshed, troops, and the long animosi-

* For details of this report with tabulated statement of all Ranger work for that period see Appendix C.

ties of years. That was his genius: to settle matters—to dispose of them—to get through and to be at other work without waste of time. Once when he was ordered to Galveston to prevent a prize-fight, he arrived at the hall where it was to take place, after the crowd had gathered. He did not bother to discuss matters with the managers or principals, but walked out on the stage and announced briefly to the audience that the fight would not take place, for the reason that it was against the law which he was there to enforce. That was a fair sample of his method—to know the law, and to enforce it, without a fire-works and without violence. No man has ever been his equal, perhaps, in that field.

It was true he was lucky, for bullets missed him, as a rule, and he steered clear of many dead-falls. Among the Mexicans, and bad men generally, there grew up a superstition that he was bullet-proof, and after the Rio Grande affair there would seem to be some reason for such a belief, for he stood up there in plain view, a tall and shining mark, blazing away, and no bullet touched him.

He has been always modest concerning his achievements, discussing them in the few words of an official report. When he has spoken at all it has been his habit to present the general result, rather than his part in it. It was this characteristic that made difficult the securing of material for these chapters. In preparing for the Rio Grande battle, for instance, I said to him:

" Of course you hit some of those Mexicans? "

" Well, you see, standing up as I was I had a good place to shoot from."

" Then you did hit some of them? "

" Well—of course, as I say, I had the best place to shoot from, and I *felt* as if I could pick the buttons off their coats."

" But, Captain, what I want to know is, if you think you *really hit* any of them."

" Oh, well, hell (very reluctantly), I don't guess I *missed* any of 'em! "

" Did you feel afraid? "

" No—I don't reckon I thought of that."

Yet every man is afraid of something. It was about the time of the conversation just noted (he was then visiting New York City), that he said anxiously to a companion who was steering him through the mess of traffic at one of the Twenty-third Street crossings:

" Look here, you'll get me killed, yet, in a place like this. I don't know the game."

The muzzle of a Colt 45, or of a Winchester, had no terrors for him, but a phalanx of automobiles and traction-cars, mingled with a medley of other vehicles, bearing down from four different directions—a perfect tangle of impending death—proved disturbing to one accustomed to simpler, even if more malignant, dangers.

With conditions of his own kind, however, he was at home, even in the metropolis. Visiting Coney

Island one night he came upon two tough individuals, clutched in a fierce grip and trying to damage each other vitally. Texas was a long way off, but it did not matter. He took hold of those men saying:

"Look here, what are you men acting so sorry for? Stop this, now, and go home!"

They were the sort of men who would have resisted a policeman—who might have killed him. What they did now was to cease their warfare and stare in a dazed way at the tall lean figure, the unusual features and the large white hat of Captain Bill.

"You fellows go on home, now," he admonished, in his slow, homely way, and the two set out in different directions, without a word.

It was on his way back to Texas that he paid his promised visit to President Roosevelt. He was a bit nervous over the prospect, but found himself altogether at ease a moment after his arrival at the White House. For he was given the sort of hearty welcome that goes with the wider life he knew best, and was introduced without formality to men who were delighted to honor him for what he was, and had been. If Theodore Roosevelt had enjoyed his visit to the plains, so no less did Captain Bill McDonald find delight amid the halls and highways of legislation.

Captain Bill McDonald of Texas—the last of a vanishing race and a vanished day; of the race to which Crockett and Bowie and Travis and Fannin belonged; of a day when a hip and a holster were made one for the other—when to reach in that direction meant, for somebody, post-mortem and obsequies. State Revenue Agent of Texas—such to-day is his title—and the work he has undertaken in his new field goes bravely on. Texas still needs his honesty, his courage, and his determination. When those qualities direct the affairs of the body politic, the prosperity and predominance of that commonwealth are assured.

THE END

APPENDIX

APPENDIX A

EXTRACTS FROM REPORT OF ADJUTANT-GENERAL
W. H. MABRY OF TEXAS; 1896. THE FITZ-
SIMMONS-MAHER PRIZE FIGHT

ADJUTANT-GENERAL'S OFFICE,
STATE OF TEXAS.
AUSTIN, Feb. 27, 1896.

Lieutenant-Governor George T. Jester, Acting Governor:

SIR:—I herewith briefly submit a few facts connected with my presence at El Paso.

Much of the views sent over the wires were all colored in the interest of the managers of the prize fight. In fact, two reporters informed me that Stuart exercised a kind of censorship over all dispatches; that he demanded they be colored in his favor, with the threat that unless it was so worded they could not see the fight. The dispatches contained the denunciatory proceedings of a city council against the Governor's order in sending the rangers, and by my action there, in having close watch kept over all that was done so far as it pertained to the bringing off of the fight, but failed, with one exception, to contain the resolutions of the Ministers' Union, who represented a large class among the best citizens approving the Governor's action and upholding my methods. I talked with many of the best citizens, among whom were district officials, who stated they believed the fight would have been pulled off on some adjacent disputed territory about El Paso. Of course, Mr. Stuart assured me that he would not bring the fight off in Texas, but the Governor of Chihuahua also informed me that Mr. Stuart assured him that he would not pull off the fight in Old Mexico, and at the same time he had the dispatches to quote him as saying he would never violate the laws of Texas. If he does not do so every day in some of his gambling establishments, then common report has woefully misrepresented him.

I had a close and constant espionage placed, not only on the principals, but also on the passenger depot and the cars loaded with paraphernalia of the ring, with instructions to follow the latter to wherever hauled. Not only did I do this, up to the 14th, but kept it up to the 21st, notwithstanding Mr. Albers' outburst of virtuous (?) indignation, because I kept a surveillance over Maher when taken to Albers' room, over the latter's place of business, on the night of the 13th, the day before the fight was to occur. I did this on the night of the 20th, when Maher was domiciled in the same room. By the way, from the report of Captains Hughes and Brooks, I find it hard to reconcile Mr. Albers' high sounding document with his action in going on the bond of some bunco men whom Captain Hughes arrested for swindling and placed in jail. They were let out of jail, and Captains Hughes and Brooks investigated the facts, and found Mr. Albers and a man by the name of Burns, a keeper of a " red light " joint, were the bondsmen. Now, the surveillance over men who were advertised to commit a crime which was a felony in Texas, made these people very mad, and much was said about the liberty of the citizen, martial law, etc. The drippings from such sanctuaries should come very seldom, and then in very broken doses. I usurped no authority, nor interfered with local officers in any duty they saw fit to perform. I was ordered there to see that no such crime as was widely advertised to come off near El Paso should be perpetrated upon any isolated Texas soil, nor even on any so-called neutral strip between Texas and Mexico. The presence of the ranger force was evidently very much appreciated by a certain business element there, when these people called on me for protection and to leave a detachment in El Paso to protect the banks, while most of my force would be out of the city on the day of the fight. The city was full of desperate characters looking for spoils from whatever source.

From the utterance of Mr. Stuart, and most of his friends, as expressed in press despatches, it would appear that the rangers and he were there for the same purpose—to prevent the fight in Texas. Nevertheless, Mr. Stuart's side kept up their misrepresentations until it became a foregone conclusion that no fight could occur on any disputed or neutral ground convenient to El Paso, notwithstanding the press dispatches reported him as having Mr. Bat Masterson and 100 men to protect his ring. I never heard of one cat squalling because another cat's tail got mashed. They began looking for another place, and Maher's eyes became very sore, and apparently remained in that condition until a secure place was found in Old Mexico, some 400 miles from El Paso. Then his eyes began to improve every day. Still, they may have been sore, but Dr. Yandell, who was reported in press dispatches as saying " Pete had acute ophthalmia," informed me that he never diagnosed his case, nor saw Maher at the time.

The prize fighters were merely dough in the hands of Mr. Stuart and the hundreds of others who were present for the money they hoped to win, and would have fought in the ring, wherever located, if unmolested by officers at that time. It is hard to believe that Mr. Stuart had so much respect for law he regarded as wrong, and which he believed was passed to affect his interests. To illustrate his great respect for laws generally, Mr. Brooks, manager of the Western Union Telegraph Company, came to me the night before the start was to be made for Langtry, and demanded protection. He stated that a representative of Mr. Stuart had come to him and informed him that unless his company paid $10,000 to Mr. Stuart, that he (Mr. B.) could not use his own office and his own wires to send off the report of the fight at Langtry. This same representative of Mr. Stuart's informed Mr. Brooks that said Mr. Stuart would place his (Mr. Stuart's) men in the office and keep him out by force. I readily granted him protection to do his legitimate business and had my rangers about the office, with the proper instructions, and no such high-handed measures were undertaken.

The statement wired, that I and the rangers crossed the river to see the fight, was palpably made to belittle the force. They knew it was false at the time.

I desire to express my approbation for the intelligent and efficient manner in which Captains Brooks, McDonald, Hughes, and Rogers executed every order and performed every duty. The rangers conducted themselves in such manner as to reflect additional credit upon the name of a ranger—always a synonym for courage and duty well performed. They were active in the execution of every order, quiet and orderly in manner, determined in mien, fearless and vigilant on duty; they thus naturally incur the displeasure of the law-breakers everywhere.

I have the honor to be your obedient servant,

W. H. Mabry, Adjutant-General.

Thanks are due Captains Orsay and Owen for the manner in which they have performed their respective duties.

I beg to here express my appreciation for the thoughtful and courteous consideration always accorded to me by Your Excellency, and my obligations for the cordial and able co-operation and advice which you have rendered to me in the administration of my department.

I have the honor to subscribe myself,

Very respectfully your obedient servant,

W. H. MABRY, Adjutant-General.

STRENGTH AND OPERATIONS OF THE FRONTIER BATTALION

As now organized, the frontier force consists of four companies, commanded by Captains J. A. Brooks, W. J. McDonald, Jno. R. Hughes and J. H. Rogers.

Three are stationed along the Rio Grande and one (McDonald) in the Pan-handle, with headquarters at Alice, Cotulla, Ysleta and Amarillo. They scout over a large section of country, and detachments are sent to different sections where needed, if it is possible to send them. Demands for rangers have been greater than this department could furnish, because of the limited number of men in the service. But every effort has been made to cover as much territory as possible.

The report of operations for the two years show that they have traveled in scouting 173,381 miles; arrested 676 criminals; returned 2,856 head of stolen stock to their owners; have assisted the civil authorities 162 times, and guarded jails 13 times.

The duties of the ranger are arduous and often dangerous. The most desperate criminals would naturally seek that isolated section, and when on the trail of the bold desperadoes, often life is the forfeit in the encounter that may follow. Praise is due the commanding officers and their men for the prompt and fearless manner with which they perform their duties. While the pay is small, none but young men of character, standing, and good habits are enlisted, and they so conduct themselves as to reflect credit upon the State in the efficient service they render.

Because of the limited force, and the great demands made upon the service, there have been enlisted 82 special rangers, who serve without pay from the State. They are almost exclusively located in the frontier sections, and are paid principally by private interests, who claim they are compelled to stand the hardship of the extra burden, or tax it imposes, because, in conjunction with the regular force as a standing menace to criminals, they are thus enabled to enjoy some of the protection which a State really guarantees to them. These " specials " are always enlisted upon the recommendation of the sheriff and the district attorney, or the sheriff and some other officer of the county or district.

APPENDIX B

PART OF TWO YEARS' REPORT OF ADJUTANT-GENERAL THOS. SCURRY

DECEMBER 1ST, 1898—OCTOBER 31ST, 1900

THE RANGER SERVICE

The fact that the State has had for some years past a force always ready to suppress disorder, arrest criminals and aid the civil authorities in the protection of courts and jails, has been the cause of hundreds of criminals taking refuge in the border States, outside of the jurisdiction of Texas, and in Mexico, who would return to Texas to continue their depredations and murders were it not for the ranger force. Instances can be shown where the moral effect of having the rangers ready to co-operate with the civil authorities anywhere in the State has been a deterrent to the commission of lawless acts, and numerous instances can be shown where whole counties have been purged of their criminal element by the presence of the rangers, who alone were able to restore peace and good order in the community.

In reality, the so-called Frontier Battalion is but four small detachments. The reports received at this office indicate that these men, while fearless and prompt in the performance of their duty, have always acted with discretion and in the most orderly manner. Their well-known reputation for courage of itself has had a most salutary and good moral effect on the lawless element of the communities where they have been stationed.

Since January 1, 1899, the officers and men of the Frontier Battalion have been very actively engaged in running down the criminal element in the west, and in subduing lawlessness in other portions of the State. The rangers have only been used in other portions of the State when a direct request on your Excellency was made by the civil authorities of cities or counties needing them. That their work has been effective and to the satisfaction of those requesting their service, it is only necessary to refer to letters on file in this office in reference to their efficiency received from citizens and officials of the various cities and towns to which rangers have been ordered. It is probably appropriate to mention some prominent features of the work of the rangers during the past two years, outside of the duties usually performed by them in the way of scouting in the sparsely settled district of the west, and the work accomplished in recovering stolen cattle, arresting thieves, murderers, etc.

During the month of March, 1899, Captain McDonald, with two men, was ordered to Columbus, Colorado county, for the purpose of preventing trouble there between the Townsend and Reece factions. Captain McDonald went alone, his men not being able to reach him in time, and his courage and cool behavior prevented a conflict between the two factions. The district judge and district attorney both informed him that it was impossible to handle the situation, but he told them that he could make the effort, and he gave the members of each faction a limited time in which to get rid of their weapons, stating that he would put those in jail who refused to comply. His order had the desired effect.

Captain McDonald was ordered by your Excellency to Henderson county to work on the cases against the lynchers of the Humphreys. In reference to this affair, I take the liberty of quoting from a letter from Hon. N. B. Morris, ex-Assistant Attorney-General:

" You will remember that at the request of the sheriff, county attorney and other local authorities of that county, Captain McDonald and Private Old were sent there to assist them and myself in the investigation of that horrible murder which was then enshrouded in a mystery that it seemed almost impossible to uncover. Before the rangers reached us the people in the neighborhood of the murder seemed afraid to talk. They said they would be murdered, too, if they took any hand in working up the case. About the first thing that Captain McDonald did was to assure the people that he and his associates had come there to stay until every murderer was arrested and convicted, and that he would see that all those who assisted him would be protected. They believed him, and in consequence thereof they soon began to talk and feel that the law would be vindicated, and I am glad to say that it was. The work of the rangers in this one case is worth more to the State, in my opinion, than your department will cost during your administration. In fact, such service cannot be valued in dollars and cents. . . .

" The rangers were at all times sober, orderly and quiet, and left that country on good terms with all factions. They paid no attention to the criticism of the mob sympathizers, but went straight along, did their duty and now have the confidence not only of the good citizens, but of the members of the mob and their friends."

Three of the lynchers turned State's evidence and eight of them were sentenced to the penitentiary for life.

In March, 1899, Company E, Captain J. H. Rogers commanding, was ordered to Laredo to assist the State health officer to enforce the quarantine laws, there being an epidemic of smallpox in that city. The Mexicans living there objected to being moved from their homes to the hospital, and the State health officer, considering it absolutely necessary for them to be moved in order to stop the spread of the disease, required force to accomplish his object. The Mexicans showed a disposition to riot on the 19th, collecting together in hundreds, some of them being armed. The city officials had a fight with them, several shots being fired, and on the 20th, Captain Rogers, followed by one ranger and a special ranger, went with the sheriff of the county to search for arms secreted in the house of an ex-policeman, it is supposed, for the purpose of making an assault upon the State health officer and his force if approached. These officers met resistance from the inmates of the house. A fight ensued in which Captain Rogers received a wound in the right arm, and one of the Mexicans was killed. The remaining detachment of Company E, having been advised of the fight, and having met Captain Rogers in a disabled condition, and presuming that the lives of the ranger and special ranger were in jeopardy, went to the scene of action without hesitation, and immediately upon reaching the street in which the Mexicans were assembled were fired upon by the latter. The six rangers proceeded up the street firing as they went, being under the impression that a man seen lying in the street, dead, was one of the rangers who accompanied Captain Rogers. Several disinterested citizens have said that these rangers showed remarkable pluck and daring in coming down the street, fighting several times their number without the slightest hesitation. Several Mexicans were wounded. After this the work of moving the smallpox patients to the hospital was an easy task.

In April, 1899, two rangers of this company were sent into

Wharton County by request, and were successful in breaking up a gang of cattle thieves operating in that locality. Several were arrested, including the recognized leader.

In September, 1899, Captain Rogers and several of his men were ordered to Orange by request of the civil authorities, on account of an organized mob killing one negro and wounding another, and sending anonymous letters to others directing them to move out of the country. Several arrests were made. Captain Rogers was removed from Orange on account of his wound, and Captain McDonald and several of his men were ordered there to relieve him. Captain McDonald succeeded in arresting and having indicted four men for murder and a great number of men for conspiracy to murder in connection with the above mob. It is to be regretted that Ranger T. L. Fuller, while in the discharge of his duty at Orange, Texas, found it necessary to shoot and kill Oscar Poole in self-defense.

On the 15th day of October, 1900, while Captain W. J. McDonald, Lieutenant T. L. Fuller and Private A. L. Saxon, of Company B, were attending court at Orange, Texas, as witnesses, and Lieutenant Fuller to answer the charge of false imprisonment (for making an arrest while a private),* the latter was shot and killed by Tom Poole, a brother of Oscar Poole, while in a barber shop talking to one of the barbers. From the information received it is certain that Lieutenant Fuller did not know of the presence of Tom Poole when shot. While this ranger was enlisted on account of his previous good record as a deputy sheriff, he enlisted with the hope of saving sufficient money to finish his education in the University of Texas, having at that time just completed his freshman year. He was a young man of temperate habits, quiet in his manner and a fearless ranger.

* This tragedy resulted in the following recommendation by the Adjutant-General, which recommendation was duly acted upon.

RECOMMENDATION

I recommend that the law governing the ranger service be so ammended " that the officers, non-commissioned officers and privates of the ranger force be clothed with the powers of peace officers to aid the civil authorities in the execution of the laws anywhere in the State; that they be given authority to make arrests, and in such cases to be governed by the laws regulating and defining the powers and the duties of sheriffs when in discharge of similar duties." That this force consist of not to exceed four companies of twenty men each. The commissioned officers to be four company commanders, each with the rank of captain, one quartermaster with the rank of captain, and four 1st sergeants. The pay of the officers and non-commissioned officers to be as heretofore prescribed, and the pay of privates to be $40.00 per month. By increasing the pay of the privates, the State will secure the service of a better class of men, who will remain in the service a longer time and do more efficient work.

In view of the fact that a number of criminal suits have been brought against privates in the ranger force for false imprisonment by reason of arrests made by them prior to the promulgation of the attorney-general's opinion advising that only the officers of the ranger force had authority to execute criminal process under the law (see General Orders No. 24, Exhibit P), I respectfully recommend that an act be passed by the Legislature legalizing the official acts of the rangers as peace officers prior to May 26, 1900.

Officers and privates have for twenty-four years been acting in good faith under the impression that all rangers had the authority of peace officers, and privates of the Frontier Battalion have, during that time, received orders from higher authority to exercise the power of peace officers.

APPENDIX C

REPORT OF CAPTAIN W. J. McDONALD, COMMANDING COMPANY B, RANGER FORCE

SEPTEMBER 1ST, 1902 TO AUGUST 31ST, 1904

The Adjutant-General, State of Texas:

SIR:—I have the honor to herewith inclose a report of the operations of Company B, Ranger Force, for the two years ending August 31, 1904:

September, 1902.—Captain McDonald, with Privates Blanton, Ryan and Taylor, scouted to Hutchinson County, from Amarillo. Private Taylor arrested James Newlin for assault to murder and turned him over to Sheriff Randal. Sergeant McCauley and Private Delling were ordered to Newlin county on a scout, and escorted a party of surveyors, who had been run out of pastures with Winchesters, and protected them from violence. Captain McDonald with Privates Blanton and Taylor went to Columbus to carry Gregorio Cortez to Karnes County district court. His life being threatened by a mob, it was necessary to secure two men from Company C and guard the jail in which he was placed. By order of the district judge we carried him back to Columbus and put him in jail there. Captain McDonald arrested S. Harvard for theft of a bale of cotton valued at $25.20 and put him in jail at Quanah.

October, 1902.—I went to Norman, O. T., to appear in cases against horse thieves previously caught by me, for theft of horses. Accompanied by Privates Taylor and Ryan, I went to Eagle Lake to investigate the attempted assassination of W. T. Eldridge and to protect Mr. Eldridge from further violence, and succeeded in finding out who did the shooting. Privates Blanton, Warrent and Ryan scouted Oldham, Moore, Hutchinson, Roberts, Hemphill, Wheeler, Gray and Carson counties during the month, locating cow thieves, reported to be in that section. Sergeant McCauley assisted Sheriff Johnson in carrying a crazy man to the asylum at Austin, Texas. During this month, 2,600 miles were scouted and traveled.

November, 1902.—Accompanied by Privates Ryan and Taylor, I attended district court at Richmond, where trouble was anticipated in connection with the attempt to assassinate Mr. Eldridge. I went to Texline and Clayton, N. M., to investigate cattle stealing.

December, 1902.—With Privates Blanton and Kenton I took Will Carr, who had turned State's evidence on the county clerk, cattle inspectors and others in Hutchinson County, to Lipscomb County to district court, where one of the cases had been transferred. By order of the Governor of the State, Company B was ordered to Fort Hancock, on the Rio Grande, which was made headquarters, instead of Amarillo.

January, 1903.—Private Smith scouted to Alpine, to Santiago and to Comstock. Arrested Joe Hammon for murder and delivered him to the sheriff at Alpine. Also arrested a man for theft.

February, 1903.—Privates Smith and Taylor arrested a man at Sanderson for burglarizing Lockhamden ranch. He recovered the stolen property and turned it over to the owner. He turned the burglar over to the sheriff of the county. Sergeant McCauley and Private Ryan arrested Joe Jones, wanted at Pecos for forgery, and turned him over to the sheriff of the county. The money in his possession was secured and turned over to the sheriff of the county, and the defendant sent to the penitentiary at once. Privates Bean and Blanton scouted to Shafter and guarded the money for the mines. I assisted the local officials of El Paso several times during the month, and went to Mangum, O. T., as witness, and to assist in the prosecution of Sid Woodring, Frank Woodring and others for stealing my horses. These men were followed by me from the line of Collingsworth County to Cleveland County, O. T., and caught with the horses. They were sent to the penitentiary for the theft.

March, 1903.—Sergeant McCauley and Privates Bean and Blanton scouted on two trips to Shafter and Marfa, and up the Rio Grande in search for the notorious Bill Taylor, the train robber and murderer, and who had broken jail on several occasions, but he escaped into Mexico. Privates Taylor and Smith scouted to Sanderson and assisted the constable in preventing trouble at a trial in court, where the defendant, a sheriff, had killed the justice of the peace. Private Taylor, at the request of the sheriff, went with him to El Paso to bring Geo. Maglovlin, who was charged with rape, to Alpine court. He also assisted in the arrest of a man for rape, one for horse theft, and one for murder, and put them in jail. Many scouts were made along the river in search of cow and horse thieves during the month.

April, 1903.—I assisted the officers and went with the sheriff of Pecos County to locate a man, but he escaped into Mexico. Sergeant McCauley and Private Bean arrested two men for theft of wood, and one for theft of a horse. Sergeant McCauley assisted the sheriff in arresting a man for threatening to take life. Privates Delling and Ryan scouted to Valentine and assisted in following horse thieves, but the thieves escaped into Mexico. They recovered one stolen horse and returned it to owner. Private Smith arrested a man for assault, and went to Sanderson to investigate the attempted burning of a hotel. He also went to Del Rio to look after several horse-stealing cases. Private Taylor went with Inspector Cook on a scout, looking for stolen cattle.

May, 1903.—I assisted in bringing to justice Gil Brice, a Mexican, charged with killing a lawyer named Tusselman several years ago, and who had escaped at Fort Hancock while shackled. Privates Ryan and Bean were sent to Sanderson to investigate the killing of a justice of peace and another man. Private Taylor arrested Thos. Chappis for attempt to murder, and succeeded in getting him in jail. Arrested R. C. McMahan for killing of Mr. Bob Smith, a justice of the peace, and Chas. Reed for lunacy.

June, 1903.—Private Ryan scouted down the river and to Sanderson. Sergeant McCauley scouted with and assisted river guards. Private Bean scouted from Sanderson in pursuit of a Mexican wanted in Tom Green County for attempt to rape. Scouted to Sanderson and arrested Tom Brown for killing Mr. Morris, the operator. Private Delling scouted to Ferlingin and investigated some cattle stealing.

July, 1903.—Privates Bean and Dunaway scouted four days down the river looking for stolen cattle. They arrested three Mexicans for shooting at Fort Hancock. Privates Delling and Ryan scouted to Sanderson to prevent trouble between factions, and to Fort Stockton to be present at the examining trial of McMahan, who was charged with murder, as trouble was expected. They also arrested a man charged with rape.

August, 1903.—Sergeant McCauley and Private Bean scouted in the northern part of El Paso County, looking after cattle and horse thieves. Private Dunaway arrested John McCain while he was in the act of robbing a T. & P. caboose. Private Taylor scouted during the month. Various other scouts were made during the month.

September, 1903.—By order of General Hulen, I took Private Dunaway and went to Marfa to investigate an attack made on L. N. Holbert, county attorney. Mr. Holbert had been taken from the hotel by a mob and seriously beaten. I found who the guilty parties were, and brought Mr. Holbert to go before the grand jury to prosecute them, but through fear he begged off from the district attorney and wanted the matter dropped. I made an investigation of some whitecappers, and furnished the grand jury with evidence of same. One man was indicted. By order of General Hulen, Sergeant McCauley and Private Dunaway went to Eagle Pass to assist in the quarantine regulations and guarded the river until the quarantine was raised. Accompanied by Sergeant McCauley, I went with Deputy Sheriff Kenton to capture a man, but failed to get him out of Mexico. Several scouts were made to Sanderson and Fort Stockton to assist the officers. Private Bean arrested two Mexicans for carrying pistols, and carried them to jail, by order of the justice of the peace. Privates Delling and Ryan arrested two Mexicans for disturbing the peace. Private Taylor went to Columbus as witness in the Cortez case. Privates Delling and Smith went with Sheriff Walton to assist him in his county for several days.

October, 1903.—Sergeant McCauley and Private Dunaway were still on quarantine service at Eagle Pass. Private Dunaway arrested a Mexican for running a night watchman from his duty, and put him in jail. Privates Ryan and Bean arrested a man for burglarizing Finley ranch; recovered the property stolen, and turned it over to its owner. The man was put in jail at El Paso. Private Smith assisted the sheriff and scouted with him over the county, and then went to Marfa and assisted the officers there. Sergeant McCauley and Private Dunaway returned from Eagle Pass, where they have been on duty for several months. Private Bean scouted after outlaws during the month. Private Ryan went to Fort Stockton to attend district court, and went to Sanderson to do some work for the sheriff in serving some papers. Privates Taylor, Smith and Delling carried prisoners from Fort Stockton to Marfa for safe keeping. Privates Smith, Taylor and Delling attended district court in Del Rio.

December, 1903.—By order of General Hulen, I went to

Walker County to look after parties who waylaid and assassinated Bob James in Kittrell's " Cut-off " on December 4th. I arrived there on the 12th, and on the 13th and 14th arrested Buck Shaw, Henry Shaw, P. Clark and Jim Alston as being implicated in the murder, carried them to Huntsville, and had them put in the penitentiary for safe keeping. Held a court of inquiry before Judge Cox, a justice of the peace, every few days. On the 24th Buck Shaw, the leader of the gang, had an examining trial, and was held without bail. Chas. Rhoden was tried on the 29th and held without bail. The defendants then sued out writs of habeas corpus before District Judge Smithers. Alston was allowed bail in the sum of $1,500. Private Delling arrived in the " Cut-off " on the 16th and has been assisting me since in the cases. Private Delling assisted in arresting two men for theft of cattle. Private Bean killed a negro porter at El Paso for knocking him down with an iron poker, and was promptly acquitted in district court at El Paso in January. Sergeant McCauley went to Marfa to investigate some stealing there and then went to investigate the killing of William Johnson.

January, 1904.—I, together with Private Delling, went to Corrigan and Livingston to look after some witnesses. I went after a bad negro for Sheriff Brooks. The negro was armed with a shotgun, and considerable shooting occurred. After the negro ran out he shot at me and I wounded him in the side. Went to Huntsville to attend habeas corpus trial of the murderers of Bob James, which resulted in holding Shaw, Roden and Clark without bail. Assisted Sheriff Brooks in arresting a bad negro, wanted for robbing. Scouted in Houston, Trinity and Walker counties during the month, continually. Private Delling went to Polk County and arrested four men for theft of hogs and put them in jail at Huntsville. Sergeant McCauley arrested C. Marsden for murder. Sergeant McCauley, Privates Ryan and Bean scouted to Love's ranch to stop an invasion of Mexicans who were coming over after parties charged with murder on this side.

February, 1904.—I went to Crockett after attached witness. Private Delling arrested a man in the " Cut-off " for theft of hogs. I was ordered to Groveton by Adjutant General Hulen for the purpose of investigating the murder of an old lady, Touchstone, who was murdered for her land and money and thrown out the door for the hogs to eat. After investigation, I found that her throat had been cut and that she had been killed outright. Assisted by Private Delling I arrested Ab Angle, who had run off, as principal, and five others as accomplices. These parties were indicted by the grand jury. I caught one of them over the line of Arkansas while running away and put him in the pen at Henderson. Private Delling arrested a man in the " Cut-off " for horse theft, and put him in jail at Groveton. Private Dunaway arrested a man for robbing a camp. Private Bean arrested five Mexicans for disturbing the peace, and one man for assault to murder. Privates Taylor and Smith attended district court at Marfa. Privates Smith and Dunaway were ordered to Groveton to assist me in holding down the toughs of east Texas. Private Ryan attended district court at Amarillo; attended district court at Huntsville; assisted the sheriff in handling prisoners. Private Delling arrested three men for shooting up the town. He also arrested one who was charged with adultery in the " Cut-off " and one for waylaying and shooting two men at Phelps with a shotgun. Private Dunaway arrested a man for carrying a pistol at Groveton, and two men for conspiring to kill Abe Hyman, the only eyewitness to the murder of Dr. Gary, and another man at Groveton. One of the men had fixed a plan to make the other believe that Abe Hyman was going to do him some violence, and succeeded in getting him to get a shotgun in order to kill Abe Hyman. Private Dunaway took the gun and landed both men in jail. The accused men admitted the whole truth. One of these men was made constable, deputy sheriff and jailer as soon as he was released from jail. The other was run off at once, but I have his sworn statements of the facts. Private Dunaway arrested a man for burglary and rape and put him in jail. Private Taylor arrested a man at Sanderson for stealing cattle. Private Taylor was ordered to report to me at Groveton. Private Dunaway arrested a man for carrying a pistol, put him in jail, but the sheriff released him soon after, pretending he was an assistant of his.

April, 1904.—I carried two of the accomplices in the Touchstone murder from Huntsville to Groveton. By order of the Adjutant General I went to Leon County to investigate the murder of Tummins, who was waylaid and killed. Two men were arrested at the house of the murderer and put under $5,000 bond, but the grand jury failed to find a bill against them. They then began shooting into houses and had the people considerably disturbed. With Private Delling, I arrested them and held them without bail at the examining trial and also in habeas corpus trial. I was ordered to San Jacinto County to investigate lawlessness there, especially wire cutting, but found some of the wire cutters on the grand jury, and it was the opinion of the district and county attorney that we could do no good under existing circumstances, and nothing was accomplished there. Private Dunaway arrested a man for assault to rape. Assisted by Privates Dunaway and Delling, I arrested four persons charged with murder. They had previously been arrested for being accomplices to the Touchstone murder. I arrested a man for theft of a horse. Sergeant McCauley scouted in different counties on the Rio Grande, and investigated the stealing of horses. I went to Waverly to investigate the poisoning of a well and cistern, but decided it was done by the parties themselves, in order to accuse others of it. I went to Palestine to assist the sheriff in hanging a negro charged with rape. Private Delling went to Leon County to investigate the murder of Bob Blackwell, and succeeded in securing the required evidence. He attended the examining trial of the two men charged with the murder, who were held without bail. Privates Smith and Dunaway arrested a man for attempting to murder A. A. Smith and put him in jail. They also arrested the same man for carrying a pistol. Private Ryan arrested two Mexicans for stealing sheep in El Paso County and another for stealing wood.

June, 1904.—Private Delling and myself scouted in Kittrell's " Cut-off," Houston and Trinity Counties. I went to Comstock; made a scout on Devil's River, to El Paso and to Fort Hancock. Sergeant McCauley arrested a man for embezzlement and started to jail with him at El Paso, but he escaped by jumping out of a window while the train was in motion. Sergeant McCauley and Private Ryan arrested two Mexicans for theft of horses and saddles, recovered the property and returned the same to its owners. Private Ryan attempted to arrest a man for theft of cattle, and had a running fight with and wounded him. He escaped across the river. Private Dunaway arrested a man and put him in jail for carrying a pistol. Privates Delling and Smith went to Centerville to court to prevent trouble between citizens there, when a malicious prosecution was filed against him. Private Delling arrested a man for carrying a pistol in the " Cut-off."

July, 1904.—Accompanied by Privates Delling and Wilcox, I went to Oakwood to investigate train robbing of the I. & G. N. We captured two of the men without a doubt. They were put in jail at Palestine and identified by the conductor as the two men that came into the sleeper, and the only two tracks that led up to where the express packages were torn open fitted theirs. They afterwards admitted them to be their tracks. While we made a strong case against them, the influence of the officers and others was too strong to find any bills. I would like to have space to add in this report the testimony taken at the examining trial.

August, 1904.—I went to Groveton to attend court, and carried Ab Angle before the grand jury, but he failed to testify, as he had been persuaded not to do so. I arrested a man for being implicated in train robbery, but he proved an alibi and was released. Private Delling went to Centerville to district court. Sergeant McCauley recovered six stolen horses and turned them over to the owners. He arrested four Mexicans for theft of cattle.

Very respectfully,

W. J. McDONALD,
Commanding Company B, Ranger Force.

Table Showing Result of Operations of the Ranger Force from September 1, 1902, to August 31, 1904.

COMMANDERS OF COMPANIES.	Letter of company.	Murder.	Assault to murder.	Aggravated assault.	Horse, cattle and other theft.	Swindling, embezzlement and forgery.	Robbery and burglary.	Mail and train robbery.	Perjury.	Rape and adultery.	Smuggling.	Carrying concealed weapons.	Seduction.	Escaped convicts (captured).	Rioting.	Minor offenses.	Total arrests.	Scouts.	Attempts at arrest.	District courts assisted.	Number days quarantine guard.	Jail guards.	Other assistance to civil authority.	Engagements with criminals.	Persons killed in resisting arrest.	Wounded in resisting arrest.	Escorts.	Rangers killed in line of duty.	Rangers wounded in line of duty.	Horses and cattle recovered and returned to owners.	Miles traveled in discharge of duty.
		Arrests Made. → (Murder through Total arrests)																													
Captain J. A. Brooks	A	26	28	5	43	15	12					17	2	2		206	344	140		19				3	2			1	1	362	47,834
Captain W. J McDonald	B	31	19	4	37	2	12	3		6		23				35	172	205		25		15	30				3			28	74,537
Captain J. H. Rogers	C	8	3	4		2	1	1	4	1		10				36	86	81		16	224	13	12	1	1		5			21	57,347
Captain Jno. R. Hughes	D	5	6		39	4	1		1	7	27		1			75	166	204		16			20							168	45,839
Totals		70	56	13	119	23	26	4	5	14	27	50	3	2		352	768	630		76	224	28	62	4	3		8	1	1	579	225,557

APPENDIX D

REPORT OF AN INVESTIGATION MADE BY HERBERT
J. BROWN, EMPLOYED BY THE WAR DEPART-
MENT IN CONJUNCTION WITH CAPTAIN W.
G. BALDWIN, WITH A VIEW OF LEARN-
ING WHAT HAPPENED AT BROWNS-
VILLE, TEX., ON THE 13TH AND
14TH OF AUGUST, 1906

WASHINGTON, *D. C., December* 5, 1908.

SIR: I have the honor to submit the following report relative
to the investigation of the Brownsville raid:

Ex-Private Boyd Conyers, of Company B, Twenty-fifth Infantry, now at Monroe, Ga., told William Lawson, a detective in
the employ of Captain William G. Baldwin, of Roanoke, Va.,
that he and three [or four] other men of the Twenty-fifth Infantry were the leaders in the Brownsville raid. This information was obtained at different dates during the month of June,
1908. (See Exhibit A.)

I submit the affidavit as presented. There are certain dis-
crepancies of a minor character, due to the fact that Lawson is
illiterate and had to depend on his memory for details. But it
should be borne in mind that Lawson was unacquainted with the
details of the Brownsville raid and was given information which
could have come only from one familiar with the secret history of
the affair. Lawson's first report included the names of Conyers,
John Holloman, John Brown, and "another man." Subsequently he supplied the name of James Powell, but I think the
original name given was that of Robert L. Collier, Company C,
one of the relief guard. This information was corroborated in
the presence of witnesses, but before Lawson could finish his
work Conyers became suspicious and would give no further evidence incriminating himself. From then on he furnished to A.
H. Baldwin, Captain W. G. Baldwin, and to myself information
piecemeal and reluctantly. The name of Carolina de Saussure,
his bunk mate, was the last one obtained.

Conyers tried to commit suicide after he found that he had made his statements to a detective, declaring that the other negroes would kill him when it got out. He finally wrote to Senator Foraker and received a reply, a copy of which is annexed. That reply he construed to mean that he should stick to his original story told before the Senate committee at all hazards, and there he stands. I have every reason to believe that his confession is genuine and gives for the first time the true secret history of the Brownsville raid.

The list of participants given in this report Conyers furnished me personally. I believe it is substantially correct, but with the influences shown to be backing Conyers to adhere to his false testimony given before the Senate committee still being exerted he cannot be relied on to support his own confession until it is thoroughly sustained from other sources.

Evidences of similar encouragement to stick to the lies told at Brownsville and before the Senate committee were found in many places, and subsequent to the date of the Foraker letter they became stronger and more obstructive than ever.

The investigation has been conducted with strict recognition of the advisability of preserving secrecy, and with discretion. No promises of immunity were made. The knowledge on the part of the ex-soldiers that the Government could not punish them after their separation from the service, coupled with the belief that by preserving silence they would aid in the passage of the relief legislation now pending in Congress, has added to the difficulty of securing information.

The issue has evidently become racial. The colored detectives would be confronted frequently in the smaller towns where these men are living with a demand from colored men for information as to their business.

We have located over 130 of these ex-soldiers, and have been in thirty States in quest of information. The appendices give statements as to the results obtained. They indicate a general knowledge on the part of the ex-soldiers that the raid came from inside the fort, and that the soldiers of Company B were the guilty parties.

We earnestly urge that we be permitted to continue the investigation. Several detectives are still in the field, and within the coming week a number of affidavits will be forthcoming.

With some repetition of matter appearing later in the report, Boyd Conyers's story is given here in narrative form:

REPORT OF T. B. SKIDMORE.

" The rumors of trouble over the assignment of colored troops to Brownsville were circulated before the troops left Fort Niobrara, and preparations were made among the men to ' get even with the crackers,' so the whites were called. Some cartridges were held out at range practice, but more en route to Brownsville. Pretense was made that they were given away at stations along the road. Some were, but a large number were secreted.

" At inspection in Brownsville, Lieutenant Lawrason, Company B, threatened punishment to the men who were short of ammunition, but nothing was done about it, and the deficiency was supplied.

" The friction with citizens of Brownsville began at once. In Boyd Conyers's language, ' Whisky made all the trouble. If we hadn't been drinking we wouldn't have had the nerve to shoot up the town.'

" It was agreed, at a gathering of a few men in the saloon of Allison, the colored ex-soldier, on the afternoon of August 13, 1906, that the raid should take place that night at 12 o'clock. It seems to have been delayed a few minutes to let Tamayo, the Mexican scavenger, get away from the B barracks.

" John Holloman, the money lender of Company B, was the chief conspirator and leader in the raid and custodian and distributor of the cartridges, but his plans could not have been carried out had not Sergeant George Jackson, of Company B, in charge of the keys of the gun racks in B barracks, and Sergeant Reid, in command of the guards, co-operated both before and after the raid.

" The four men who led the raid were John Holloman, John Brown, Boyd Conyers, and Carolina de Saussure, all of Company B (and probably R. L. Collier, of Company C). Holloman was in barracks, Brown in the bake shop, Conyers and De Saussure in the guardhouse. The two latter were in the same detail, and had been relieved at about 11 o'clock, De Saussure on the post at the guardhouse, and Conyers on No. 2, around the barracks and facing the town. Holloman got the party together. Conyers and De Saussure slept on the same bunk in the guardhouse, claiming that they wanted to get under the mosquito net, and they had the trick of taking their guns into the bunk instead of placing them in the open rack, on the excuse that they didn't rust so badly under cover, but really so the absence of the guns from the open guardhouse rack would not attract attention, and their own absence would be ascribed to a visit to the closet, which was back of the guardhouse. These two men slipped out the rear door of the guardhouse, passed through the sally port, and joined Holloman and Brown.

" The party crossed the wall of the fort down near the end of A barracks, went up the roadway to the entrance to the Cowen alley, where the signal shots were fired. These shots were immediately tallied onto by the alarm shots of Joseph B. Howard, guard on No. 2, and formed the series testified to by Mrs. Katie E. Leahy, of Brownsville. Her testimony is further borne out by the statement that not over thirty seconds elapsed before a number of men of Company B swarmed out on the upper gallery and opened a fusillade on the town.

" It is an absolute certainty that it would have been impossible for Sergeant Jackson to have opened the gun racks, for the men to have assembled, secured their guns, loaded them, gone out to the gallery, and started firing, all after the first shot was fired; all aroused, as they testified unanimously, from sound slumber, in less than two minutes, in the confusion of a dark barrack room. Beyond the possibility of a doubt, the racks had been opened and the inside conspirators were ready to pour out on the signal shots. The testimony is ample that there were scarcely twenty seconds between the last of the signal shots and the first general volley from B barracks.

" The number firing from the barracks is unknown, but perhaps 20 men were involved. A smaller number went to the ground and followed the leaders up the alley. It will be remembered that one of the witnesses testified to hearing some one of the group of soldiers exclaim, ' There they go! ' Whereupon these men leaped over the wall and ran up the alley.

" Boyd Conyers is the man whose gun jammed at the exit of the alley by the Cowen house, testified to by Herbert Elkins, and it was taken from him by De Saussure and fixed in the street where the light from the street lamp at the corner of Elizabeth Street shone on them.

" Less than five minutes elapsed from the time the first shot was fired until these men were all back inside the fort.

" Conyers stated that Reid was told that they were going to shoot up the town, and he had laughed and said, ' Don't go out there and let the crackers get the best of you.'

" When Conyers and De Saussure reached the guardhouse they ran in the back way and got into their bunks. Sergeant Reid came in and swore at them, but Conyers was so excited and out of breath that he could hardly stand, so Reid stationed him at the rear of the guardhouse in the dark where he could not be scrutinized so closely.

" Holloman came around with extra cartridges about daybreak and Reid passed them out. The guns were all cleaned before daylight."

This day personally appeared before me William Lawson, who, being duly sworn, deposes and says:

" On June 5, 1908, I was sent to Monroe, Ga., to interview Boyd Conyers, one of the soldiers who was stationed at Brownsville, Tex., in August, 1906. I was sent by Mr. Baldwin to get in with Conyers and ascertain if he knew who did the shooting at that point. I was not given the names of any of the members of either of the companies stationed at that point, nor was I given any other information, except the fact that a shooting occurred at the time and place above mentioned, and that Boyd Conyers was suspected of knowing who did same.

" I arrived at Monroe, Ga., on June 5, and stopped at the home of Esther Crews, colored. I met Boyd Conyers, who is known as ' Buddie ' Conyers, on the morning of June 6, but had very little conversation with him, but was introduced to him as an old soldier. On the morning of June 8, between 8 and 9 o'clock, I met Conyers about halfway between the station house and Main Street. We talked some twenty or twenty-five minutes. I broached the Brownsville case, and mentioned the fact that the soldiers had shown their good sense by keeping their mouths while at Washington. I then asked him what the motive was for the shooting. He told me that the ' crackers ' at Brownsville had made threats that they would have no negro soldiers at Brownsville, and the soldiers had made it up in their minds that if they bothered them that they would go in and clean up the ground. He also said that they mentioned this to Sergeant Reid, who was commander of the guards, and that Reid said, ' All that I have to say is to take care of yourself and the boys when you go down there.' S. H. Parker, whose home is at Charleston, S. C., was present and heard the same conversation.

" About then a gentleman called Conyers to come and clean some clothes, and Conyers left, and nothing further was said about the matter at this time. I was with Conyers nearly every day, and went to Gainesville, Ga., on an excursion with him on the 15th of June. I did not mention the Brownsville matter to Conyers again until on the 29th of June, when I returned from Atlanta, having gone there on June 27. On this date I met him at Joe Blassingame's and had a pint bottle of liquor, offered him a drink—he would not drink in the house, but we went up the street and we stopped under a storehouse porch, near Main street. We took a drink or two, and I started the Brownsville case again. He told me that he was doing guard duty at the time of the shooting at Brownsville, and was stationed at the outlet toward the town. He said that when the guard was called the night of the shooting they mentioned to Sergeant Reid what had occurred downtown, and he said, ' Boys, if you are not satisfied, you will have to go and get satisfied,' and they remarked that they were going to get satisfaction that night. Reid then laughed and said, ' Boys, don't you go down there and let them get the best of you.' He then assigned the guard and went away.

" In this conversation Conyers told me that John Brown, J. H. Holloman, and a man named Powell, and several others, came down where he was on guard, and that they went downtown and just gave them hell, and after they shot out all of their cartridges they ran back to the barracks, and when they got back to the barracks they found that the alarm had been sounded and the officers were calling the roll. Holloman, Brown, and himself were late for roll call, but that some one answered for Brown and Holloman, but that he was late, and that Reid told him that they had gotten themselves and himself in a hell of a hole, and told him to go to the guardhouse and pretend to be asleep, which he did.

" He told me that they had slipped a few cartridges when at target practice and that before inspection, after the shooting, Reid gave him some cartridges to replace the ones he had used. He further said that they had all agreed before they went out that they would keep their mouths, and that he would have told them at the investigation at Washington all about the shooting, but that he was afraid. I had no further talk with Conyers, because I saw that I was being suspected by the negroes around Monroe, Ga.

" WILLIAM (his x mark) LAWSON."

Witnesses:

    H. J. BROWNE.
    GEO. W. MADERT.

This day personally appeared before me Herbert J. Browne, of Washington, D. C., who, being duly sworn, deposes and says:

" I was employed by the War Department in May, 1908, in company with Captain William G. Baldwin, of Roanoke, Va., chief of the Baldwin Detective Agency, to investigate the conduct of the battalion of the Twenty-fifth Infantry, stationed at Brownsville, Tex., which conduct resulted in the Brownsville raid, so called, on the night of August 13-14, 1906, wherein one Frank Natus was killed, Lieutenant of Police Dominguez badly wounded, and the houses of several citizens were shot into. Captain Baldwin has charge of the secret work for the Norfolk and Western Railway, the Chesapeake and Ohio Railway, the Southern Railway, and the Atlantic Coast Line, and is one of the best known and most responsible detectives in the country.

" In conjunction with him I have been continuously employed upon this work since its inception in May.

" The facts set forth in my report addressed to General George B. Davis, Judge-Advocate-General, War Department, under date of December 5, 1908, are true to the best of my knowledge and belief.

" In particular I visited Monroe, Ga., to corroborate the investigation at that point of William Lawson, a colored detective in the employ of Captain Baldwin, whose affidavit and reports are annexed to and made a part of my report of December 5, 1908, above referred to.

" I had several interviews at Monroe with Boyd Conyers, ex-private of Company B, Twenty-fifth Infantry, one of the guard on the night of the Brownsville raid, and found that William Lawson's statements regarding Conyers were substantially and essentially correct. I personally obtained from Conyers further information detailing how the cartridges used in the raid were surreptitiously and illegally obtained and distributed, how the principal raiders proceeded, when and by whom the gun racks in Company B were unlawfully and secretly opened for the purpose of the raid, how the raiders were protected during and subsequent to the raid and given opportunity to clean their guns, and, in particular, was furnished by Conyers with the names of eight participants in the raid other than the three named by him in his statements to William Lawson, a total of eleven, including himself, the said Conyers, all members of Company B, Twenty-fifth Infantry.

"The leaders of the raid, as named by Boyd Conyers, were John Holloman, John Brown, Carolina de Saussure, and himself. Following them were William Anderson, James Bailey, Charles E. Cooper, William Lemons, Henry Jimerson, James 'Rastus' Johnson, and Henry 'Sonny' Jones. Sergeant Reid, in charge of the guard, was accused by Conyers of knowledge before and after the raid. Sergeant George Jackson, in charge of the keys of the gun racks of Company B, was accused of opening the racks for the raiders, and of again opening them subsequent to the raid in order that the guns might be removed and cleaned.

"I found Boyd Conyers in a disturbed frame of mind. No claim is made that his original declarations to William Lawson were other than those of a criminal boasting to one of his own race of his crime and of his success in escaping discovery. His subsequent declarations to me were given partly during moments of contrition and in a desire to unload his conscience by a confession and partly as the result of careful and persistent questioning.

"I found the effect of the letter from Senator Foraker to Conyers extremely obstructive. He seemed to regard it as a mandate to adhere to the false story told by him before the Senate Committee on Military Affairs, and as absolving him from any and all obligations to aid in uncovering the truth. Similar influences were encountered at many points, adding largely to the difficulty of obtaining admissions of even the most obvious facts relative to the raid.

"HERBERT J. BROWNE."

Subscribed and sworn to before me this 9th day of December, 1908.

[SEAL.]   J. B. RANDOLPH, *Notary Public.*

APPENDIX E

REPORT OF T. B. SKIDMORE,

PRESIDING JUDGE OF ELECTION, PRECINCT NO. 1, RIO GRANDE CITY, NOVEMBER, 1906

RIO GRANDE CITY, TEXAS, 11/12/06.

Hon. Jno. R. Hulen, Adj.-Gen.,
City.

SIR:

As the presiding judge for this Precinct, No. (1) one of Starr County, Texas, at the late general election held in this city on the 6th day of November, 1906, in the upstairs room at the court-house, used by the district judge as the court-room, permit me to make the following report of the proceedings had that day:

Having had no call nor communication from the Republicans of this place for representation among the (4) four clerks of the election subject to appointment by the presiding officer, they had already been named, taking care that one man who had theretofore voted the Republican ticket was chosen and also one man whom I knew to favor Mr. Gregorio Duffy, the ruling spirit locally of the opposition to the Democrats.

Also, having heard ugly rumors of threats accredited to the Republicans, I had notified eighteen (18) law abiding citizens to be present at the polls as early as half-past seven A.M. on the 6th of November, 1906, then and there to take the oath of office and act as the peace officers during the election. Of these only 12, I think, appeared and were sworn in.

As soon as the election judges assembled they and those of the peace officers present and the supervisors were sworn in.

At this point the presiding officer stepped to the front door and noting that a body of armed men on horseback and afoot had assembled on the outside at the 100-foot limit from the polling place, asked who had dared come to the polls thus armed and was told they were the Republican voters.

Immediately Mr. F. W. Seabury called me to the foot of the first flight of steps and introduced me to a Mr. Creager, who, after replying that the armed men outside were Jose Pina's peace officers, demanded representation among the clerks of election. I told him that all parties had representation, but when he insisted on some of the names he suggested, it being agreed to by the person, I put Domingo L. Garza in the place of the Duffy representative I had called to act as clerk.

From the names Mr. Creager suggested as inside officer, I also chose Mr. Jose Pina, believing that by having him under my direction, the agreement between Mr. Seabury and the presiding judge on the one hand and Mr. Creager on the other, that the voters should come up stairs in pairs—one Democrat and one Republican together—could best be maintained, for the reason that the said Jose Pina had been the agency who, through his magisterial capacity incident to him as county commissioner for this Precinct, had appointed the (40) forty peace officers that Mr. Creager said the Republicans had at hand to preserve the peace and insure a fair and quiet election.

Thereupon Mr. Garza and Mr. Pina and the balance of the peace officers called by the presiding judge were sworn in, and word reaching me that threats of breaking in the front door below were being made by the Republican crowd outside, the janitor was ordered to open it; the polls were declared open and the timepiece set at eight o'clock A.M.

During the course of the first half hour—possibly it was that long—the agreement of pairing the voters coming up to the vote was observed. Then, noting that for some minutes nearly all the voters had been Republicans, inside peace officer, Jose Pina, was directed to see why there were no Democrats coming in.

On his return he told me it would be all right and that there were no Democrats at the door just then, but another of my deputies from below in response to my call came up and told me the Republicans had taken possession of the staircase and lower door and would only let such Democrats in as forced their way by them at peril of their lives.

At the end of about (2) two hours the disorder became so great that repeated demand had to be made on Mr. Jose Pina and the other inside officers to regulate the people outside the rail. On seeing that even Mr. Pina could not control his Republican friends I had to threaten the crowd with closing the polls if they did not preserve order, and remain in line instead of filling the area outside the railing to such an extent as to threaten to tear it loose from the floor.

Immediately after the fourth threat of this kind, I was informed and could see from the faces of the crowd that only trouble would ensue if I tried that method to handle them, so I let them have their own way and thereafter they did break the railing supports loose from the floor. Thereafter, I repeatedly called on Mr. Juan Hinajosa, the Rupublican challenger, to enforce order and refused to receive any more votes until his people should get into line.

On entering the polling place, my only object was to see that a fair election should take place, and I do not think that I neglected any precaution to have it so. I repeatedly sent word to my peace officers below, after about half-past ten A.M., to clear the stairs and lower corridor of all who had already voted, but none of them could be found generally, and when one was found he would send back word that he could do nothing with the crowd and that Democratic voters were being turned away from the lower door and only Republican voters were being allowed to enter.

I have since been told by the peace officers of the election, that fear for their lives led them to desist from trying to enforce the entry of Democrats into the line going to the polls.

I have also since learned that Democratic voters who were business men of the town, left their places of business as many as three and four times and went to the polls to vote, but were denied entrance by Mr. Pina's armed deputies and other Republicans and their sympathizers. And also that four desperate characters with Winchesters in their hands were picketed in front of the lower entrance to the court-house, and that when asked if they were voters Mr. Gregorio Duffy replied, " No, they are only some posts driven in the ground there for a rear-guard to keep out the Democrats."

Also on examination of the certified list of poll-tax payers of this precinct after the election, I find that 126 of them did not vote, and nearly all were Democrats. Why, I have not had time yet to inquire, but you will note that this failure to vote bears out the statements of the peace officers appointed by the presiding judge.

During the course of the election 160 out of the 367 voters who deposited their ballots were sworn, and I believe that if the legal voters only of those 160 had been permitted to vote and the Democrats of the 126 poll-tax payers who did not get to vote had been permitted to do so that the majority would have stood about 40 in favor of the Democrats instead of 103 against them, as it did result.

Permit me to explain in closing that I had reasons to believe before the election that the Republicans intended to appear in force and with arms at the election, but, under the advice of Judge Welch, I had made no arrangements up to the evening before the election for peace officers of my appointing, but that, when I told him about five o'clock P.M. on November 5th that 30 or 40 strangers from Mexico were in town, Judge Welch told me to appoint whatever number I thought proper to guarantee a peaceable election, but especially admonished me not to have so many as to give the semblance of an armed force at the polls.

Such being my course beforehand, I felt myself morally responsible for the lives of the men I had appointed as peace officers, and therefore never sent them any command during the day to use force in handling the crowd, and that they were all men of good enough sense to see the futility of such a course is shown by the fact that they did not in any instance act arbitrarily.

In conclusion let me add that I had no interest to serve and none at stake in this election, and that my only interest now in submitting this report is to help, as best I may, in maintaining the majesty of American law and the purity of the ballot box, and the sanctity of the elective franchise thereunder to the utmost confines of this American Union.

I am, Sir, yours sincerely,

T. B. SKIDMORE,

Late Pres. Judge of Election in Precinct No. 1 of Starr Co., Tex., on Nov. 6, 1906.

Duffy has since been murdered.

APPENDIX F

PORTION OF A MESSAGE FROM GOVERNOR T. M.
CAMPBELL, REFERRING TO RECENTLY
ENACTED LAWS AND THEIR
ENFORCEMENT

AUSTIN, January 14, 1909.

To the Senate and House of Representatives:

As members of the Thirty-first Legislature, you have each voluntarily undertaken an important task. Your duties are important and your responsibilities are serious. You have assembled under favorable conditions. The State Treasury is on a cash basis. The State is generally prosperous, and the people are contented and happy. The law is supreme in Texas, and all the laws are now very generally enforced and obeyed.

There is no substantial reason to doubt that the welfare of the State and the happiness of the people will be promoted by the intelligence of your work, and by your fidelity to the people with whom you made a covenant at the ballot box. You need make no serious mistakes, as the will of the people has been ascertained upon all important matters which demand the attention of the Legislature at this time.

Organized avarice, though in attempted disguise, can hardly be expected to override the popular will. Selfish interests and those seeking special advantages and exclusive privileges will have their ready advocates on every hand, and wholesome legislation heretofore enacted for the protection of the people will doubtless be assailed. A word of caution is therefore offered to the end that the chosen representative of a confiding constituency may be on his guard. It is not unlikely that designing forces have organized and will be maintained at the Capitol which will test the wisdom, integrity and patriotism of this Legislature.

The laws enacted and the reforms wrought under the present administration in behalf of the great masses of the people of Texas have been under fire for nearly two years, and have repeatedly received the emphatic endorsement of the Democratic voters of our State, and have been approved and re-affirmed by the organized Democracy in convention assembled. The platform of the opposition party demanded the repeal or modification of many of these important laws, and that party, its candidates and its platform were repudiated and defeated by about 150,000 majority. Desperate efforts have been employed by sinister agencies to discredit these laws, and to defeat the operation of these reforms, but the people have willed otherwise, and the laws have come to stay. Such changes as may be sought by the friends of the laws to strengthen them, and which may be dictated by experience, may, with propriety, be made, but these laws were demanded by the people; they were enacted by their trusted representatives, and in spirit and substance they should stand.

They are just and right and ought to stand. The result of the recent political contests involving these laws and reforms strikingly demonstrate that the agencies of corrupt and sinister special interests can not dominate and control in Texas. The patriotism of our people and the freedom of speech which obtains in Texas make it certain that her incorruptible electorate can be safely trusted to uphold the public official who keeps the faith and redeems his pledges made to them. Those who have contended that modifications and exceptions in their interest should be made in the laws enacted by the last Legislature might have placed their propositions upon the Democratic primary election ticket, and thus tested them at the ballot box, or they could have uncovered their schemes in the last Democratic convention, and these plans were suggested time and again as open to them. This course was open under the law, but they chose rather to undertake the defeat of candidates who stood for these laws. In this they signally failed in every instance. The State Democratic Convention, following the lead of nearly all the county conventions, endorsed the laws as they stood, and placed the party candidates upon a platform committed to their perpetuation. The enemies of the legislation and reforms enacted by the last Legislature chose to submit their demands for repeal, changes and modifications thereof in the Republican State platform, which of course binds all representatives of that party faith. Democrats are bound by party action, by the verdict rendered at the polls, and by the platform made by its convention.

The Democratic platform declaration with respect to the laws enacted during this administration is as follows:

" We heartily endorse * * * the acts of the Thirtieth Legislature enacted in obedience to platform demands, and we rejoice at the emphatic endorsement given said laws and administration by the Democratic voters of Texas in the recent primary election."

The measures of commanding importance enacted during the present administration are in the interest of justice, equality, good government and decency. They have resulted in no harm or injustice to any man or to any legitimate business enterprise within this State. The truth of this statement has already been demonstrated, and any effort to emasculate, destroy or weaken them would be a fraud upon the people and a betrayal of the Democratic party. These laws became effective in the midst of a great national panic, and Texas has been and is in a better financial and economic condition to-day than any State in the Republic.

To effect needed reforms and to check evil tendencies, laws were enacted by the last Legislature to the following effect:
1. The keeping of gambling houses and the exhibiting of gambling devices was made a felony.
2. The practice of drinking intoxicating liquors on railroad trains was prohibited.
3. A law passed requiring contests of local option elections to be promptly instituted, and providing that otherwise the legality of such elections should be conclusively presumed.
4. Authority was granted district judges, on proper showing, to prevent by injunction the sale of intoxicating liquors in prohibition communities.
5. A tax of $5,000 was levied on express companies shipping intoxicating liquors into prohibition districts, the effect of which was to take the express companies out of the liquor and saloon business.
6. An effective bucket shop law which prohibits gambling in cotton and other futures, thereby guarding against depression in the prices of the farmers' crops, as a result of unnatural speculative or gambling transactions.
7. To encourage and promote agricultural development, a separate Department of Agriculture was created, and has been organized, and is at this time actively promoting, with the facilities at hand, our agricultural interests.

8. The occupation tax on useful occupations was repealed.

9. A law prohibiting the free-pass evil was enacted.

10. A law against nepotism was passed.

11. Charter fees of corporations were increased in a just and fair amount.

12. The depository law enacted keeps in circulation State funds and the rates of interest secured yields a return largely in excess of the entire expenses of the State Treasurer's office, and provides a handsome yield in interest on county funds heretofore deposited in banks without interest.

13. Laws increasing franchise taxes, and gross-receipts taxes, and securing the listing, rendition and assessment of the railways' intangible values for taxation, were enacted, and their operation has resulted in shifting a large portion of the burden theretofore unjustly borne by the individual property taxpayers to those who had been evading and escaping taxation.

14. A mine inspection law for the protection of laborers engaged in mining business, a law against black-listing, and a law lightening the labors of trainmen, enginemen, and telegraph operators and to protect the public, and other just laws, were passed for the benefit and protection of workingmen.

15. The law known as the " Robertson Insurance Law " having for its object the better protection of the policy-holders in Texas, and to promote investments in our State, was passed. The practical operation of this law is to require the investment of seventy-five per cent. of the Texas reserve of life insurance companies doing business in Texas, in Texas securities, and to require the deposit of such securities in the State Treasury, or other depository designated by the law. It is also provided that the deposit and investment features may be waived by the Commissioner of Insurance upon substantial showing under the terms and conditions of the law.

16. The " Full Rendition Law," as it is called, and the " Automatic Tax Law," having for their respective objects the rendition and assessment of all taxable property at its full value, greater uniformity and the adjustment of the tax rates and tax burdens in keeping with the absolute requirements of the government.

17. A uniform text-book law, providing for the adoption of a uniform system of text-books for all the public free schools of the State was passed.

18. A law prohibiting insolvent corporations from doing business in Texas was enacted.

19. A law prohibiting lobbying, and many other useful laws, were passed in the interest of the people.

In the administration of the State government during the past two years, an earnest effort has been made by the Executive and all other departments of the public service, to give the people a clean, efficient, and economical government.

That the full measure of our success may be ascertained, and the people more fully informed, the most careful and rigid investigation into the administration of every department of government and into the management of each State institution is invited and suggested. That the laws should be properly enforced upon all alike, no law-abiding man will deny. The Constitution provides that " the Governor shall cause the laws to be faithfully executed," and every means and power that could be appropriately exercised has been brought into requisition to meet this mandate of the Constitution. No one should be strong enough to escape the power of the law, and none too weak to receive its protection.

The mandate of the Constitution is clear and the duty of the Governor, with respect to enforcing the law, is plain, but the Governor's powers are not adequate, and adequate statutory powers as contemplated by the Constitution should be promptly provided by legislation suited to present conditions as well as for future contingencies.

Obedience to all criminal laws should be a condition in liquor dealers' bonds, and jurisdiction for suits for breach thereof should be given to the district courts of Travis County.

The transactions of the Treasury Department are set out in detail in the State Treasurer's annual report for the fiscal year ending August 31, 1908. The report, together with the tables accompanying the same, contain much useful information, and it is suggested that an examination of the same will be useful and profitable to the legislators.

At the beginning of this administration, the Comptroller estimated the deficit for the fiscal year ending August 31, 1907, to be approximately $300,000, and possibly more. However, as a result of careful and, we believe, efficient administration, aided by more effective revenue legislation, the deficit was avoided, and the State has been able to meet all of its current obligations for the past two years, and at all times to maintain an adequate working surplus in the State Treasury. Instead of a deficit, as predicted, on August 31, 1907, the State had met all of its obligations, and had a cash balance of $692,612.81 to the credit of the general revenue, and at the close of the fiscal year, August 31, 1908, after paying all claims when presented, the State had to the credit of the general revenue fund a balance of $888,985.61.

This very satisfactory financial condition was secured and has been maintained under the operation of the present tax system without additional tax burdens upon the individual property-tax payers. Interests theretofore escaping and property theretofore unrendered have been required, under the new laws, to contribute more to the support of the government, thereby lessening the burden upon those who were under the old laws bearing more than their just share.

To illustrate: Under the operation of the intangible tax law, $173,698,318 of intangible values of railways and bridge and ferry companies were listed for State and county taxes for the year 1908. The physical values of the railways increased under the new rendition law from $100,166,782, in 1906, to $157,822,790, in 1908. The intangible tax law, and the full rendition law has added to the tax rolls more than $250,000,000 of railway and other corporate values theretofore escaping taxation. The credits of money of banks and bankers and of others than banks and bankers are not now being properly listed for taxation; still there has been a great improvement, as the tax rolls show that they were increased from $42,112,424, in 1906, to $80,717,825, in 1908; an increase of more than 91 per cent. These are prominent illustrations of property values heretofore escaping, which, under the new laws, have contributed to the reduction of the ad valorem tax rate of 20 cents on the one hundred dollars in 1906, to the low rate of 6¼ cents on the one hundred dollars in 1908. The average tax rate in the counties throughout the State for 1906 was 55 cents on the one hundred dollars. This average rate of 55 cents was reduced in 1908 to an average rate of 40 cents on the one hundred dollars for county purposes by the operation of the new laws. The individual citizens who have been paying taxes upon their homes and farms at a fair valuation will pay less taxes in 1908 in proportion to value than they have paid for the support of the State government in any year since 1860, and as the receipts from other sources to the credit of general revenue increases, the ad valorem tax rate for State purposes will be reduced in proportion.

Under the operation of the tax laws of the last Legislature, the property values on the tax rolls increased from $1,221,-159,869, in 1906, to $2,174,122,480, in 1908. The amount of taxes paid in 1906 on the tax rate of 20 cents on the one hundred dollars, amounted to $2,435,412.92, and in 1908, with the tax rate of 6¼ cents, the total tax amounts to $1,358,826.55; an increase in assessed values of $952,935,411, and a reduction of $1,076,-586.37 in the total amount of ad valorem State taxes levied for 1908 as compared with 1906, and a much more equitable distribution of the taxes has been secured.

The valuation of property assessed for taxes, the rates and the amounts of State ad valorem taxes for the years 1906, 1907, and 1908, are as follows:

1906—Valuation, $1,221,259,869; rate, 20 cents; amount of taxes, $2,435,412.92.

1907—Valuation, $1,635,297,115; rate, 12½ cents; amount of taxes, $2,040,625.58.

1908—Valuation, $2,174,122,480; rate, 6¼ cents; amount of taxes, $1,358,826.55.

Receipts to the credit of the State's general revenue for the year 1906, 1907, and 1908, from special corporation taxes and from all other sources, not including the ad valorem taxes on tangible and intangible values, is shown below; $375,418.94 received from the United States government in 1906 not included:

> 1906—Amount of receipts.......$1,826,682.26
> 1907—Amount of receipts....... 2,024,434.80
> 1908—Amount of receipts....... 2,416,218.46

The county tax rolls for 1906, 1907, and 1908 disclose the gross inequalities obtaining throughout the State prior to the recent tax legislation, and they further show that an earnest effort was made in the large majority of the counties to comply with the laws respecting rendition, assessment and equalization. In a few counties, however, the law was ignored, and the conduct of the tax officials of such counties was little short of unconscionable. These counties received the full benefits of the reductions in the State ad valorem tax rate from 20 cents to 6¼ cents, and the State school ad valorem rate from 20 cents to 16⅔ cents, and received the full benefit of the increase in the apportionment of the available school fund, but by the dereliction and disregard of duty on the part of their trusted tax officials they contributed practically nothing to the increase of values resulting in such general good. This is so manifestly unfair and unjust that an effective remedy should be speedily provided by law. It is inconceivable that the oath of office prescribed by the Constitution, to say nothing of the oath prescribed by the new statute, and to which all tax officials must solemnly subscribe, should be so lightly considered by some men who have been honored with official station. Each county and each citizen and corporation of the State should contribute a just share and no more of the taxes necessary to support the State government and to maintain the public free school system, and no county, citizen or corporation through the dereliction of tax officials should be permitted to share in the benefits of reduced rates, and the increase of school funds when they fail to do their part. They should not be allowed by official dereliction to shift their just share of the taxes to the taxpayers of other counties and communities. It is just to say that the people of some of the counties where the law was disregarded repudiated the derelict tax officials upon their first opportunity.

Article 5124e, of Chapter XI, of the Acts of the First Called Session of the Thirtieth Legislature should be amended so that suits for removal from office may be instituted and prosecuted either in the county of such officer's residence, or in the district courts of Travis County, at the option of the Attorney-General. Laws should also be enacted providing that resignations or expirations of terms of office shall not abate action for removal from office, and the law should further provide that county officers who are removed from office for malfeasance or misfeasance or for any dereliction shall not thereafter hold office in this State until their eligibility is established and restored by act of the Legislature.

In this connection, I invite your attention to the respective annual reports of the State Tax Commissioner and the State Revenue Agent. The data and the difficulties encountered in the laws enforcement, and the suggestions made by these faithful officials, will, I believe, be of much value to the Legislature in improving our system of taxation and in enacting legislation to secure equality and more uniformity in the distribution of its burdens.

APPENDIX G

ADDRESS OF THE HON. W. D. WILLIAMS IN REFERENCE TO THE FULL RENDITION LAWS

I am altogether sensible, gentlemen, of the honor which you have done me by inviting me to discuss before you that act of the Thirtieth Legislature of Texas commonly known as the Full Rendition Statute. I am fully aware of the honor done me, as I have said, and yet I am not averse to accepting the invitation. I have heard so much said about this law; I have heard it so wildly praised and so extravagantly denounced; I have heard its promoters and all who were concerned in the enactment so severely condemned on the one hand and so unreservedly lauded on the other; I have read so many editorials in favor of full rendition and so many more against it, that the fever of strife has been set to circulating in my own blood, and I have come at last really to desire to speak my own thoughts on this subject. And especially is this true when I am afforded to-day the opportunity of addressing upon this issue the body of distinguished citizens which is assembled here before me, and which represents the opinions, the aspirations and the sentiments of the commercial classes of my own State. For this too is true, gentlemen, that however much I may in some particulars and on some occasions dissent from the prevailing beliefs of what is called the business world, I am now and always compelled to admit that the leaders of commerce are not only keen of intellect, but that they are full of courage, ready to give weighty reasons for the faith that is in them, loyal and patriotic citizens, commanding the respect and admiration of the world, true and sincere friends and generous adversaries.

That statute, which is generally called the Full Rendition statute, was enacted at the Regular Session of the Thirtieth Legislature, and is published by official authority as Chapter XI on page 459 of the General Laws of 1907. By provisions of this act, assessors are required to list the property for taxation at its reasonable cash market value or, if it has no market value, then at its real and intrinsic value.

Practically this is what is meant by the words "full value rendition," that the rendition shall be at the reasonable cash value of the article or thing which is listed. But it is well settled by repeated decisions of appellate courts that where the word "value" is used in a statute and is not limited either by qualifying words or by the context of the statute, it has the same meaning as if it had been written "reasonable cash market value," or "real and intrinsic value."

So that, as respects its actual intent, the Full Rendition statute brings into operation no new principle and does nothing more than to deprive our assessors of a common excuse, sometimes honestly made and sometimes not, of misunderstanding the meaning of the word "value," as used in former statutes upon the same subject. The act was not intended to and did not introduce a new practice in the assessment of property for taxation, but on the contrary, was aimed at persuading or compelling obedience to methods already established by law, but fallen into partial or total disuse.

The Constitution of 1876, which is now in force, commands that "all property in this State shall be taxed in proportion to its value," and, as already explained, the word "value," as used in this connection, means fair cash market value, or if the article has no market value, then its real and intrinsic. The Constitution fixes the same standard of compensation as does the Act of 1907, and if the latter is correctly designated as a full rendition law then is the Constitution itself also a full rendition Constitution.

Now, when we are inclined to complain of the trials and hardships of the present, it is sometimes the part of wisdom for us to recall for a moment the conditions and circumstances which surrounded us in the past. For it is by such a comparison alone that we may truly know whether our situation has indeed changed for the worse, or whether our complaints are justified.

We have had an ad valorem general property tax in Texas since the beginning of the Anglo-Saxon government within our boundaries. The Constitution of 1836 gave to the legislative department of the Republic an absolutely free hand to shape laws for the raising of a public revenue at its sole will and pleasure. "Congress," so it was written, "shall have power to levy and collect taxes and imposts, excise and tonnage duties." Article 2, Section 1. This authority was sufficiently broad to enable the Legislature of an independent sovereignty, such as Texas then was, to determine what persons and what property should be burdened for the support of the government and what persons and what property should be exempted. There was no limitation upon the power, nor any restrictions to prevent whatever discriminations Congress should see fit to enact.

With this unlimited charter in its hands, the first Congress of Texas met together in October, 1836, the founders of a new nation, a truly representative body, great in intellect, great in character and courage, but greater than all in devotion and loyalty to the eternal principles of right and justice, which are now, always have been and always will be the principles of Democracy also. And those ancient heroes in home-spun, being thus the sovereign legislative body of an independent people, legislating as well for the planter, with his broad and fertile lands, tilled by his hundreds of slaves, as for the wandering hunter and scout, whose Kentucky rifle and pouch of bullets and horn of powder constituted his sole possessions, passed that act, entitled " An Act to raise a public revenue by direct taxation," approved June 12, 1837. And, after this manner, there came into being the first " full rendition " statute, which was also the first statute for the direct taxation of property enacted under Anglo-Saxon domination in Texas.

For, by this act, Congress required all property owners and all agents and representatives of such owners, to make out and deliver to the proper assessing officers inventories showing the value of all their properties, and to swear that same were just, true and faithful valuations and lists. If the assessor believed any valuation offered to him was too low, it was made his duty, summarily and without notice or formality, to call to his assistance two neighboring citizens, to be selected by himself, and the three of them were required to persuade and encourage the reluctant property owner into those straight and narrow paths where duty leads and virtue is its own and only reward. From the assessor and his chosen helpers there was no appeal. That which they said was the full value was the full value, both in law and in fact, and there was an immediate end of the controversy.

In these modern days of frock coats and silk stockings and peace and comfort, we would incline to think that the Act of 1837, which put a " big stick " in the hands of the assessor, would have been sufficiently strenuous to have satisfied even that most strenuous of officers, our worthy President Theodore Roosevelt. But there were mighty men in those old days, when Sam Houston was at the head of the Lone Star Republic, and this problem was as meat between their teeth. They enjoyed it to the uttermost. They enjoyed it so much that they could not keep their minds occupied with other things, and, in 1838, Congress amended and strengthened the original "full rendition" bill so as to require every property owner to swear a still harder swear, to wit, that his list was a true and perfect inventory and account of his property and its value. A true and perfect valuation! Think of it, O ye who strain at gnats in these meek and modern days! A most vigorous oath, indeed, was that. Strong and bitter, like the medicines they took in those good old times. And yet I must own to it, gentlemen, that I have nowhere heard or read that either the oaths or the medicines did them any harm.

I have recalled to your recollection those old days of the golden age of Texas for one purpose only, which is that you may be reminded how, in the words of Solomon, "there is nothing new under the sun." There is nothing new, not even our troubles, and I can imagine that, even in the time of the Republic, our citizens desisted momentarily from the fighting of Mexicans and the pursuit of hostile Indians to hold indignation meetings all the way from Nacogdoches to Matagorda Bay, where fierce protests were drawn and adopted, condemning Houston and Lamar and the members of the First Congress for their wickedness in procuring the enactment of a "full rendition" statute with which to oppress and impoverish the Lone Star people.

I, myself, am reminded in this connection of the solemn utterances of some of the daily newspapers, most excellent oracles of Democracy, warning us in editorial columns long that this is a new country, where a continuous stream of bottoms is dropping out of our real estate booms, and that it is a great big mistake to assess our new and fragile values at anything approaching their face. And in my mind's eye, I can see right now one of those ancient and beloved heroes, recently companion to the immortal Davy Crockett, the tails of his coonskin cap fluttering in the wind, addressing an indignation meeting in the days of the First Congress, arousing unlimited enthusiasm with the very same argument which is now so commonly used, founded upon the newness, three-quarters of a century ago, of this country of ours, which some of us profess to believe has not yet grown sufficiently old to tell the truth for purposes of taxation.

The statutes of Texas have always been "full rendition" statutes, and our Constitutions, except for that one which was adopted in 1836, have always been "full rendition" Constitutions. And, in my judgment, there can be no honest attempt at a fair adjustment of the burdens of a direct tax upon the general property of this or any other country which does not make a decent effort at an equalization in proportion to the true value of each article which is taxed. The true value of an article is necessarily its fair, full value, nothing more and nothing less. If we levy general property taxes, we are compelled to require by law that all property subject to the levy shall be taxed in proportion to its value, and such a rule is inevitably a law for a "full rendition."

If a government were to command that its taxables should be listed at one-fourth their full value, and that a tax of $1 on the $100 should be levied on the values so listed, it would in substance have enacted a law for the taxation of its property, at full value, at 25 cents on each $100, and no amount of figuring can make out of it anything less or anything more.

The proposition that property shall be taxed at one-fourth, or at one-fifth, or at any other fractional part of its true and full value is wholly inadequate to meet any of the objections which are urged against the "full rendition" bill. If a tract of land be assessed at $100 an acre at its full value, January 1, 1908, and by reason of any change in conditions, the value has diminished before the arrival of the taxpaying season, say December 31, 1908, to $50 an acre, and, if it be assumed that it would be an injustice under those circumstances to require the owner to pay a tax in December which is based upon such a valuation, still the slightest reflection will convince you that this injustice has not been obviated by assessing the land at $25 an acre and, at the same time, multiplying the tax rate by four. In either case precisely the same amount of money is exacted from the owner, and, in either case, the tax is in truth based upon the full value January 1st, which we have assumed to be $100 an acre, and no account is taken of any subsequent depreciation.

But, if it be urged that the owner will be better satisfied to pay 25 cents an acre if his land be valued at $25 an acre than he will be to pay the same 25 cents on the same acre upon a valuation of $100, then I can only answer by saying that the Texans with whom I am acquainted are so well fixed with brains that you can not fool them with a trick so transparent as this. If a citizen pays a tax of $50 on a 200-acre farm, he knows that he is out just $50 in good, common, hard cash, and all the assessors and collectors in the State can not fool him into the belief that he has paid only $40 by showing him how low his land was assessed and how high it was taxed. Having paid his money, he will feel neither better nor worse because of the valuation put upon his property, provided only that he has had a square deal as compared with the other taxpayers.

This is the whole of the tax question, as I see it—to deal justly with every man in the sight of God—to tax every person as nearly as possible in proportion to his ability to pay. And under any ad valorem system the measure of the ability of each individual and the only approximately fair measure which the ingenuity of man has ever been able to devise is found in the reasonable, full value of the taxable property of every owner.

No revenue law is wholly bad which tends in this direction and, on the other hand, every such law is good and valuable in direct proportion as it is so drawn that it will aid in bringing about this all-desirable equality in the imposition of public burdens.

Granting that taxes are apportioned with reasonable fairness, there is but one way whereby an impartial reduction can be had and the benefits of such reduction distributed proportionately and honestly among the taxpayers, and this way is by cutting down the expenses of the government. Every other effort is either the pursuit of a ghost, leaving the pursuer empty handed if he were to succeed in catching it, or it is an effort at tax dodging. The average taxpayer is no shirk, and the very best for which he can hope and the things for which he should always be demanding are, first, an economical administration of public affairs, and, second, the utmost fairness in the distribution of public burdens.

The Constitution of Texas, as I have already shown, has always commanded an equality in taxation, to be attained by levying upon all property in proportion to its value. The laws of Texas have been enacted in obedience to the constitutional mandate, as full rendition laws, but have until the late session of the Thirtieth Legislature failed in one respect, at least, for they provided no adequate means by which they might be enforced. And under these laws, which on the face required a fair assessment, but did not undertake to compel obedience to their provisions, a practice of evasion was begun and spread all over the State, until a condition prevailed which was anarchy, pure and simple. County strove against county and neighbor against neighbor, each one trying unjustly to shift some portion of his rightful burden to the shoulders of another. It was a reign of lawlessness, gentlemen, when, as some of you members have demonstrated, the average assessment in one county was only 24 per cent. of the value of the property assessed, while the average in another county was as much as 75 per cent. And the remaining counties of the State ranged themselves anywhere you please between these two extremes.

Equality in taxation was a thing dead and forgotten, and honorable people were being taught to look with contempt upon the affidavits which were required to be made before the assessors. A strong and manly people who throughout their history had held the vice of lying in peculiar detestation, were made accustomed to falsehoods, uttered for profit, under the supposed sanction of an oath. A condition prevailed which would in time have compelled the moral deterioration of all citizens.

Now, it is certain that it is one of the most important of the functions of government that it shall secure justice and fair dealing as between all those who are subject to its jurisdiction. But more than this, and more than all else, it is the duty of those who are in control of public affairs that they shall permit no condition to continue which threatens to undermine the moral character of its people. For I venture the opinion that civilization is not builded of capital and labor alone, but that its chief component parts are the love of virtue and the sense of honor and the devotion to truth and integrity which are in the hearts of all persons, and if these good attributes are no longer actuated by these high ideals, then I predict that mankind will have become from that moment forward incapable of maintaining social order.

The practice of undervaluing property for purposes of taxation, which had become common and almost universal in Texas, was destructive of all possibility of justice as between the respective owners, and had in addition thereto a distinct tendency to debase the morals of an uncontaminated and virtuous people. The movement for what I will venture to call purer and better laws did not begin in the Thirtieth Legislature, but years and years ago, and the so-called Full Rendition act of 1907 is merely a milestone in the forward march of a progress which has continued throughout the ages, and which will never end.

The statute for the taxation of banks and banking capital is a "full rendition" statute, designed to enable and to require assessors to list at full value the stocks or property of such institutions and all funds employed in that particular business. The act for the taxation of the intangible assets of railroads, an act which I had the pleasure of assisting to pass in the Twenty-ninth Legislature, is another " full rendition " law, under the operations of which nearly $174,000,000 of additional railroad values is exposed to view and listed and taxed. These and other statutes of the same kind, which I have not the time to mention, are just and fair, if all other property is also assessed approximately at its value, but they become discriminatory and oppressive as soon as undervaluations of other taxables are purposely allowed.

I am fully aware that there are certain vices which appear to be necessarily inherent in any system that can be devised for the direct taxation of both real and personal property. And while I am not inclined to believe that these vices render this character of tax more difficult of fair apportionment than is any other, yet I would not for a moment attempt to render blind either myself or you to those imperfections and weaknesses of human nature which make it apparently impossible entirely to effect the purpose of any law, no matter how just or wise it may be. But I would remind you that we can not give ground in the face of this argument without abandoning all effort at an orderly rule of society and plunging headlong into the deadly chaos of anarchy. If our inability, entirely and in all cases, to enforce a full rendition law is just cause for the abandonment of the full rendition principle, then, in the same way and for the same reason, we shall be driven from any other plan that we may adopt. Indeed, if we once admit the force of this objection, we must abandon all law, for in no case are we able satisfactorily to enforce any statute which is upon our books.

Remember, gentlemen, I make no pretense that perfection has been attained in the act of the Thirtieth Legislature, or that the act is incapable of improvement. What I am contending is that it is a step forward, and that this body, standing as it does for the ideal aspirations of the business men of Texas, must take no step backward. To repeal this statute, setting up nothing better in its place, retreating to a condition of which you, as thoughtful and patriotic citizens, must have been sick at heart, may bring us to have " fewer laws," but I am not able to persuade myself that those laws which are left will thereby have become any the better.

In my judgment, *ex parte* affidavits, which have the effect of making the truth cost money and of rewarding falsehood as if it were a virtue and not a vice, ought not to be exacted in any but the rarest of cases, and only where no other source of information can reasonably be found. And, for this reason, I have long preferred that the visible property of the State should be valued and assessed by the assessor rather than by the owner. But I am greatly in the minority in my opinion of this subject, and because that opinion is of absolutely no consequence, I refrain from enlarging upon it.

Proceeding, then, along the only road which is open for travel, and assuming that each owner shall continue to fix the *prima facie* value of his own assets, it can not be successfully denied that the interests of society demand that such valuation shall be made under oath, and that the value stated in every affidavit shall be the true, full value and not an arbitrary, assumed and fictitious proportion of the same.

The " full rendition " law, considered in connection with other statutes in force upon the same subject, provides an admirable system of local equalization, and tends in a very considerable degree toward equalization throughout the limits of Texas.

But this is a State of vast areas and of prodigious distances, and in any such widely extended territory it seems to me that the physical conditions alone are sufficient to demand the enactment into law of some method of apportionment which will not depend entirely upon local views and local sentiments. It must be kept in mind that, while the Attorney-General may sue to remove from office any assessor or member of a board of equalization whom he believes to be guilty of intentionally accepting undervaluations, yet, convictions for such offenses are always difficult to secure and the prosecution of the vast majority of such cases would be no better than a farce. The State government is practically without power to compel reasonable assessments in any county or section where the citizens are largely opposed to full rendition. The administration has no legal authority which it can effectually use, but must confine itself to moral suasion alone, and in controversies where interested parties are arrayed upon opposite sides, we, as a people, have never regarded moral suasion and merely moral responsibilities as a sufficiently effective force to be worthy of serious mention. We will not permit a judge to hear a case in court, or a juror to sit on a jury where either the plaintiff or the defendant is related to him within the third degree, either by blood or marriage. Arbitrators must be without interest and not related to the parties, and, in general, wherever an act is authorized which may affect the rights of others, the law is vigilant in requiring that the officer or person acting shall be disinterested and impartial. Everyone will agree that these precautions against injustice are right and necessary, and yet I can conceive of no good reason why interested parties or their relatives may not be permitted to adjudge any other disputed claims quite as well, and with just as large a probability that justice will be done as when they were asked to determine what amount of State taxes they will pay.

A compulsory equalization of some character seems to me the next step to be taken in the forward march toward fairer taxation in Texas. We have come a long way from that original plan of 1837, by which an assessor and two neighbors arbitrarily determined what a property owner should pay, but we are still very far from home. Nor should this occasion surprise, for if the law is to be worthy of respect, if it is to be in any way effective as a force for the right, it must not be fixed and unchangeable, but, on the contrary, must be capable of infinite variety and infinite development, growing with the growth of the people who are its creators and enforcers, eternal in seeking justice, but flexible in adapting itself to the present.

In conclusion, gentlemen, permit me to call to your attention very briefly a few of the effects of the new tax laws. For if we are to return, as at least one candidate for high office is insisting, to the old order of things, we are abandoning not merely the so-called Full Rendition law, but all other of the recent enactments upon the same subject. We are to abandon the intangible tax law, the franchise tax law, the law taxing the gross receipts of certain corporations, and all other of the statutes of the Twenty-ninth and Thirtieth Legislatures by which a fairer adjustment of the burdens of government was sought to be secured. And if we abandon these laws we must abandon their undeniable benefits as well as their doubtful disadvantages, and pay taxes as we paid them in the good old times.

Now, in 1906, when these laws were either tied up in court or not yet in force, the property owners of Texas were called upon to pay a total ad valorem tax for the expense of the State government of $2,443,637, but in 1907 the ad valorem tax for State expenses was reduced to $2,044,566. The operation of the new tax laws reduced the burdens put upon property owners by $400,000, and of the amount which property was still required to pay, something near $214,000 was levied upon railroad intangibles. The saving upon the general property, aside from railroad and corporation taxes, was $614,000 for that single year, for State expenses alone. In the same way, the saving for the year 1908 will not be less than $900,000 on State expenses, not including the school fund.

It can not be successfully denied that the new tax laws have tended largely toward an equitable distribution of tax burdens and that in doing this they have diminished the amount paid by the average citizen. The intangible assets tax alone brought in a revenue for 1907 of $1,470,000 to the State and its counties, and cost for its administration the insignificant sum of $2,650, a result which can not be surpassed in the history of governmental finance.

These are the triumphs which we are asked to abandon by returning to that system where "the assessors under the commissioners courts made the assessments as under former laws."

Now, gentlemen, I for one am not disposed to retreat. I am intending to go forward, not backward. And in the course which I am determined to pursue I am expecting to go arm in arm in the company of the most of those who are here to-day as the representatives of commercial Texas.

Index

Abernethy, John R., 278, 280
Abilene, Texas, 168
Aley, Texas, 252, 255
Alice, Texas, 362, 364
Alley, Sheriff John, 56, 58
Amarillo, Texas, 142, 143, 145, 170
Angle, Ab, 268, 269
Angle, George, 268-270
"Anti-Democrats", 153
Askew, C. W., 335, 336
Athens, Texas, 250-259
Austin Colony, 127
Austin, Texas, 323, 374

Bailey, Senator, 320
Bailey, Al, 177
Baker, _____, 317
Barker, Sheriff, 60, 64, 65
Barker, Dud, 223, 225, 233, 235, 240
Bates, _____, 317
Bay City, Texas, 293
Baylor County, 48, 49, 176
Bean, Ed, 38-41
Bean, Jim, 38-41
Bean, Roy, 196, 197
Beaver Creek, 72, 79
Beckham, Sheriff Joe, 166-168,
    176-178, 208
Bell, Ranger, 233, 261
Bell, Sheriff Tom, 252
Bellevue, Texas, 123, 200
Bellville, Texas, 373
Bishop, John, 143
Blanton, John, 262
Blocksom, Maj., 325, 329, 333,
    340, 342
"Blues", 361

Boger, Mart, 207
Bowie Knife, 33
Bracken, John, 143
Brittain, Grude, 262
Brittain, Sgt. J. M., 143
Brooken, Bill, 58, 68
Brooken, Bood, 68
Brooken Band, 55-58, 64-68
Brown, Jim, 227, 237
Brown's Bluff, Texas, 30-31
Brownsville, Texas, 315-356
Buck, Red, 176-178
Burford, J. C., 246
Burke, Texas, 137
Burnett, Burke, 273, 274, 277, 278
Burnett, Tom, 277, 279, 283
Burson, Lon, 78-94
Buzzard's Water Hole, 222-240

Cabell, Sheriff Ben E., 252
Camp, W. B. (letter), 163, 164
Campbell, Bob, 136-139
Campbell, Dan, 136-139
Campbell, Gov. T.M., 373
Camp Mabry, 323
Canadian River, 159
Canadian, Texas, 83, 89
"Car-shed Convention," 151-153
Carter, Rhoda Isabel, 31
Casita Ranch, 366, 369
Cattleman's Association, the, 96
Cherokee Strip, 99-105
Cherokee Strip Livestock Assn.,
    115
Childress, Texas, 165
City National Bank (Wichita Falls,
    Texas), 199

Clark, George, 152, 153
Clay County, 123
Coffer, Sheriff Dick, 171, 172
Colorado County, 244-249
Columbus, Texas, 245
Comanche County (Okla.), 273
Comb, Mayor, 325, 348
Conditt, J. F., 290-303
Conditt, Mildred, 290-292
Cook, _____, 167
Cook, Sheriff, 176
Cook, Bill, 121, 123, 124
Corinth, battle of, 20
Corpus Christi, Texas, 363, 364
Corpus Christi Crony, 359
Crawford, _____, 199-213, 302
Crook, Jerry, 252
Crutcher, _____, 170, 171
Cuero, Texas, 314
Culberson, Charles A., 30, 189-195,
    212, 213, 226, 320
Culberson, Dave, 29, 30, 189
Cunningham, Sheriff, 168

Dallas, Texas, 220, 323
Dalton, Bill, 121n
Dalton Gang, 121n
Davidson, John, 59-64
Deep Red Creek, 277
DeKalb, Miss., 17
Delling, Blaze, 262, 266, 270, 322,
    326, 327, 365, 367, 369
Democratic State Convention, 323
"Diamond Tail" (brand), 97
Diaz, President, 186-187
Diggs, Augusta, 310
Dillon, Buck, 112
Doan's Store, 189
Donnelly, Ed., 240
Dorsey, Frank, 199
Dowell, Sheriff Pete, 34
Dunnaway, Ranger, 271

Durham, Eunice, 16

Edna, Texas, 290-303, 308-314
Edwards, Forrest, 240
Egg, Sheriff, 293, 297, 308
Electra, Texas, 177
El Paso, Texas, 194
Erath County, 216
Evans, Mrs., 318

Farias, _____, 371
Fitzsimmons, Bob, 194, 196, 198
Fitzsimmons-Maher Prizefight, 194
Fortescue, Lt., 277
Fort Brown, 316-356
Fort Griffin, 284
Fort Parker, 127-129
Fort Reno, Oklahoma, 355
Fort Sam Houston, 355
Fort Sill, Oklahoma, 287
Fort Smith, Arkansas, 124
Fort Worth, Texas, 181, 211, 212, 216
Fort Worth & Denver RR, 214-216
Frederick, Oklahoma, 277, 287
Fuller, Ranger, 261

Galveston, Texas, 393
Garner, Congressman, 348
Gibbs, Hunter, 272
Gibson, John, 292
Gibson, Monk, 292-303, 308-314
Golden, _____, 33
Good, Mr., 145, 216
Gordon, George, 33-35
Green, Guy, 251
Green, Jim, 143
Greene, Colonel, 26
Greene, Charley, 27-29
Greenhaw, Arthur, 255, 259
Greenhaw, John, 255, 259
Greenville, Texas, 307
Greer County, 189, 391, 392

Grimes County, 127
Groveton, Texas, 265-267, 271, 272
Guthrie, Okla. Terr., 106, 114

Hall County, 145
Hallettsville, Texas, 294
Hamilton, Mack, 334
Hammond, Johnny, 51
Hansford County, 71, 82, 83, 85
Hardeman County, 53-71, 171, 284
Harlingen, Texas, 322, 364
Harrold, Texas, 48, 55, 137
Harwell, Jack, 177, 178, 200-213
Hemphill County, 83
Henderson County, 250-259
Henderson, Texas, 22, 27
Hennessey, Okla. Terr., 115, 120,
   121n
Henrietta, Texas, 78, 207
Higgins, Texas, 80, 81, 91
Hill, Judge, 382
Hogg, James S., 31, 32, 41, 42,
   139-142, 151-153, 166, 182, 187
Holiday Creek, 200
Holly, Bill, 52, 53, 254, 255
Holly, Buck, 52, 53, 253-255
Holly, Buck, Saloon, 51
House, Edward M., 163
Houston, Temple, 82
Houston, Texas, 152, 166
Houston County, 265, 266
Howard, Henry, 298, 300, 310
Hughes, Capt., 371
Hulen, Gen., 294, 297, 320, 323,
   324, 346
Humphrey, _____, 250
Humphrey, George, 253
Humphrey, Willie, 259
Hunter, Col., 217
Hutchinson County, 71, 158-162
Hutto, Hill, 268-269

I. G. & N. RR, 35

Inman, _____, 365, 368
Iowa Park, Texas, 136
Jackson, Sergt., 331, 339
Jackson County, 290-303
Jefferson, Texas, 28, 29
Johns, _____, 257
Jones, Ranger, 261

Kansas City Journal, 156n
Keeton, Jim, 262
Kelley, _____, 325
Kemper County (Miss.), 17
Kennon, Judge, 244-247
Kingfisher, Okla. Terr., 106,
   114-116, 120
Kittrell's Cut-off, 265, 266
Kleiber, _____, 329, 338, 341, 342,
   348, 350, 360, 361
Knight, Marshal George A., 67,
   70, 108

Lacy, L. L., 356
Lambert, Dr. Alexander, 277
Langford, H. H., 199
Langtry, Texas, 196
Lanham, Gov., 266, 271, 295, 320,
   323, 346, 350, 354, 362, 370
"Law West of the Pecos.", 197
Lazarus, Sam, 58, 96, 97
Lewis, Kid, 176-178, 199-213
Limestone County, 127n
Lipscomb County, 80
Llano County, 239
Loftus, Hill, 176-178, 209
Longview, Texas, 31
Lynden (District Atty.), 239
Lyon, Capt., 326, 332, 335, 337,
   344
Lyon, Cecil, 149, 277, 281

Mabry, Gen. W. H., 134, 187, 195
McCarthy, Jeff, 227, 237
McCarthy, Jim, 227, 228

452

McCauley, W. J., 123, 124, 143, 177, 178, 200-213, 233, 261, 322, 324, 327-329, 339, 363, 364, 367

McClure, Bob, 123, 167, 168, 200, 203, 240

McCormick, Josh, 233, 236, 238

McDonald, Enoch, 16, 19, 20

McDonald, Eunice Durham, 20, 21-25

McDonald, Rhoda, 236, 304-307

McKenzie, Sam, 322, 326, 327, 365-367

Macklin, Capt., 326, 331, 332, 334, 335, 337, 338

McMurray, Capt. S. A., 66, 136, 139, 140

Madison County, 272

Madisonville, Texas, 271, 272

Maher, Peter, 194, 195, 198

Mangum, Oklahoma, 190

Margaret, Texas, 56

Marsden, _____, 364

Masterson, Bat, 195, 198

Matador, Texas, 155

Matador Ranch, 155

Matamoras, Mex., 316, 317, 333

Matthews, John Pierce, 165-175

Melvin, Judge, 49-52

Meridian, Miss., 19

Mexico, 182-188

Meyers, Charley, 120

Miller, Corporal, 326, 331-335, 339

Miller Hotel (Brownsville), 319, 350

Mineola, Texas, 31-43, 251

Mississippi (State), 16-22

Monasco, _____, 254

Monasco, Bill, 254

Moore, "Bony", 279

Morris, Asst. Atty. Gen. Ned, 250, 252, 259n

Moses, Sheriff, 168

Motley County, 166, 167, 176

Nacona (Comanche), 284-286

Natus, _____, 319

Neil, Edgar, 224, 233, 240

New Orleans, Louisiana, 30

No-Man's Land, 69-77, 87-94

Ogle, Bill, 227, 242

Oklahoma Territory, 176-178

Olds, Ranger, 255, 261

Orange, Texas, 260-262

Osuna, _____, 371

Panhandle City, Texas, 160

Panhandle of Texas, 154-178, 189-193

Parker, Benjamin, 128

Parker, Cynthia Ann, 126-129, 283-286

Parker, Rev. James W., 128

Parker, John, 128

Parker, Quanah, 126, 278, 282, 283, 285, 286

Pease River, 150

Penrose, Maj., C. W., 316-356

Perez, _____, 371

Perry, Ollie, 240

Platt, John, 143

Platt, Sam, 55

Platt, Tom, 143

Plemons, Texas, 160

Plummer, Mrs., 128, 129

Port Arthur, Texas, 262-264

Potter County, 142

Powell, Felix, 292, 297-301, 316-356

Powell, Irene, 309

Powell, Warren, 297, 308

Prairie Flower (Comanche), 285, 286

Pretty-nicey (Comanche), 283

453

Quanah, Texas, 55, 59-64, 100, 136, 142, 150, 167, 169, 182, 189, 191, 192, 212
Queen, Ranger, 200-213
Quite-nice-enough (Comanche), 282
Quitman, Texas, 31

Rankin, D. C., 359
Ray, Jim, 270
Red River, 178, 189
"Reds", 361
Reece-Townsend Feud, 244-249
Reed, _____, 309
Reed, Bethel, 310
Reeves, Marshal George, 35-37
Rice, Joseph, 149
Rio Grande City, Texas, 357-372
Robb, H. L., 267, 271
Roberts County, 88
Rogers, Capt., 260
Rogers, Col., 20n
Roosevelt, Theodore (letter), 11
Roosevelt, Theodore, 273-289, 315, 395
Ross, Gov. L. S., 66, 284, 285
Rusk County, 22
Ryan, C. T., 322, 324, 327

Sabine Pass, 262
Sabine River, 31, 39, 260, 262
Salisbury, Texas, 145, 146
Sam Fordyce, Texas, 358, 364
San Antonio, Texas, 301
Sand Creek (Okla. Terr.), 106
Sand Creek Gang, 114
Sanderson, Texas, 197
San Saba County, 221-242
San Saba River, 226
Saxon, Ranger, 261
Scurry, Adj. Gen., 262
Scurry, Thomas 249n, 259n

Seabury, _____, 361
Simpson, Sloan, 277
"Skeeter" (outlaw), 121, 123, 124
Smith, Jasper, 23
Smith County, 38
Soule's Commercial College, 30
Some-nicey (Comanche), 272
Sowell, A. J. (quoted), 130-132
Sparks, Eli, 257
Starr County, 358-372
Stuart, Dan, 195, 196, 198
Sullivan, Sgt. J. L., 123, 143, 200, 202
Sullivan, John, 223, 225, 226

Talking John Creek, 284
Tate, Mr., 317
Tehaucano Indians, 127
Terry, Wright, 272
Tesca, Okla., 278
Tex, Charlie, 116, 117
Thurber, Texas, 216-219
Too-nicey (Comanche), 282
Topeka, Kansas, 107
Touchstone, Mary Jane, 267-269
Trans-Cedar Bottoms, 250
Trinity County, 265-267
Tullis, Joe 268
Tullis, Wash, 268-270
Tummins, _____, 272
Turkey Creek (Okla. Terr.), 115, 116, 159
Turkey Creek Gang, 115-121
Turkey Track Ranch, 71, 77
Turner, Bull, 58, 96
Twenty-fifth Infantry Regt. (U.S.), 315
Twenty-seventh Infantry Regt. (U.S.), 336

U.S. Marshal, So Dist. of Kansas, 67

U.S. River Guard, 365

Vernon, Texas, 189, 276, 277
Victoria, Texas, 314
Vincia, _____, 371
Volz, William, 356

Waggoner, Tom, 273, 277
Waggoner's Ranch, 178
Walker, Marshal, 107, 108, 114
Walker County, 265, 266
Wanderer's Creek, 55, 95, 100,
   149
Weeks, Polk, 256, 259
Welch, Judge Stanley, 324, 338,
   340, 342, 344, 348-350, 352,
   353, 357-372
Wells, James B., 340, 342, 347, 348
Wichita Falls, Texas, 48-55, 81, 82,
   85, 124, 137, 166, 199-216, 275,
   276
Wichita County, 43-55
Wichita River, 200
Wichita, Kansas, 114, 115
Wilbarger County, 59, 177, 189
Wilkerson, Joe, 252
Willacy, Sen., 348
Williams, Bill, 62-64
Wise County, 41
Wolforth, Pat, 59, 61, 96-98
Wood County, 31
Woodring, Frank, 391
Woodring, Sid, 391

XIT Ranch, 155

Young, John, 298, 299
Young, Lt. Gen. S. M. B., 277, 278